D0784912

Short Introduction to Strategic Management

The *Short Introduction to Strategic Management* provides an authoritative yet accessible account of strategic management and its contemporary challenges. It explains the roots and key rationales of the strategy field, discussing common models, tools, and practices, to provide a complete overview of conventional analytical techniques in strategic management. Andersen extends the discussion to consider dynamic strategy making and how it can enable organizations to respond effectively to turbulent and unpredictable global business environments. There is a specific focus on multinational corporate strategy issues relevant to organizations operating across multiple international markets. Written in a clear and direct style, it will appeal to students and practicing managers and executives alike.

TORBEN JUUL ANDERSEN is Professor of Strategy and International Management at the Copenhagen Business School where he teaches an MBA course in Strategic Management, and he is Associate Dean of the MBA Program. He has held positions as Vice President at Citibank/ Citicorp Investment Bank, London, Senior Vice President at Unibank A/S, Copenhagen, Managing Director of SDS Securities A/S, Copenhagen, and Senior Consultant at PHB Hagler Bailly, Arlington. He is the author of numerous articles and books including *Strategic Risk Management Practice* (Cambridge University Press, 2010), *Perspectives on Strategic Risk Management* (2006), and *Global Derivatives: A Strategic Risk Management Perspective* (2005).

Cambridge Short Introductions

Series editors: Cary L. Cooper CBE, Lancaster University

Thomas G. Cummings, University of Southern California

The purpose of this innovative series is to provide short, authoritative, reasonably priced books for students taking a first course in Management, particularly at MBA and Masters level. The books include concise coverage of the key concepts taught in the core subjects, as well as suggestions for further study. Written by a team of experts from the world's leading business schools, these books are highly recommended for anyone preparing to study for an advanced management qualification.

For supplementary materials, visit the series website: www.cambridge.org/csi

About the series editors:

Cary L. Cooper is Distinguished Professor of Organizational Psychology and Health, and Pro Vice Chancellor at Lancaster University. He is the author/editor of over 120 books and is a frequent contributor to national newspapers, TV, and radio. Professor Cooper is past President of the British Academy of Management, is a Companion of the Chartered Management Institute, and one of the first UK-based Fellows of the (American) Academy of Management. In 2001, Professor Cooper was awarded a CBE in the Queen's Birthday Honours List for his contribution to occupational safety and health.

Thomas G. Cummings is a leading international scholar and consultant on strategic change and designing high-performance organizations. He is Professor and Chair of the Department of Management and Organization at the Marshall School of Business, University of Southern California. He has authored over 70 articles and 22 books. Professor Cummings was the 61st President of the Academy of Management, the largest professional association of management scholars in the world with a total membership of over 19,000.

Also in this series:

Short Introduction to Accounting by Richard Barker

Short Introduction to Strategic Human Resource Management by Wayne F. Cascio and John W. Boudreau

Forthcoming books:

Short Introduction to Entrepreneurship

Short Introduction to Operations Management

Short Introduction to Leadership

Short Introduction to Strategic Management

Torben Juul Andersen

CAMBRIDGE
UNIVERSITY PRESS

CAMBRIDGE
UNIVERSITY PRESS

University Printing House, Cambridge CB2 8BS, United Kingdom

Published in the United States of America by Cambridge University Press, New York

Cambridge University Press is part of the University of Cambridge.

It furthers the University's mission by disseminating knowledge in the pursuit of education, learning and research at the highest international levels of excellence.

www.cambridge.org
Information on this title: www.cambridge.org/9781107671355

© Torben Juul Andersen 2013

First published 2013

Printed in the United Kingdom by Bell and Bain Ltd

A catalog record for this publication is available from the British Library

Library of Congress Cataloging in Publication data
Andersen, Torben Juul.
Short introduction to strategic management / Torben Juul Andersen.
        pages   cm. – (Cambridge short introductions to management)
Includes bibliographical references and index.
ISBN 978-1-107-03136-4 (Hardback) – ISBN 978-1-107-67135-5 (Paperback)
1. Strategic planning.   2. Management.   I. Title.
HD30.28.A516 2013
658.4′012–dc23   2012042149

ISBN 978-1-107-03136-4 Hardback
ISBN 978-1-107-67135-5 Paperback

Additional resources for this publication at www.cambridge.org/csi

"Til Mette, den sejeste pige jeg kender, og hendes to fantastiske børn, Christine og Christian."

Contents

Figures

Preface

The aim of this book is to provide a concise presentation of the theory and practice of strategic management, with particular emphasis on effective, responsive strategy-making processes. The scope is comprehensive and research-based and yet presents the content in an accessible manner, ready to be applied in management practice. The book presents conventional and newer tools for practical strategy analysis and considers the associated strategy process expressed in an integrative strategy model, where strategic responsiveness is a necessary precursor for organizational adaptation. These themes are anchored in the core elements of strategic management, together with inputs from current research efforts. Hence, the book can be used as a general strategy textbook in contemporary MBA programs where there is a need for a succinct overview of the field. By adding selected reference articles and related case studies, it can form a solid base for graduate classes in strategic management. It may also serve as a useful foundation for different executive programs where participants want to probe the strategy field, challenge their current thinking, and consider approaches to effective strategy making that can be applied to their own organizations. With a general grounding in the strategy literature including key references, it might even serve as a useful core text for PhD students with a general interest in the strategic management field.

   In retrospect all organizations can ascertain the realized strategic outcomes, both positive and negative, and try to ascribe them to particular circumstances and activities pursued over time. However, there can be a great deal of dispute about how things actually came about the way they did in the organization. When things go well and favorable outcomes are observed, there might be a tendency to rationalize executive decisions and interventions that led the way and the story might assume slightly heroic undertones, giving undue credit to managerial foresight and leadership skills.[1] Conversely, when things turn out for the worse and go awry, it is not uncommon for executives to blame unfavorable outcomes on unforeseeable circumstances that were beyond their control.[2] It is even argued that the introduction of the "black swan" phenomenon, in some cases, has become a convenient way of excusing shortfalls in the fiduciary obligations of senior executives during periods of extreme events and crisis.[3] The rational perspective on strategy making has been criticized at times for being a somewhat old-fashioned and false way to approach and understand how strategy comes about.[4] As the world becomes increasingly dynamic and complex, the strategic plans conceived in the board room and their underlying assumptions become outdated before it is possible to take the necessary steps to realize the strategy.

Some of the most prominent scholars in the field invested much effort in a heated debate about whether planned strategy or ongoing learning processes constitute the better way to approach effective strategy making.[5] Of course, we now know that this was a futile debate, although useful at the time, where neither side could win (or lose) because they both were right (and wrong). In other words, effective organizations reflect upon their future strategy development in advance, involve key decision makers in these deliberations, and use various analytical techniques to help them in this strategic thinking process. However, these organizations are also aware of ongoing changes in their competitive environment, they communicate widely about these observations, and they allow responsive initiatives to emerge from within the organization to deal with unforeseen developments that represent new risks and opportunities for the firm. Hence, the reality is that firms engaged in rational planning efforts fare better than those that do not and even more so among firms operating in highly turbulent business sectors, such as computer products, information technology, and the like. And those that are able to combine their strategic planning efforts with ongoing responsive initiatives throughout the organization fare better still.[6]

While this might appear comforting to some, it begs the question as to how organizations can combine a strategic planning approach with ongoing learning in responsive activities to achieve this idealized state. Here we are short of precise answers. The contemporary views on effective strategy making pay tribute to the firms' so-called *dynamic capabilities* broadly understood as their ability to observe environmental changes and adapt to accommodate these changes – in other words, how the organization is able to sense emerging risks and opportunities and respond effectively to them. This ability hinges upon the observations of many organizational members engaged in different and often specialized activities, where the information somehow is channeled through a central function that interprets what is going on and uses these insights to deploy initiatives that enable the organization to adapt over time.[7] However, the discussion of possible ways in which this might be carried out remains somewhat illusive and is typically explicated through a variety of corporate anecdotes and case-based illustrations.[8] In short, we are on the right track, but continue the search for more concrete proposals regarding effective approaches to responsive strategy making. In this book, we try to frame this challenge in the context of what is known about strategic planning as a rational analytical approach to strategy making and combine this with current insights about emergent strategy processes. Our intention is to outline the contours of such an integrative strategy-making process and thereby hopefully create a better understanding of what it takes to combine planning and emergence in effective strategy development.

The book is organized around six distinct chapters. The first chapter introduces *the strategy concept* and traces the origins of various perspectives from past scholars and learned practitioners that have shaped the strategy field. The second chapter describes *strategy formulation* as a rational analytical process to determine a future strategic path based on prescriptive use of tools for environmental analyses and strategy evaluation. This pretty much outlines what may be referred to as conventional planning, or strategic management, including key theories and model frameworks. Chapter 3 is focused on *strategy execution* and takes a closer look at how corporate entrepreneurship, business venturing, innovation, autonomous initiatives, and power dispersion may help furnish strategic responsiveness that drives strategic emergence as an updating complement to the central planning activities. Chapter 4 outlines *integrative strategy* as a combination of formal planning, ongoing responsive business execution, and interactive strategic control processes. The model is specified across different hierarchical management levels as a set of processes with different clock speeds that interact over time. It explains how short-term lower-level experiential learning processes are convoluted within longer-term tactical and strategic learning processes and how these processes interact with each other. It also introduces regular war-room meetings and strategic issue management as potentially effective interfaces between the long-cycled planning process and short-term responsive strategy initiatives. Chapter 5 focuses on *multinational corporate strategy* where the complex strategic issues associated with diversity of geographical scope and corporate business activities are discussed. Here, the integrative strategy model is extended to consider the challenges associated with headquarter planning and dispersed strategic initiatives in local business entities. Chapter 6 is devoted to *strategic leadership* and considers the executive role in the integrative strategy-making process. The executive influence on corporate values and organizational structure is recognized, as is the responsibility to create a moral impetus that guides corporate activities.

The writing of this book has been inspired by my interest in the strategy field over the past decades and is undeniably influenced by my managerial and executive experiences. Much of the academic heritage is owed to a string of fantastic mentors, scholars of the highest caliber and great human beings, at UNC – Chapel Hill (my alma mater). Many ideas have evolved further through my scholarly engagements at a number of great institutions, and more recently I have been blessed by my association with the productive research environment at the Copenhagen Business School – one of the most dynamic university settings in Europe. Here, I have benefitted from discussions with inspiring colleagues and received valuable feedback from smart students at the acclaimed MSc Programs, the CEMS International Management Program, and the prestigious MBA Program. Many of the underlying themes in the book have been discussed with scholars and executives around the world at various encounters over the years. I truly appreciate all these inspiring conversations and the invaluable feedback derived from them. However, any flaws and errors are all of my own doing.

Notes

1 See, for example, R. M. Pascale, Perspectives on strategy: The true story behind Honda's success, *California Management Review* 26(3): 47–72, 1984, for an account of what really took place as Honda entered the US market in contrast to a report drafted by the Boston Consulting Group (BCG) for the UK government. R. M. Pascale, *Managing on the Edge*, Simon & Schuster: New York, 1990. R. M. Pascale, Reflections on Honda, *California Management Review*, 38(4): 112–117, 1996.

2 See, for example, J. Collins, *How the Mighty Fall: And Why Some Companies Never Give In*, Random House: London, 2009; S. Finkelstein, *Why Smart Executives Fail: And What You Can Learn from Their Mistakes*, Penguin Books: New York, 2003.

3 N. Roubin, S. Mihm, *Crisis Economics: A Crash Course in the Future of Finance*, Penguin Books: London, 2010; N. N. Taleb, *The Black Swan: The Impact of the Highly Improbable*. Allen Lane, Penguin: London, 2007.

4 H. Mintzberg, *The Rise and Fall of Strategic Planning*, Prentice Hall: Upper Saddle River, NJ, 1994.

5 H. Mintzberg, The Design School: Reconsidering the basic premises of strategic management, *Strategic Management Journal* 11(3): 171–195, 1990; I. Ansoff, Critique of Henry Mintzberg's The Design School: Reconsidering the basic premises of strategic management, *Strategic Management Journal* 12(6): 449–461, 1991; H. Mintzberg, Learning 1, Planning 0, Reply to Igor Ansoff, *Strategic Management Journal* 12(6): 463–466, 1991.

6 T. J. Andersen, Strategic planning, autonomous actions and corporate performance, *Long Range Planning* 33(2): 184–200, 2000; T. J. Andersen, Integrating decentralized strategy making and strategic planning processes in dynamic environments, *Journal of Management Studies* 41(8): 1271–1299, 2004.

7 D. J. Teece *et al.*, Dynamic capabilities and strategic management, *Strategic Management Journal* 18(7): 509–533, 1997; D. J. Teece, Explicating dynamic capabilities: The nature and microfoundations of (sustainable) enterprise performance, *Strategic Management Journal* 28: 1319–1350, 2007.

8 See, for example, Helfat *et al.*, *Dynamic Capabilities: Understanding Strategic Change in Organizations*, Blackwell: Malden, MA, 2007.

1 The strategy concept

Learning points

- Discuss diverse strategy perspectives
- Trace the roots of strategic management
- Outline the analytical foundation of the field
- Provide a basis for further studies

Strategy is important. The term *strategy* or *strategic* is used every so often to give things a more imposing flair. Just think about terms such as strategic marketing, strategic operations, strategic human resource management, strategic finance, etc. So, something being "strategic" is supposed to indicate that this thing is more important than every other thing. How this came about is possibly worth a thought. After all, the academic field now commonly referred to as *strategic management* started out as something as mundane as "business policy."

If we ask a group of intelligent people with managerial experience, say a class of MBA students, what their understanding of the term "strategy" is, a substantial portion of them will most likely answer: a plan. While this implies that strategy arises from conscious human deliberation, and that strategy makers think before they act, there are many other ways to interpret how strategy comes about. A reference from a prominent dictionary explains that strategy is "the art of planning operations in war, especially of the movement of armies and navies into favorable positions for fighting." By comparison, a tactic is an "expedient; means of achieving an object".[1] A comparable source notes that strategy is "the art of planning and moving forces, etc. especially in war, politics, etc."[2] Or, strategy is "the science or art of military command as applied to the overall planning and conduct of large-scale combat operations" where a tactic is "an expedient for a goal; a maneuver."[3] The dictionary may also explain that strategy derives from the Greek word *stratēgia*, office of a general, and *stratēgos*, general. In other words, strategy is something that takes place around the highest management echelons, anchored at the general's office and administrative staff, and deals with the ability to move entire armies around for (hopefully) victorious outcomes and (positive) long-lasting effects.

Claus von Clausewitz refers to war as "an act of violence intended to compel our opponent" where "the compulsory submission of the enemy to our will is the ultimate object."[4] This is very much seen from the commander's perspective where military genius and leadership skills support the men under command and help them accommodate unruly battle conditions. He distinguishes between *strategy* as "the use of combats for the object of the war" and *tactics*, which refers to "the use of military forces in combat." Hence, the commander develops the *strategic plan* that settles "when, where, and with what forces a battle is to be delivered." The forces should be disciplined and maintain "a certain strength of body and mind" but otherwise ordinary soldiers are not seen to play any strategic roles in battle. The commander motivates and scales efforts for the battle as "the sum of available means and the strength of the will" are assessed in view of the enemy's position. Similarly, the ancient Chinese warrior philosopher Master Sun argues that the one who uncovers many favorable strategic factors at headquarters before battle will win. Or, as expressed by the classical Taoist *Book of Changes*: "Leaders plan ... consider problems, and prevent them."[5] From this summary discussion, we may discern the contours (and origins) of a strategic planning perspective that to a large extent prevails under the present-day conditions. Hence, we can trace the war-like aspirations to outmaneuver and displace market opponents in contemporary competitive analysis.

Strategy interpreted from the commander's perspective considers the effect of military genius where alert commanders in instantaneous decisiveness can change the course of events. The implied importance ascribed to individual managerial intervention and entrepreneurial initiative is also reflected in the earlier economic literature. Frank Knight ascribes the ability of entrepreneurs to deal with the uncertainty of future business activities as the underlying reason for residual income, or profit, consisting of excess rents obtained over the market price paid for different production inputs. As he explains: "When ... the managerial function comes to require the exercise of judgment involving *liability to error* … the nature of the function is revolutionized; the manager becomes an entrepreneur."[6] And he argues: "His income will normally contain in addition to wages a pure *differential* element designated as 'profit' by the economic theorist."

The importance of individual entrepreneurs to industrial development is echoed by Joseph Schumpeter, a pre-eminent economist in the first half of the twentieth century, who saw economic growth as deriving from innovation and entrepreneurial activities. He explained how industries and organizations continue to change and to challenge stability with profits falling to those who instigate change and build new rewarding businesses. In his own words: "They have … employed existing means of production differently, more appropriately, more advantageously. They have *carried out new combinations*. They are entrepreneurs."[7] In short, the importance of entrepreneurial spirit in corporate leadership has been recognized for quite some time.

The strategy perspective of the supreme commander, or the chief executive in the corporate jargon, continues to permeate the strategy view. The corporate historian Alfred Chandler, who is considered one of the initial founders of corporate strategy, reinforced such a rationalistic top-down logic.[8] He defined strategy as "the determination of the basic long-term goals and objectives of an enterprise, and the adoption of courses of action and the allocation of resources necessary for carrying out these goals."[9] He distinguished between *formulation*, where top management deliberates and outlines the strategy, and *implementation*, where lower-level managers engage to carry out the strategy. This distinction between initial executive strategic considerations and subsequent execution by managers throughout the organization remains a feature of the strategy models depicted in most strategy textbooks today. In his studies, Chandler described how large corporate conglomerates evolved in the US economy during the late nineteenth and early twentieth centuries and noted that the strategic decisions seemed to determine how corporate structures were established to achieve the expected economic payoffs. This observation laid the foundation for the so-called SSP dictum stating that organizations develop strategy before they make structural adjustments to accommodate the strategy, and that the adopted organizational structure subsequently affects performance outcomes. That is, Strategy–Structure–Performance (SSP), and in that order.

Igor Ansoff was a contemporary scholar and another pioneer in early conceptualizations of corporate strategy making and is often considered the "father" of strategic planning. Somewhat inspired by decision theory, he made normative descriptions of the strategy process as it ought to be carried out in large organizations. Ansoff's depiction of strategy was ascribed to "decision rules and guidelines, which guide the process of development of an organization" and he argued that "strategy is one of several sets of decision-making rules for guidance of organizational behavior."[10] Accordingly, he outlined a formal *strategic decision-making process* with sequential steps of objective setting, using gap identification between current and intended firm positions, while assessing alternative solutions to reduce identified *gaps*. He proposed a *cascading approach* whereby preliminary decisions deal with overarching issues, such as corporate purpose, and then decide on business, product, and customer choices before specifying organizational structure, systems, processes, etc. This logical sequence of increasingly detailed analytical steps also implies that the firm eventually specifies functional strategies, e.g., in marketing, operations, finance, etc. Ansoff shaped the idea to assess future growth opportunities along dimensions of geography, market needs, and product/service technologies. He also subtly pointed out that everyday operational problems attract management attention automatically whereas strategic issues remain in the background and thus need conscious effort to attract high-level attention. Hence, strategic focus and initiative is something that must be assumed by (top) management itself, and gaining this is crucial unless the firm wants to be mindlessly driven by events that happen in the surrounding business environment.

The view of strategy as something that derives from the executive echelons is contrasted in Chester Barnard's earlier discussion of the executive role.[11] He defined a *formal organization* as "a system of consciously coordinated activities or forces of two or more persons" and noted that the "willingness of persons to contribute efforts to the cooperative system is indispensable." So, people matter for the way business is carried out in the organization and those people need an acceptable purpose to motivate collaboration and individual contributions. The *informal organization* formed by personal contacts and their operating interactions was deemed equally important for the creation of supportive social norms. That is, authority can be gained only when the internal communication is consistent with an overarching acceptable corporate purpose. This in turn makes strategy making a function of the *morality* in executive governance. Philip Selznick backed this view when he argued: "The setting of institutional *goals* cannot be divorced from the enunciation of governing *principles*. Goal-setting, if it is institutionally meaningful, is framed in the language of character or identity, that is, it tells us what we should 'do' in order to become what we want to 'be'."[12] In short, mission, purpose, and values constitute cornerstones of effective strategy-making processes.

Business policy

The era of *business policy* developed during the 1950s and 1960s from essential management courses that confronted students in business administration with managerial issues involving the entire organization. The business policy classes required students to apply insights from different fields of study, including decision making, organizational behavior, accounting, marketing, operations, corporate finance, etc., in dealing with overarching organizational challenges and complex business problems. This required inclusion of insights from different topical fields across essential functional areas handled in different parts of the firm, often supported by case studies developed for teaching purposes to consider different competencies and concerns, including human resource management and general leadership challenges.[13]

In the words of Kenneth Andrews: "Business policy is the study of the functions and responsibilities of the senior management in a company, the crucial problems that affect the success of the total enterprise, and the decisions that determine its direction, shape its future, and produce the results desired."[14]

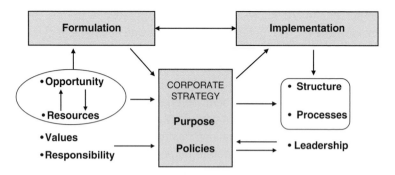

Figure 1.1 Andrews' corporate strategy model. Source: adapted from Andrews (1971/1987)

This implies that it is a primary task for top management to impose coordinated policies that tie the organization together for successful business outcomes and high performance. Hence, Andrews argued: "Corporate strategy is the pattern of decisions in a company that determines and reveals its objectives, purposes, or goals, produces the principal policies and plans for achieving those goals." Here we can trace the relationship to corporate decisions noted by Ansoff as well as the role of purpose emphasized by Barnard. Andrews placed these decisions within a more structured model of corporate strategy making that is quite consistent with the SSP dictum introduced by Chandler. He clearly distinguished between *formulation* as a distinct activity deciding what to do and *implementation* where the decisions subsequently are carried out through concrete actions (Figure 1.1). Strategic alternatives to be decided upon are determined through identification of opportunities and risks in the business environment held against available competences and resources assessed by strengths and weaknesses. This constitutes the precursor to the well-known SWOT analysis. The adaptation of organization structure and internal processes then follows from the execution of strategic decisions as proposed by Chandler. Andrews' original model recognized the importance of personal values and social responsibility and he reasoned: "It is increasingly clear that government regulation is not a good substitute for knowledgeable self-restraint."

The business policy teaching at the Harvard Business School was leading the way at the time and offered one of the dominant textbooks by Learned *et al.*[15] They defined strategy as "the pattern of objectives, purposes, or goals and major policies and plans for achieving these goals, stated in such a way as to define what business the company is in or is to be in and the kind of company it is or is to be."[16] This view of strategy recognized the importance of organizational purpose while emphasizing the conscious development of corporate policies and plans as the means by which to achieve the overarching strategic aims.

Strategic management

By the end of the 1970s two established business policy scholars, Dan Schendel and Charles Hofer, argued that the field needed a new paradigm to advance research and practice in an increasingly dynamic business environment.[17] The business policy perspective was too limiting and they argued: "It is good strategy that ensures the formation, renewal, and survival of the total enterprise." To deal with this, they organized a conference with leading policy scholars at the time to outline the contours of a new field of study they called *strategic management*.[18] The proposed paradigm defined strategic management as "a process that deals with the entrepreneurial work of the organization, with organizational renewal and growth, and more particularly, with developing and utilizing the strategy which is to guide the organization's operations." This paradigm set out a sequential structure of tasks in the strategic management process: goal formation, environmental analysis, strategy formulation, strategy evaluation, strategy implementation, and strategic control (Figure 1.2).

Their main argument for the formal strategic management process was that businesses were facing major environmental changes and therefore needed a more structured approach to better deal with the potential effects of change. As they noted: "Enormous, almost calamitous change has taken place in the rate at which technological, social, political, and economic events occur." So, dynamic changes in surrounding market conditions and higher interdependencies in environmental relations combined with increasingly complex organizational contexts would call for

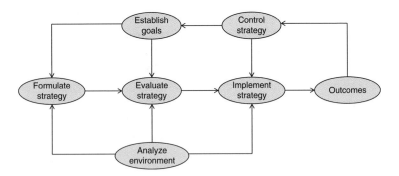

Figure 1.2 A model of the strategic management process. Source: adapted from Schendel and Hofer (1979)

more stringent environmental analysis as a necessary prerequisite to identify alternative strategic choices. Schendel and Hofer observed a need to consciously consider all those environmental factors that are beyond corporate control. In other words, the initial model had more of an external than internal emphasis even though strategy implementation was considered paramount for eventual success.

The areas of social responsibility and governance as well as strategic control were consciously toned down at the conference due to time constraints where only the more central elements of the strategic management process could be accommodated. It is interesting to note that these aspects of the strategic management model have remained relatively subdued areas of research in the strategy field. Different approaches to strategic control have frequently been addressed by scholars in management accounting whereas corporate governance and corporate social responsibility (CSR) gradually have evolved into rather specialized academic disciplines in their own right. However, the corporate strategy model promoted by Andrews (1987) already had a strong focus on purpose, ethics, and responsibility as central areas of concern. He argued: "The presidential functions involved include establishing or presiding over the goal-setting and resource-allocation processes of the company, making or ratifying choices among strategic alternatives, and clarifying and defending the goals of the company against external attack or internal erosion." Similarly, the rational analytical model of the strategic management process outlined by Schendel and Hofer emphasized the importance of strategic control as a way to monitor and assess strategy development in a dynamic business environment. So, while these areas may have received relatively limited attention as the scholarly strategy field evolved, they constitute central elements of the overarching strategy framework.

Another outcome from the discussions at the strategy conference was to identify a clearer distinction between different levels of strategy that remains in use among many scholars today. This strategy framework distinguishes between four strategy levels: enterprise strategy dealing with the overarching role of business in society, corporate strategy dealing with the issue of what business activities the firm should engage in, business strategy dealing with questions about how to compete in a given product market, and functional strategies dealing with the specific strategic requirements imposed on different functional entities (Figure 1.3).

The systematic approach to the strategy-making process formed the basis for a generic strategic management model that continues to be taught in business schools around the world (Figure 1.4). Look to any MBA curriculum in strategic management and you will find this model as a core element of the course that figures prominently in all major strategy textbooks in some version or the other. That is, we typically teach strategy making as deriving from a systematic, orderly process where we first set ambitions and goals, then determine the best strategic position for the firm to achieve these objectives based on rational analytical efforts, stake out and plan the actions required to realize the aims, and then monitor outcomes and adjust actions as required to stay on course. The general perception is that the formal process will integrate all aspects of forthcoming decisions aimed to achieve the overarching goals, i.e., "strategy is a timed sequence of internally consistent and conditional resource allocation decisions that are designed to fulfill an organization's objectives." The process is seen as a way to coordinate future organizational activities and optimize the ability to achieve desired outcomes. Hence, "a strategic planning system (SPS) is a set of interrelated organizational task definitions and procedures for seeing that pertinent information is obtained, forecasts are made, and strategy

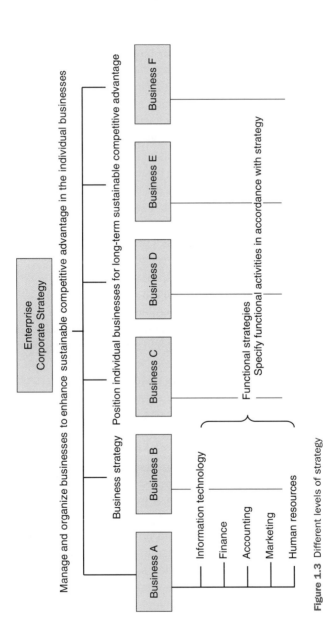

Figure 1.3 Different levels of strategy

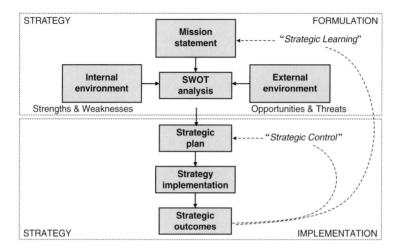

Figure 1.4 The strategic management model

choices are addressed in an integrated, internally consistent, and timely fashion."[19]

Indeed, it is a nice way of presenting strategic management because it sets out a very orderly, logical, and generally accepted way of perceiving how the strategy-making process ideally should proceed (see Box 1.1 *The basic elements of the generic strategic management model*). It is also convenient for teaching because it is possible to gather information about the business environment that allows for a lot of shrewd analyses adopting a variety of models and analytical techniques that can point to new solutions for a future strategy (see Chapter 2). However, everybody who has been involved in practice knows that achieving real results hinges upon an ability to execute and take actions that eventually can realize the strategic intentions. Furthermore, reality is typically more ambiguous than foreseen at the time of planning. The often very intricate dynamic, complex, and interrelated decision processes associated with business execution during implementation are simply too complicated to reproduce in a classroom setting. So, it is often omitted from the learning process and consequently quite a few students graduate in the belief that the generic strategic management model tells the whole truth. As we will see later, the strategic management model has a lot of merit, but it is only part of the story. Strategic planning as a rational analytical approach to strategy making works and it creates value. So, we can teach this strategy approach with a good conscience, realizing, however, that it is not a sufficient condition for effective strategy making that will achieve successful outcomes and superior firm performance.

The strategic management model builds around rational analyses of the external environment and the internal environment to identify potentially superior positions in the market place and to find ways in which firm competencies can be used effectively to assume these positions. This approach also incorporates the Andrews tradition to consider corporate values and guidelines as instrumental in the development of an overarching mission statement. While this generic model has formed the basis for much of the conventional classroom teaching, many nuances and alternative perspectives on the strategy process have emerged to strengthen the underlying analyses.

Market position and resources

Michael Porter introduced his path-breaking analytical frameworks on competitive forces and market positioning around the same time and shaped a period dominated by analyses of industry conditions and their competitive context.[20] Porter's insights were deduced from industrial economics where differences in industry profitability could be explained by the competitive structure within those industries. By extension, managers should try to exploit the underlying economic forces and devise strategies to position the firm in the industry in ways that could improve returns. This arguably entailed basic choices between generic strategies of *cost leadership* based on low prices and *differentiation* based on unique products (Figure 1.5). Cost leadership was aimed at a market posture where the firm exploits superior volume-driven operating efficiencies as lower average costs provide a more powerful competitive position. Differentiation was aimed at a market posture where the competitive position is enhanced by developing unique product and service features, albeit at the expense of standardization economies. The analytical framework was refined

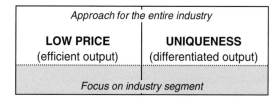

Figure 1.5 The generic strategies proposed by Porter. Source: adapted from Porter (1980/2004)

by outlining a cohesive practical approach for *competitor analysis* and identification of *strategic groups* adhering to comparable strategies. The strategic considerations were extended to consider the effect of *industry life cycle*, arguing that the underlying competitive dynamic depends on whether the industry is under emergence, is in transition to maturity, or is in a phase of decline. This cohesive analytical apparatus was instantaneously adopted as a core element of formal strategy analysis and has proven its durability over time.[21]

In the ongoing development of an analytical framework, Porter deliberated about internal firm conditions that could support *competitive advantage* defined as an ability to outperform close competitors in the industry. In this context, he introduced the *value chain* concept and specified the different components of a linked production process, ranging from purchasing, manufacturing, distribution, marketing, and sales, to after-sales service. He argued that competitive advantage could be associated with specific value chain activities whereby the firm might gain specific economic efficiencies or differentiate its market offerings. In other words, the value chain perspective could be linked to the generic strategies of cost leadership and differentiation.[22]

The idea of firm-specific advantages has some resemblance to Philip Selznick's work on *organization character* where habitual responsive actions are shaped over time as the firm relates to the environment. In this work he coined the term *distinctive competence*. He states: "In studying character we are interested in the distinctive competence or inadequacy that an organization has acquired" and this constitutes an examination of "the commitments that have been accepted in the course of adaptation to internal and external pressures."[23] That is, Selznick entertained the now well-established idea that firms adapt by considering both external and internal environmental conditions as reflected in the strategic management model. He also considered what may be seen as a precursor to the concept of competitive advantage, which is an engrained element of the strategy vocabulary today. The firm perspective on strategy development can also be traced to Edith Penrose, who introduced resources as the essential corporate building blocks. Her basic view was that an organization is comprised of a collection of resources used to supply goods and services in accordance with internal plans. The resources can be tangible things, including land, buildings, equipment, raw materials, semi-finished goods, waste, by-products, and finished goods in stock. However, they also comprise human resources, such as unskilled and skilled labor, administrative and technical staff, and management. The resources can be combined in different ways to serve the firm but Penrose argued: "It is never the *resources* themselves that are the 'inputs' in the production process, but only the *services* that the resources can render. The services yielded by resources are a function of the way in which they are used."[24] This fits neatly with Porter's contention that the way the firm organizes, structures, and manages its internal processes can create competitive advantage. Hence, according to Penrose, the organization uses its own internal resources together with various inputs acquired from outside the firm to produce and sell goods and services in the market at a profit.

This *resource-based view* was revived by Birger Wernerfelt as he introduced a basic framework that links internal resources to different product markets and vice versa as a fundamental way to assess the firm's strategic situation (Figure 1.6).[25] He defined resource as "a strength or weakness of a given firm" and thereby linked the assessment of firm resources to the core element of the strategic management model where internal resources are contrasted to external market threats and opportunities. The new thing was the inside-out perspective that contrasted with the outside-in perspective enhanced by Porter's work. However, the combination of the two views essentially corresponds to and extends the SWOT analytical approach practiced by Andrews and others. This internal look at corporate value creation was developed and refined

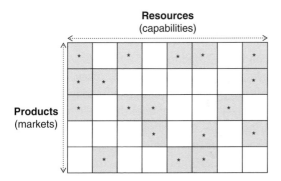

Figure 1.6 The firm's resource–product matrix. Source: adapted from Wernerfelt (1984)

by Jay Barney. The positioning view assumes that the firm can maneuver around the competitive forces in the industry and thereby create durable excess return conditions for the firm. However, this depends on how effectively the needed resources are deployed to this end. Hence, it is argued that the efficient acquisition and deployment of resources from the so-called *strategic factor market* to implement a given strategy is a source of competitive advantage (see Box 1.2 *The economic logics of the market positioning and resource-based perspectives*). If the underlying resources are valuable, relatively rare, hard to imitate, and can be organized for economic exploitation, then the competitive advantage becomes easier to *sustain* over time. Therefore, the analysis of the firm's internal skills and competencies provides a good basis for assessing the firm's long-term strategic viability.[26]

The focus on firm resources has been extended with a *knowledge-based* perspective considering that the increasing need for specialization and development of organizational capabilities depends on knowledge and an ability to integrate and deploy this knowledge within the organization. To the extent specific knowledge as an essential resource resides with individual employees, knowledge management as a strategic discipline will pose new governance challenges for corporate executives because the employees then effectively control important parts of the knowledge base that supports the value-creating activities in the firm.[27]

Alternative views

The preceding sections include and refer to a number of scholarly contributions that have provided essential inputs toward the development of the strategy concepts that prevail today. This should provide general insights into some of the basic roots of the field and its evolving nature. It outlines the core elements of the generic strategic management model that continues to be practiced and explains how it evolved over time. This model represents a cohesive approach to strategy formulation and implementation that suggests a dynamic process of ongoing monitoring and updating of activities in a strategic control process. The generic model framework can be presented in different ways, often guided by a genuine aim to discuss the strategy process more eloquently or to personalize the presentation of strategy making. In most cases, however, the proposed framework remains true to the basic principles of the strategic management model. Hence, an alternate form of the strategy process could look like the model shown in Figure 1.7.[28] Whereas this model may appear different from the generic strategic management model, it pretty much contains the same elements. The real difference is that the sequential steps of the model are presented sideways, left to right, as opposed to horizontally, top to bottom. So, the models

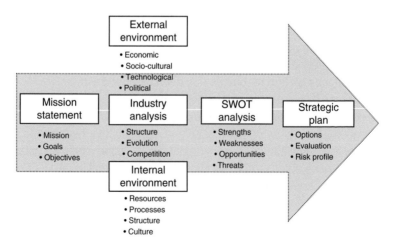

Figure 1.7 Alternate forms of the strategy model. Source: inspired by De Kluyver (2000)

are largely identical and merely represent variations of the same basic framework. When studying other strategy textbooks, it is noticeable that most of them adopt the generic strategy model and discuss the strategy process from that same vantage point. This book is no exception, but we will extend this framework later.

The strategic management model follows a logical sequence of steps analyzing the environmental context and formulating an "optimal" strategy for subsequent pursuit through orderly implementation as organizational members execute the strategic steps outlined in the strategic plan. That is, we assume that top management is in a position whereby they can stipulate a future strategic path and devise a series of corporate actions that will make the planned intentions come true. Similarly, when we try to analyze organizational developments after the fact, we often assume that the observed corporate actions arose on the basis of an initial grand plan brought to life in the executive suite. However, when strategy development has been studied as *a pattern in a stream of decisions* it has often uncovered a less orderly amalgam of strategic events.[29] Hence, the reality is that much of the strategy as developed in the strategic planning process is never realized by the organization because environmental conditions change or initial assumptions turn out not to hold true as the organization starts to execute the strategic action steps. That is, a substantial part of the *intended strategy* may end up as *unrealized strategy* (Figure 1.8). Yet an observant and responsive organization will be able to react to

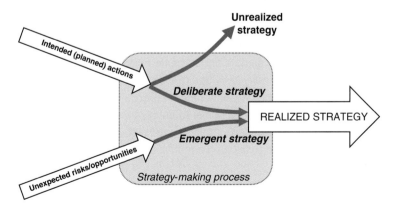

Figure 1.8 Deliberate and emergent strategy. Source: adapted from Mintzberg (1978)

new environmental developments as they unfold, which often may occur rather abruptly and unexpectedly. To the extent the firm is able to respond to the changing circumstances and exploit new business opportunities that arise from shifts in competitive conditions, the effects from these responsive actions can be referred to as *emergent strategy*. Hence, the strategic outcomes observed after the fact, i.e., the *realized strategy*, will comprise elements of the *deliberate strategy* devised in the strategic planning process together with strategic initiatives that emerged from implementation or ongoing execution of business activities. This interplay between intended and realized strategy may help us better understand the complexity of the strategy-making process.

By perceiving strategy as a pattern of decisions and ensuing (resource-committing) actions, we allow for a more nuanced view of how strategy actually happens. One might argue that the distinction between *formulation* and *implementation* is a false or at least an incomplete depiction of what is going on, because once the organization starts to take action to fulfill and realize the strategic intentions, the underlying assumptions and expected effects are confronted with the reality of a dynamic market place. The environmental context often turns out to react and behave differently from expectations and thereby provides opportunities for the organization to observe, learn, and experiment along the way. Hence, an *organizational learning* perspective could be a relevant approach to complement the conventional planning model considering the fact that specialized knowledge residing among the human resources in the firm might be paramount for effective execution. It tries to explain how an organization can learn about and adapt to changing conditions and unexpected events, probably entailing an ability to sense weak signals about subtle environmental changes and using them to modify activities in the organization in ways that accommodate the new conditions. This may suggest an *information-processing* perspective to better understand how organizational actors absorb, analyze, interpret, monitor, store, and disseminate knowledge flows in effective strategic decision-making processes that drive responsive actions in the firm.

In other words, strategy can also be interpreted as the result of *managerial decisions* taking place across different hierarchical levels and functional areas in the firm where the resulting actions have consequences and generate organizational outcomes over time that can be observed in retrospection. From this perspective it is apparent that the underlying decision-making processes are likely to be influenced by the views and beliefs held by the various organizational decision makers, i.e., the *cognition* of influential managers will make a difference. This provides a basis for studying effective decision making in a strategic management context. It also provides the foundation for *institutional theory*, where cognition and culture explain organizational (and strategic) behavior based on the idea that to succeed, firms must conform to prevailing norms and beliefs in a given business environment.[30] This relates to a *resource dependency* perspective that sees organizations as embedded in interdependent networks of social relationships where managers act to gain and preserve access to resources important for the firm.[31] The analysis of organizational actions as a way to secure needed resources considers effects of power structure, political influence, negotiation strengths, etc., and thus provides a link between concerns for market positions, internal competencies, and managerial behaviors. The perspective discards the idea of strategic decision makers as rational actors often subsumed in classical economics and normative strategy models.

Herbert Simon, the influential social scientist (and so far the only non-economist to receive the Nobel price in economics), coined the term *bounded rationality*. The term reflects the view that decision makers usually act on incomplete information where emotions can cloud their judgment as they act under circumstances that are a far cry from the perfect information or actuarial clarity implied by rationalistic decision models. That is, strategic decisions are circumscribed by many uncertainties. When decisions are based on anticipated future consequences coupled with a poor understanding of the alternatives available to the firm, it becomes difficult and possibly meaningless to optimize decision outcomes. Instead, decision makers engage in *satisficing* behavior with an aim of reaching acceptable interim decision outcomes that satisfy or exceed predetermined performance hurdles. So, Simon is confronting us with the reality of organizational decision making and proposes a theoretical framework to understand and describe these situational contexts. In his own words: "It is precisely in the real world where human behavior is *intendedly* rational, but only *boundedly* so, that there is room for a genuine theory of organization and administration."[32]

Another issue related to strategic decision making is the fact that managers act on behalf of business owners, or policy communities, that often are distant from the specific organizational decision situations. In financial economics this frames the so-called *principal–agent problem* created by the separation of shareholders in limited companies from the day-to-day managerial decisions taken by professional managers in the firm. The separation between ownership and resource-committing decisions can give rise to *asymmetric information flows*, where hired managers in principle can exploit insights gained on the job for their own benefit at the expense of the owners, thereby creating potential problems of *moral hazards* and conflicts of interest.[33] In finance, this issue is typically discussed as a concern between corporate executives and the shareholders.[34] However, from a strategy perspective, the potential *agency conflicts* can be extended to include several other managerial layers, including the board of directors, line and middle managers, functional managers, and indeed any employee in charge of essential tasks and possessing important knowledge. A common solution is to try to align the interests of the agents that act on behalf of the firm with those of the actual owners (principals). This might comprise commissions, performance pay, profit sharing, stock ownership, and other incentives as well as performance monitoring and behavioral supervision by managers in the corporate hierarchy. Hence, the agency problem is relevant in most employee relationships and particularly so in situations where authority and decision power is delegated.

Considering the many potential limitations to rational decision making and optimal strategic behavior, some organizational views give limited credence to models of conscious strategy making as executives often seem to adhere to prevailing norms in their business environment. Instead, strategy development might be better understood in the context of evolutionary theory as applied in the natural sciences to uncover the dynamics of populations as they interact with the environment over time. This *population ecology* perspective adopts a longitudinal view of organizations characterized by firm *births* (start-ups, spin-offs, etc.) and *deaths* (bankruptcies, restructurings, etc.) within a given industry (population). It can also be extended to consider *migration* of firms between different industries (populations). Hence, new firms arise from entrepreneurial activities where the "genetic code" consists of competencies, routines, market offerings, and knowledge elements, possibly developed in other organizations, and then agglomerated in start-ups pursuing new business concepts. This may happen, for example, when an experienced employee becomes frustrated with corporate reluctance to use his innovative concept and therefore starts his own firm to pursue this business opportunity. If the venture is well received in the surrounding environment, it will be successful and will continue to be so as long as the concept satisfies basic needs in demand. If the business runs into trouble because the products, services, or operations become obsolete and outdated, the firm may cease to exist as an independent entity. However, the assets of the restructured firm usually prevail where many resources and competencies are carried forward and become part of existing corporate businesses or form new start-ups. Strategic renewal is thus shaped by entrepreneurial activities and the competitive environment acts as a selection mechanism where only the successful firms survive as time goes by.[35] That is, strategy as conscious decision making plays a limited role here.

This diversity of perspectives has inspired a particular view of strategy as something people do in organizations in some form or another possibly circumscribed by behavioral rituals around annual planning sessions, strategic retreats, and the like. Here strategy derives from complex processes that often involve many individuals throughout the organization rather than from one-off decisions by top management that will then permeate down through the organization. This view is often referred to as *strategy as practice* and has as a central aim to uncover how strategy actually happens in organizations and thereby creates a better description of the often highly convoluted organizational processes we refer to as corporate strategy making.[36] In short, strategic management is not simple but more often than not a complicated amalgam of activities influenced and affected simultaneously by many different factors. Hence, the alternative ways to see strategy can provide greater nuance as we try to interpret what is going on, and it may thereby help the analyst better understand what it takes to make strategy happen by considering different views.

Conclusion

Strategic management is conceived from the perspective of top management to consider how business and functional entities can work together to achieve sustainable, long-term results for the entire organization. We trace the historical roots of strategy from military affairs where the general uses his armies to dominate his adversaries. Strategy as a field evolved from business policy courses where management students were challenged in a last integrative course before graduation to think about the challenges associated with organizational success where many specialized entities and individuals must work together. This will typically require the integration of functional activities toward a common goal and coordination of organizational activities in efficient execution.

Hence, strategic management is introduced as a rational analytical process aimed at identifying viable market opportunities and deploying company resources to exploit those opportunities and thereby gain a stronger market position for the firm. While market positioning can be seen as a major strategic aim, the deployment of company resources toward that end will challenge the involvement of people across the organization to take the actions necessary to achieve the overarching strategic goals and in doing so they must gain new insights and learn about what can work and adapt activities to ensure that the organization is effectively moving toward the stated objectives. The complexity of this strategic adaptation process has inspired a variety of alternative views to understand many particular aspects of the strategy-making process.[37] By engaging alternative views and considering different angles to the strategy-making process, we may be able to triangulate our analysis by incorporating multiple aspects to better understand how things work.

While this chapter has provided a general background for strategic management, the next chapter will focus on how different types of analyses can support the strategy-making process, including appropriate tools and model frameworks for effective strategy analysis.

Box 1.1 The basic elements of the generic strategic management model

Mission statement: The mission statement should give direction for all organizational activities and arguably contains three things: (1) a basic corporate purpose explaining why the organization exists, (2) aspirations and goals to ideally be achieved by the organization, and (3) a set of values and guidelines setting a yardstick for preferred organizational behavior.

External analysis: Tries to understand the environmental context typically construed at three levels: (1) the macro-environment with political, economic, social, and technological trends that can affect general business conditions, (2) the competitive dynamic in the specific industry (or network of industries) where the firm conducts business, and (3) assessing performance compared with that of close (and potential) competitors. This will be able to say something about how the competitive position can support economic value and how this may change over time under uncertain external conditions.

Internal analysis: Takes an inward look to understand the conditions under which the firm performs its business transactions and may include an overview of organizational structure, governance, management and decision practices, operational and innovation processes, support functions, information and communication systems, reporting and control frameworks, etc. The analysis may provide an overview of productive assets, competencies, and know-how (*resources*) essential to corporate value creation.

SWOT analysis: Combines internal analysis (strengths, weaknesses) with external analysis (opportunities, threats) and provides a basis for understanding how the competitive context and deployment of firm resources may support high performance over longer time for *sustainable competitive advantage*. It can also identify gaps between strengths/weaknesses and between opportunities/threats that need attention while serving as an analytical framework to identify alternative strategies and their requirements. It can serve as a platform for strategic decisions and the choice of a particular strategic path.

Strategic plan: Once the corporate decision makers have chosen a specific strategic path, the ensuing planning process should outline the necessary steps to be taken by the organization to reach the new strategic position. The plan can contain detailed actions for functional entities and may contain time schedules, goal specifications, and expected outcomes from actions.

Strategy implementation: Once the plan is developed it must be executed by the organization as relevant actors in the firm take concrete actions. The plan is communicated and actions are taken in accordance with the plans, although modifications must be envisioned if prior assumptions need reconsideration and if environmental conditions develop in a direction different from initial expectations.

Strategy outcomes: The initial planning and subsequent execution of decisions taken during implementation lead to strategic actions that affect the firm's market position and operating efficiencies. The performance effects of these actions constitute the outcomes of the preceding strategy process.

Strategic control: The strategic outcomes registered after the strategic implementation phase has been accomplished can be compared with the initial strategic aims in the strategic plan to identify discrepancies and assess the possible causes for them. This follow-up process can be used to consider whether there is a need for adjustments to the strategic action plans, with the aim of getting closer to the strategic aims established from the outset.

Strategic learning: If the strategic outcomes are substantially different from the planned aims due to fundamental changes in assumptions and expectations it may lead to rethinking of the entire strategy. This way the organization can learn from potential discrepancies between realized and expected outcomes to adjust the strategic path.

Box 1.2 The economic logics of the market positioning and resource-based perspectives

According to classical economic theory, the price (P) and quantity (Q) of a product exchanged in the market are determined by aggregate supply and demand in the market. The downward-sloping demand curve (D) reflects the collective trade-off between the desired quantities of the good at different price levels. The upward-sloping supply curve (S) reflects diminishing returns of resource inputs and that firms have different production efficiencies. A higher quantity of the supplied good requires delivery from the next most efficient supplier, i.e., as the supplied quantity increases, so does the price because more and more marginal producers are invited into the market. That is, under *perfect competition* the least efficient firm supplying the industry will not make any excess returns but will receive only revenues sufficient to pay for the productive inputs, e.g., land, labor, and capital, required in the production process. However, under *monopolistic conditions* the only firm in the industry to supply the good can set the price so as to optimize its profit. That is, where the marginal cost (MC) is equal to the marginal revenue (MR). The latter position is clearly more attractive.

Industry structure and competitive forces: The *market positioning* strategy is based on the idea that the firm can deal with counterparts in the economy to enhance the monopolistic traits of the firm's competitive position. For example, securing sole access to an important input for production may create such an advantage, while devising the product in ways that make customers more dependent is another way, as is reducing compatibility with alternative products. Similarly, the firm could try to *differentiate* its products and make them truly unique, which would tend to make the firm a sole supplier of a particular good or service. In these cases, the firm would try to create conditions of a distinct demand curve that resembles monopoly with the purpose of gaining a higher return.

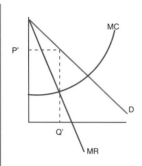

The value creation of resources: The *resource-based* strategy is supported by the idea that the firm can hone its resources and thereby realize excess returns through unique economic efficiencies that create a durable position of excess returns beyond that of most other firms in the industry. The acquisition, development, and deployment of firm-specific resources are often part of a *path-dependent* process where the generation of new resources evolves from a prior set of resources in use. So, a strong resource position with positive economic efficiencies can be extended to subsequent periods into the future. If the underlying development process is complex and hard to emulate, it can lead to sustainable effects of excess economic returns.

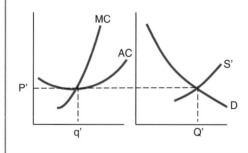

Notes

1 A. S. Hornsby, *Oxford Advanced Learner's Dictionary of Current English,* Oxford University Press, 1974.
2 T. McArthur, *Longman Lexicon of Contemporary English,* Longman: Harlow, 1981.

3 W. Morris (ed.), *The Houghton Mifflin Canadian Dictionary of the English Language*, Houghton Mifflin Canada: Markham, Ontario, 1980.

4 C. von Clausewitz, *On War*, Wordsworth Classics: London, 1997 (written until his death in 1831).

5 Sun Tsu, *The Art of War*, Shambhala Publications: Boston, MA, 2005, translated by Thomas Cleary (first compiled well over 2,000 years ago).

6 F. H. Knight, *Risk, Uncertainty and Profit*, Dover Publications: Mineola, NY, 2006 (originally published in 1921).

7 J. A. Schumpeter, *The Theory of Economic Development: An Inquiry into Profits, Capital, Credit, Interest, and the Business Cycle*, Transaction Publishers: New Brunswick, NJ, 2008 (originally published in 1934).

8 R. Whittington, Alfred Chandler, founder of strategy: Lost tradition and renewed inspiration, *Business History Review* 82(2): 267–277, 2008.

9 A. D. Chandler Jr., *Strategy and Structure: Chapters in the History of Industrial Enterprise*, The MIT Press: Cambridge, MA, 1990 (first published in 1962).

10 I. Ansoff, *Corporate Strategy* (update edition), Penguin Books: London, 1987 (first published by McGraw-Hill in 1965).

11 C. I. Barnard, *The Functions of the Executive* (thirtieth anniversary edition), Harvard University Press: Cambridge, MA, 1968 (first published in 1938).

12 P. Selznick, *Leadership in Administration: A Sociological Interpretation* (California Paperback Edition), University of California Press: Berkeley, CA, 1984 (first published by Harper & Row in 1957).

13 The *business policy and planning* division became an active disciplinary home base for members of the Academy of Management in the 1970s within this scholarly area and has soared in popularity and importance ever since.

14 K. R. Andrews, *The Concept of Corporate Strategy* (custom edition), McGraw-Hill: New York, 1987 (originally published in 1971).

15 These case-based course activities became the role model for many educational institutions where business policy was included as a required capstone course to be completed by all business students before graduation.

16 E. Learned *et al.*, *Business Policy: Text and Cases*, Irwin: Homewood, IL, 1965.

17 D. Schendel, C. Hofer, *Strategic Management: A New View of Business Policy and Planning*, Little, Brown: Boston, MA, 1979.

18 The group included many scholars who have had a profound influence on the strategic management field, e.g., Igor Ansoff, Joseph Bower, John Child, Yves Doz, John Grant, Peter Lorange, Ian McMillan, Henry Mintzberg, James Utterback, and Richard Rumelt, among others.

19 J. H. Grant, W. R. King, *The Logic of Strategic Planning*, Little, Brown and Company: Boston, MA, 1982.

20 M. E. Porter, How competitive forces shape strategy, *Harvard Business Review* 55(2): 137–145, 1979.

21 M. E. Porter, *Competitive Strategy: Techniques for Analyzing Industries and Competitors* (export edition), Free Press: New York, 2004 (first published in 1980). M. E. Porter, The five competitive forces that shape strategy, *Harvard Business Review* 86(1): 78–93, 2008.

22 M. E. Porter, *Competitive Advantage: Creating and Sustaining Superior Performance*, Free Press: New York, 1985.

23 P. Selznick, *Leadership in Administration: A Sociological Interpretation* (California Paperback Edition), University of California Press: Berkeley, CA, 1984 (first published by Harper & Row in 1957).

24 E. Penrose, *The Theory of the Growth of the Firm* (fourth edn.), Oxford University Press: Oxford, 2009 (first published in 1959).

25 B. Wernerfelt, A resource-based view of the firm, *Strategic Management Journal* 5: 171–180, 1984.

26 J. B. Barney, Strategic factor markets: Expectations, luck, and business strategy, *Management Science* 32(19): 1231–1241, 1986; J. B. Barney, Firm resources and sustained competitive advantage, *Journal of Management* 17(1): 99–120, 1991; J. B. Barney, *Gaining and Sustaining Competitive Advantage*, Addison-Wesley, Reading, MA, 1997.

27 R. M. Grant, Toward a knowledge-based theory of the firm, *Strategic Management Journal* 17 (winter special issue): 109–122, 1996.

28 Partially inspired by a strategy model presented in C. A. De Kluyver, *Strategic Thinking: An Executive Perspective*, Prentice Hall: Upper Saddle River, NJ, 2000.

29 H. Mintzberg, Patterns in strategy formation, *Management Science* 24(9): 934–948, 1978; H. Mintzberg, J. A. Waters, Of strategies, deliberate and emergent, *Strategic Management Journal* 6: 257–272, 1985.

30 W. R. Scott, G. F. Davis, *Organizations and Organizing: Rational, Natural, and Open Systems Perspectives*, Pearson Education: Upper Saddle River, NJ, 2007.

31 J. Pfeffer, G. R. Salancik, *The External Control of Organizations: A Resource Dependence Perspective*, Stanford Business Classics: Stanford, CA, 2003 (first published in 1978).

32 H. A. Simon, *Administrative Behavior: A Study of Decision-Making Processes in Administrative Organizations* (fourth edn.), Free Press: New York, 1997 (first published in 1945).

33 M. Jensen, W. Meckling, Theory of the firm: Managerial behavior, agency costs, and ownership structure, *Journal of Financial Economics* 3(3): 305–360, 1976.

34 In fact, there is potentially a two-tiered conflict because the board of directors act on behalf of the shareholders, and the executive management act on behalf of the board of directors. See, for example, T. Clarke, *International Corporate Governance: A Comparative Approach*, Routledge: London, 2007.

35 H. Kaufman, *Time, Chance, and Organization: Natural Selection in a Perilous Environment* (second edn.), Chatham House: Chatham, NJ, 1991.

36 G. Johnson *et al.*, *Strategy as Practice: Research Directions and Resources*, Cambridge University Press, 2007.

37 H. Mintzberg *et al.*, *Strategy Safari: Your Complete Guide through the Wilds of Strategic Management* (second edn.), FT Prentice Hall: Harlow, 2009.

2 Strategy formulation

Learning points

- Outline the core elements of a mission statement
- Discuss how to assess the environmental dynamics
- Deploy the conventional strategy-formulation process
- Extend the generic strategic management model
- Prepare the strategy-execution plans

The previous chapter explained the historical roots of the strategy concept and gave the background for the generic strategic management model that continues to permeate the field. One of the essential premises of this strategy model is that management is normative and so managers will try to engage in rational decision making. Accordingly, the formal strategy-making process first engages in thorough analyses of business conditions to identify a favorable strategic position to aim for and subsequently develops a plan intended to move the organization toward that position. This set of activities is often called *strategy formulation*. For this purpose we use an analytical approach to uncover alternative strategic options available to the firm as the basis for choosing a suitable path forward.[1] Once a decision is made about a desired strategic position, management will plan the actions necessary to achieve the desired strategic outcomes. Once such a plan of action has been deliberated, the organization supposedly takes action in accordance with the plan to realize the specified aims. This phase is often referred to as *strategy implementation*. The underlying assumption here is that we can make a clear distinction between the advance thinking that goes into the forward-looking planning activities and the subsequent execution of actions as stipulated in the plan. We will address and challenge this assumption in Chapter 3. However, the current chapter will confine discussions around the so-called formulation phase, where various analytical techniques can help assess the business environment that circumscribes the firm.

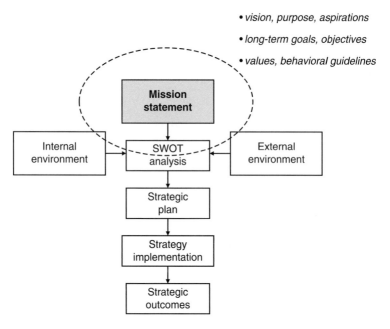

Figure 2.1 Developing the mission statement in the strategy model

As shown in the strategic management model introduced in Chapter 1, formal strategy formulation is made up of a number of sequential analytical steps that include developing a mission statement, completing an analysis of the external competitive environment and the firm's internal organizational environment, SWOT (and TOWS) analyses to assess market opportunities, and related risks to outline viable strategic alternatives for executive consideration (Figure 2.1). The outline of a future strategic direction should lead to a strategic plan that stipulates the actions required to implement the strategic choice successfully throughout the organization and move the firm toward the desired position. We will discuss each of these steps.

Mission statement

It is argued that organizations should develop a mission statement comprised of a number of core elements: (1) an overarching vision for the business and *purpose* for the activities pursued by the organization setting aspirations for future effort, (2) a set of long-term *goals* that focuses on organizational activities with tangible objectives to aim for, and (3) a summary of essential corporate *values* that serve as guidelines for appropriate behaviors and business conduct when individuals in the firm interact with important stakeholders.[2] The prescriptive content of the mission statement is at times embedded in rather imprecise wording and is somewhat equivocal in its form. Accordingly, one can find a variety of mission statements when searching across official company websites, but they usually reflect and capture some of the essential ingredients mentioned above. Similarly, there is no clear recipe for the development of a mission statement, although the contents typically arise from deliberations among a relatively narrow group of corporate executives where some parts may be exposed to open hearings and wider discussions throughout the organization.

The theoretical foundation for a formal mission statement can be found in the concept of *values-based management* where moral principles provide the foundation for core values and standards that can guide organizational tasks, particularly when the company is dealing with complex and unexpected situations.[3] A major premise for this view is that the values heeded by organizational members will have a significant impact on outcomes from organizational activities as individual employees deal head on with the firm's many counterparts when they carry out the daily business transactions. The wider implications of this are outlined in the ideas around stakeholder theory, where a *stakeholder* is defined as "any group or individual who can affect, or is affected by, the achievement of a corporation's purpose."[4] From this perspective all activities pursued by the firm are embedded in co-evolutionary developments with customers, suppliers, employees, owners, government, and society at large. Strong customer relationships evolve when the firm can provide incremental value in its products and services, suppliers engage because they value the relationship, employees become engaged and receive a steady salary, owners are rewarded with a fair return on investment and take pride in corporate achievements, while the firm benefits from public investments in infrastructure, education, health care, etc., and the government receives tax revenues from income and profits. Hence, the various stakeholders gain from interdependent relationships with no real conflicts between these groups because they rely on each other for fruitful business interaction. In short, "business is about how customers, suppliers, employees, financiers (stockholders, bondholders, banks, etc.), communities, and managers interact and create value."[5] Hence, good performance outcomes very much depend on the firm's ability to make appropriate consideration for and build strong relationships with its core stakeholders.

We can think of a number of rationales that can explain why a mission statement may have a positive influence on corporate performance:

- It clarifies the overarching organizational aims that motivate and inspire employees by setting attractive aspirations for individual efforts.
- It sets a clear direction for organizational activities and establishes a focus that facilitates joint efforts toward predetermined long-term goals.
- It provides a stronger basis for informal coordination through mutual adjustment of functional activities in accordance with overarching goals.
- It reduces emphasis on organizational activities that otherwise might develop into digressions from the general purpose of the firm.
- It provides guidance for frontline employees to act in ways that ensure strong and valuable stakeholder relationships and avoid costly conflicts.
- It provides general direction for adaptive responses taken throughout the organization when confronted with unexpected and unforeseen conditions.

While no conclusive empirical studies can show that use of mission statements will always create value, there is a great deal of evidence to suggest that successful firms have been driven by strong ideologies. Their core values were shared throughout the organization and could help them adapt during periods of environmental change.[6] We recognize some of these traits from established firms, such as A. P. Moller – Maersk, Bayer, Mars,

Novo Nordisk, and many others (see Box 2.1 *Corporate value statements – three examples*). For example, the Maersk Principles of Conduct were introduced as the company continued its global expansion to support employees located in different places around the world when they interact on a day-to-day basis with local colleagues, customers, suppliers, investors, and communities.[7] The core argument is simply that *good behavior is good business*. In the words of Nils Smedegaard Andersen, CEO: "We believe that high business standards play a significant role in ensuring our continued growth and success."[8] Successful firms seem to have strong values that are widely shared among employees throughout the organization and many of the underlying attitudes and beliefs about good business conduct and strategic goals have been passed on from one generation to the next. As an example, the A. P. Moller – Maersk Group recognizes that their core values "are closely linked to our founder, Mr. Arnold Peter Møller, and his son, Mr. Mærsk McKinney Møller, and they form our guiding principles for behavior, decisions and interaction."[9] Yet, while this characteristic is associated with successful firms, it obviously cannot guarantee future success.

Hewlett-Packard is another global company in a completely different industry that historically has shown a remarkable ability to transform itself successfully as business conditions have changed in the dynamic technology industry. The apparent success of this innovation-driven adaptive capability may rely on the fact that the company adhered to "high ethical standards, humane treatment of employees, and a commitment to innovation as the source of growth."[10] The unique beliefs that permeated the company were probably conducive to employee involvement and a willingness, possibly a drive, to strive toward new and better opportunities for the firm. As explained by Packard himself: "We feel our objectives can best be achieved by people who understand what they are trying to do and can utilize their own capabilities to do them." At the same time, the corporate leadership promoted responsible behaviors: "Whenever we discuss overall company objectives, we touch our responsibility to the community at large. Those things which the institutions in our community provide, the general sense of moral values, the general character of people … are things which we accept and are extremely important in the operation of an organization like this."[11] Also, a minimum required financial return was not considered a corporate goal in its own right but was the fruit of good products and services. In Packard's own words: "Profit is the measure of our contribution to our customers – it is a measure of what our customers are willing to pay us over and above the actual cost of an instrument." So, corporate values seem to matter a great deal: "Enduring great companies preserve their core values and purpose while their business strategies and operating practices endlessly adapt to a changing world."[12]

The mission statement should have durable qualities and thereby serve as a foundation to guide corporate activities over longer periods of time. The implication is that the contents should lay out the foundation that explains the firm's overarching purpose, or raison d'être, and the core values that drive the business toward admirable goals and aspirations for noble outcomes. The general purpose, principles, and goals should be expressed in fairly broad terms, without detailing specific actions, and thus allow for redirection of activities when needed while retaining flexibility to respond if and when conditions change. This captures some of the ideas behind the concept of *logical incrementalism* where strategy making remains flexible and adaptive to new challenges.[13] Here the firm expresses its goals in general terms that can be interpreted fairly broadly, which will allow senior management to discuss a wider set of innovative solutions with key people in the organization and take appropriate actions in response to threats and opportunities as and when they arise. The ability to maintain a longer-term focus in the organization's general aspirations and at the same time retain an ability to generate innovative responses is particularly important for firms operating in turbulent environments. For example, in knowledge-intensive, innovation-based industries, new products, services, practices, and technologies appear with high frequency and often unexpectedly, and the industry structure at times may change rather abruptly. It is argued that the professionals in knowledge-intensive firms execute the strategy and therefore must buy into the core values of the firm so they permeate all decisions and actions.[14] Under these circumstances the mission statement may play a particularly important role (see Box 2.2 *A mission statement – an example*).[15]

However, the writing of formal mission, vision, and value statements is not sufficient to ensure corporate success – it must be an engrained part of all organizational activities and embedded in the way every employee behaves in daily interactions. Making official statements without true anchoring within the organization is superficial and serves only to mislead the public. According to Edgar Schein, the corporate culture is formed by common sharing of beliefs, attitudes, values, and assumptions among organizational members that distinguish them from people in other groups and firms.[16] It is difficult to change embedded corporate values and requires that senior management challenges the validity and relevance of shared beliefs, e.g., by introducing troubling data and facts, and thereby opens up for new interpretations. Similarly, the introduction of new corporate values requires the direct involvement and support from senior management to create common understanding and a vision to be shared by all employees. This may be reinforced by frequent references to the mission and use of illustrative anecdotes at internal meetings throughout the organization.

Hence, the values and beliefs that undergird organizational behaviors are part of a corporate culture possibly with deep historical roots that are hard to change and mold. As a corollary to this, the true corporate values may be hidden underneath the surface and could differ substantially from claims in official documents and public remarks made at special occasions. So, one should be cognizant of the fact that occasionally there can be wide discrepancies between official claims and what actually happens in the organization (see Box 2.3 *Failing corporate conduct – three examples*). Whereas it can be difficult to change corporate values, it is probably worth striving toward a high degree of correspondence between official policies and the actual doings within the organization.

External analysis

We know that firm performance is affected by the conditions provided by the surrounding business environment.[17] Hence, the next step in the strategy-formulation process is to assess the firm's location in the external environment as it forms the conditions under which the business operates and uncover threats and opportunities that can affect performance outcomes and thereby point to possible future strategic actions (Figure 2.2). We can conceive of the external environment as consisting of two analytical spheres: (1) exogenous environmental conditions made up by the macro-economic trends and socio-political developments that affect business activities in general, and (2) industry-specific conditions pertaining to the firm's particular competitive context.

The assessment of *exogenous environmental conditions* considers the potential influences of political, economic, social, and technological developments, popularly referred to as PEST analysis. Political factors encompass government policies, legislative initiatives, confrontation, and divergence among lawmakers that may affect the conduct of business and economic prospects in general. These considerations will include areas such as new institutions, political unions, international trade agreements, currency interventions, national elections, transnational conflicts, civil unrest, and so forth. By economic conditions we mean things such as demand for goods and services, growth prospects, factor cost developments, relative price changes, and volatility of financial rates. By social conditions we think of developments in demographics, demand patterns, lifestyles, social structures, age distributions, educational levels, and so forth. By technological conditions we mean the ways in which products and services are developed, produced, and delivered, and ways of organizing and conducting business, as well as inventions and scientific progress, e.g., in biotechnology, chemicals, medicine, digital processing, internet-based facilitation, etc. This framework constitutes more of a checklist of environmental areas that one should remember to consider in the analysis than a formal analytical model. Sometimes the list is extended by environmental (or ecological) issues, including economic externalities such as pollution, greenhouse gasses and CO_2 emission, global warming, sustainability and concerns for biodiversity, recycling, sustainability, etc.[18] In this case the framework is typically referred to as STEEP analysis where the acronyms are expanded and reshuffled a bit. At other times the

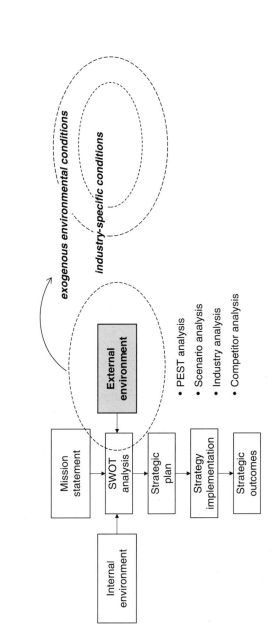

Figure 2.2 Analysis of the external environment in the strategy model

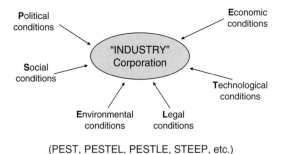

(PEST, PESTEL, PESTLE, STEEP, etc.)

Figure 2.3 Analyzing the exogenous environmental factors

framework is further detailed to also consider legal conditions as a separate area of focus to specifically consider the role of legislation, legal systems and law enforcement, public and semi-public regulatory initiatives, adherence to international conventions, etc. In this case we may refer to a PESTEL or PESTLE frame of analysis (Figure 2.3). These analytical frameworks are by and large comparable and subscribe to the same basic idea of assessing important developments in the external macro-environment and the various exogenous factors that could exert a material influence on the business conditions in major markets and the global economy as a whole.

The overarching rationale in this phase of the strategy-formulation process is to consider the major trends in potentially influential exogenous environmental factors so as to devise strategic actions that may drive the firm toward a more favorable position in view of these developments. In this context, it is important to identify the most important factors that could affect the business potential of the firm where observed trends and expected effects on performance should be validated as far as possible against facts. It is a major challenge to assemble and feed sufficient amounts and relevant pieces of information into the analyses. One way to accomplish this could be to create a special entity, e.g., a unit for market intelligence, planning, budgeting, or risk management to search for relevant sources of information. Among other things this search might consider a broad range of environmental analyses made available by various advisors, consultancies, interest groups, research institutions, and universities, often published with indicative headings, such as "international outlook," "global trends," "business prospects," "executive sentiments," "management surveys," and the like. Obtaining informational inputs from a cross-section of providers gives a diversity of views and a good basis for discussing and validating the information. Another approach would be to survey important organizational decision makers within the firm, possibly including some of the important external stakeholders, about what they consider to be significant developments that can challenge the future business.[19] A third approach could be to engage a range of middle managers representing different functional areas in discussions around an initial list of proposed exogenous influencers and inquire about its validity and whether something has been overlooked.

The information-gathering process can provide a structured way of collecting diverse views and obtaining more broad-based environmental intelligence that can fuel essential thinking about prevailing trends in the macro-environment and their potential effects. It may also form the basis for a consistent way to monitor key developments on an ongoing basis and include those in regular discussions about the strategic progress. The underlying analyses should be supported by reliable data and facts, which are not always easy to get and are difficult to project into an uncertain future. However, a major rationale for this exercise is not necessarily to gain exactitude in predictions but rather to facilitate a more qualified understanding of the strategic situation and possible developments for use in ongoing strategic decisions. Of course, the reality is that in many instances we are dealing with inherently unknowable future conditions where thorough analyses nonetheless may help uncover areas that otherwise would be ignored or discarded and thinking through the consequences of unlikely but not impossible future scenarios. As expressed by Nassim N. Taleb: "Many Black Swans can be caused by and exacerbated by *their being unexpected.*"[20] In other words, it is worthwhile to think through what might happen in the external environment and how the firm can deal with these events. To the extent managers have thought about the unthinkable, they are less likely to be taken by surprise when the future unfolds. Hence, good analytical processes may help managers avert the common tendency to disregard important signs that could have a major influence on business conditions and future firm performance.[21] We will revert to these issues in subsequent chapters.

The assessment of *industry-specific conditions* closer to the firm's operational task environment is concerned with the often dynamic changes that take place in the competitive situation. Some changes are obviously imposed by exogenous factors in the macro-environment, but a great number of them derive from the specific industry context in which the firm operates. One particular strand of industry analysis considers the competitive dynamic that circumscribes the firm and its close competitors where market share and organizational size are identified as significant predictors of performance. Hence, industrial economics explains how the market structure characterized by the number and distribution of firms in a given market, e.g., expressed by a concentration measure, will affect industry profitability.[22] A high market concentration with few dominant industry players is associated with higher prices and profitability. For example, Microsoft's dominant position in computer software and recognized brands such as Coca-Cola and Pepsi in the global market for soft drinks are more profitable than, say, American Airlines or Delta in a crowded airline industry. So, industries display significantly different return characteristics over time. Hence, the industries for soft drinks and prepackaged software have consistently outperformed the airline industry over the past decades. However, other economic forces are also at play, such as mobility barriers that make it difficult for new firms to establish a foothold in the industry and prevent existing business counterparts from doing business with competing firms.[23] These economic rationales were incorporated into a cohesive strategy analysis by Michael Porter in his celebrated book on competitive strategy.[24] The cornerstone of his analytical framework is captured in the *five forces model*, so called for obvious reasons (Figure 2.4).

The model explains why some firms generate superior returns due to a particular competitive dynamic in their industry. In Porter's words: "Understanding the competitive forces, and their underlying causes, reveals the roots of an industry's current profitability."[25] Hence, the intensity of *rivalry* among industry participants will influence the ability to generate a profit. An

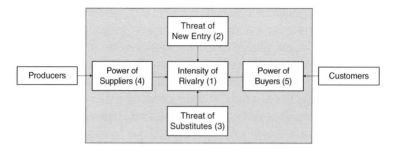

Figure 2.4 The five forces model. Source: adapted from Porter (1980)

industry with one or only a few participants (monopoly, duopoly, or oligopoly) will be less competitive and thus more conducive to higher prices. The competitive dynamic is influenced by the development stage of the industry, e.g., embryonic, growth, maturity, or decline, and the level of innovation pursued by market participants. The intensity of rivalry can be affected by the threat of *new entry* to the industry or the introduction of close *substitutes* to existing products and services. If the industry has strong barriers to entry, the intensity of rivalry is held at bay and existing returns are relatively safe. Such barriers may derive from high capital intensity, scale economies, legal restrictions, reputation, brand loyalty, strong relations, preferential resource access, a steep learning curve, unique know-how, patents, etc. Competitive pressures are also affected by the number of immediate substitutes available to compete against the products and services offered in the industry. The performance characteristics of potential substitutes, the price elasticity of existing products, and the value-for-price ratio of alternative offerings all point to the possible threat of substitutes. The intensity of rivalry is further affected by the relative power of *suppliers* to and *buyers* from the industry. If there are few alternative suppliers to the industry and they assume favorable positions, they can dictate prices and conditions to gain economic advantage at the expense of industry participants. The same arguments apply to situations with few dominant buyers. The power of suppliers and buyers can be affected by the specific characteristics of these commercial relationships, including trade volumes, number of alternative input–output channels, preferential sourcing and distribution systems, dependencies, switching costs, etc. Here we make a slight extension to the traditional model as we realize that supplier and buyer relationships can be channeled through major wholesalers, distribution companies, or retailers as intermediaries that then exert the true power of suppliers and buyers.

In essence, the five forces model provides a framework to assess how much of the value creation is retained by firms within the industry and how much is sifted away due to supplier and buyer powers and threats of new entry and substitutes. These analytical insights can then be reverse engineered to pinpoint strategic moves and actions that will reduce some of the adverse powers and threats to increase returns in the industry or the value-creation potential of individual firms operating in it. As such, the most influential competitive forces identified in this analysis become important elements to consider in the strategy-formulation process. However, it should be kept in mind that industries vary and display different competitive dynamics and that good analysis therefore requires detailed insights about industry-specific conditions. Above all, the analysis hinges upon appropriate identification of the industry where participants compete on comparable terms, e.g., are exposed to the same suppliers, buyers, entrants, and substitutes. So, the trick is to focus on relevant product/service markets where firms compete on similar terms across a certain geographical region, if not globally.

The intensity of rivalry in the industry can be better understood by undertaking an analysis of the firms that compete in the particular product market. Managers often make assumptions about the competition and base corporate decisions on beliefs influenced by prior experiences that may vary in reliability and relevance to a given situation.[26] Thus, a comprehensive analysis of the peers in the industry backed by evidence and validated information can provide useful inputs to the analytical exercise that stand against prevailing perceptions. The competitor analysis can be construed in a systematic manner by considering the basic elements that drive competitive actions, such as the firm's goals and assumptions, as well as what it does, e.g., its strategies and capabilities (Figure 2.5).[27]

A competitor analysis may help reveal how peers in the industry will act in various market situations and respond to different

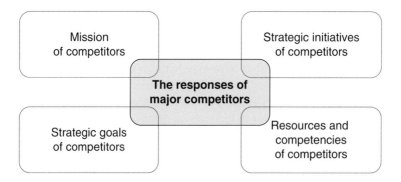

Figure 2.5 Competitor analysis. Source: adapted from Porter (1980)

competitive moves. The formal goals expressed by the firms say something about the purpose, aims, and strategic targets they pursue while the corporate values indicate how management prioritizes different activities and stakeholders. The assumptions held by agents in the firm capture their perception about the market position of the business and what drives the ability to create value in the market place. The strategy reflects the actual position held by the firm in terms of products and services, sourcing and distribution channels, organizational structure, incentive systems, actions pursued, etc. The capabilities determine what the firm can actively pursue and accomplish with its existing assets, technologies, operations, processes, skills, human resources, etc. To be complete, the analysis should also consider potential entrants into the market from other industries to obtain a more realistic picture of the competitive situation. Much of the information about close competitors can be collected from public sources made available by the firms in official reports, on company websites, etc. The things firms do in terms of new initiatives, actions, investments, etc. are often communicated in official press releases and reported by the business press. At times there can be a discrepancy between official statements and the actions taken by the firms, which then should be considered in the analysis. The official information can also be validated by accessing information from a broader set of internal and external contacts, for example, through interviews, questionnaires, and probing conversations.

It is a challenge in industry and competitor analysis to define the industry neither too narrowly nor too broadly. A narrow definition can discard potential entrants and miss important aspects of the industry dynamic that otherwise might predict future changes. Adopting a broad definition will catch too many nuances of competitive behaviors that make cohesive analysis highly complex. So, competitor analysis is focused on firms with market offerings that cater to some of the same customers and compete on comparable dimensions such as pricing policy, product features, quality, service enhancements, business and geographical scope, degree of specialization, operating costs, etc. Industries may span across different types of products sold in different geographical locations and here *segmentation* can help narrow in on the appropriate competitive context. Identifying the characteristics of different types of buyers and products tailored to these market segments can identify relevant sub-markets. For example, one would quickly be able to identify distinct market segments for wristwatches, e.g., luxury-fashion-quality versus low-cost mass market, where identifiable firms cater specifically to these segments. Each of these market segments should be considered as appropriate for competitive analysis because the industry participants compete on comparable terms. To the extent the industry can be clearly segmented by geographical regions, e.g., due to particular national customs, then regional markets would be appropriate for analysis. However, limiting the focus to include a relatively narrow group of close competitors can also limit the scope of the analyst. Hence, an alternative approach is to use the customer as the focal point and consider how basic needs can be satisfied in new and different ways to seek out potential competitors and new offerings. For example, in the global market for handheld mobile phones, customers have generally appreciated ease of handling in a user-friendly design and the ability to integrate different informational sources in the same products, which carved out a significant market position for Apple's iPhone in a market otherwise dominated by giants such as Nokia, Samsung, and Motorola. Hence, it is important to retain a broad view of the competitive environment to avoid delimitations along conventional market perceptions. Here a diverse network of internal and external

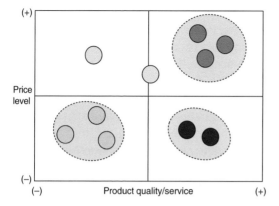

Figure 2.6 Strategy groups

contacts and informants can be useful to spot new developments and gain access to a more nuanced perspective.[28]

The analysis of close competitors should reveal some of the essential competitive dimensions that can be used to differentiate between groups of firms that compete on comparable terms. For example, firms may differentiate themselves in the market by the prices they charge and quality of product offerings. The relative position adopted by the firms on these essential dimensions can be mapped in a two-by-two graphic to reveal similar strategy approaches to the market (Figure 2.6). A low-price policy would normally correspond to a simpler offering of lower durability and with few service features, whereas more advanced product features typically would correspond to a high-price policy. Think of firms in the industry for wristwatches, where Rolex is considered a high-priced, luxury/quality brand, whereas Citizen provides a broad range of reasonably priced watches for everyday use. Firms may pursue either of these generic strategies or assume interim forms that can identify more or less favorable strategic positions. For example, firms able to create a high perceived product quality while charging lower prices could represent serious future competition to keep an eye on, learn from, and respond to. Hence, Swatch was able to successfully redefine the concept of what a wristwatch is to introduce durable and price-competitive products but with many unique and colorful models for different types of buyers. The strategy groups can obviously be identified based on other important dimensions, including level of innovation, production technology, sourcing patterns, distribution channels, internet sales, etc., depending on the specific industry context. An industry with multiple strategy groups will generally display higher competitive pressures with more intense rivalry among the firms that adopt comparable strategies, particularly if there is relatively high concentration within the group.

Understanding the way major rivals think, behave, and act is a good foundation for analyzing potential business games, which is an area covered by *game theory*. Game theory is a systematic approach to analyzing situations where the position of one firm depends on choices made by another firm (or other firms) and to model the competitive behavior of interacting firms. The games can be described over a sequence of decisions to assess the potential consequences of tactical moves. Under competition we often envision *zero-sum* games where players try to gain their maximum share of a given amount of available resources and benefits. So, the gain of one is a loss for another. This can lead to intriguing *prisoner's dilemma* situations where self-interests can lead both players to become worse off than if they had not acted in pure self-interest. The games can also be *cooperative*, whereby the players gain mutual benefits from initiatives and thus enhance the total gains available. The game might reach a *Nash equilibrium* where none of the players can benefit further from a change in their strategies, but might also lead to multiple solutions or ambiguous outcomes.[29] In short, anticipating future competitive moves and thinking about responsive behaviors can be a useful exercise. Game theory as a formalized analytical framework can be particularly relevant in situations where there are two major rivals, such as Boeing and Airbus dominating the global market for large passenger aircraft. However, it has been applied in many other cases, for example to analyze the US–Soviet positions during the Cuban missile crisis in 1962.[30] The analysis can consider reactions to tactical decisions and assess their competitive repercussions and consequences. This can be extended to consider more players or strategy groups, but analysis of multiple players can quickly become a complicated affair. The game-theoretical approach implies that the analyst can foresee possible future moves, responses, and their consequences. So game theory reaches its limitations in complex situations with mixed competitive and cooperative plays with ambiguous outcomes.[31] Yet, the underlying idea of orchestrating competitive scenarios to understand the consequences of different decision patterns can be a very useful exercise.

The five forces model looks at the important players in the competitive game that comprise existing firms in the industry, their customers, and their suppliers where new entrants and substitute products and services can change the competitive situation over time. However, it is argued that the competitive analysis also should include so-called *complementors*, i.e., those firms that provide complementary goods and services to the buyers or customers the market participants compete for. For example, the existence of good tire manufacturers and companies in oil-extraction and petroleum-refinery businesses is pretty crucial for the global automobile industry. Hence, Brandenburger and Nalebuff introduced the concept of a "value net" where value creation is influenced not only by competitive forces but also by collaborative activities referred to as *co-opetition* (Figure 2.7).[32]

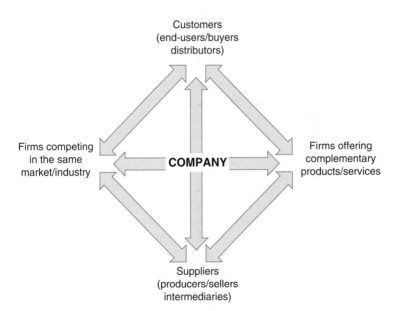

Figure 2.7 The value net. Source: adapted from Brandenburger and Nalebuff (1996)

That is, when we assess the competitive dynamic of an industry it is not just a question of finding areas where returns can be increased by managing the firm's power position, it is equally important to identify the essential value-creating relationships with the purpose of developing those further. Hence, there may be situations where it pays off to collaborate in friendly competition and expand a joint market rather than compete head on by exploiting relational power positions. Therefore, complementors together with suppliers and customers can be conceived as cooperative partners and allies in the business process and as such may constitute important counterparts to be taken seriously. Porter argues, however, that the role of the complementors will affect each of the five forces and thus the core model can still be used as the basis for industry analysis. In short, complementors should be taken into consideration in analyses of the industry competitive dynamic and value-creation potential. Similarly, the potential for collaborative engagements with suppliers and buyers as suggested by the stakeholder perspective should be considered in the industry analysis.

Competitor analysis based on basic rationales about the economic power of market players requires a focus on close competitors within a well-defined product-market context. This can obviously mean that the analyst becomes too narrow minded and assumes a static view of competitive developments. The level of rivalry in an industry is also influenced by the life-cycle stage of the industry, i.e., whether it is a new industry going through an initial growth phase or is a mature industry moving toward stagnation and depletion. The competitive dynamic may be affected by other external factors that can change the rules of the game. Hence, Andy Grove accepts the usefulness of conventional competitive analysis but emphasizes the need to consider rule-changing developments in the industry. The relative influence of competitors, customers, and suppliers affects business conditions in the industry, but the complementors and the way they interact with these same constituents to offer new business constellations can, in his experience, play a central role. He refers to the *six forces* of existing and potential competitors, existing customers, suppliers and complementors, and the possibility that business can be done differently, i.e., current approaches

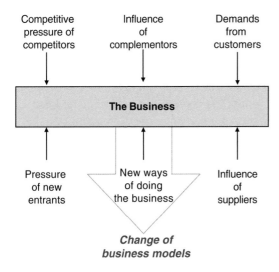

Figure 2.8 The six forces model. Source: adapted from Grove (1997)

can be substituted by new ways of conducting business in the industry (Figure 2.8).[33]

The possibility that business can be done differently, e.g., by creating, delivering, and managing a product/service offering in new ways, may resemble the substitution construct in the five forces model. However, changes in technology, essential product features, production processes, etc. may lead to dramatic changes in the way business is organized and could eventually drive monumental shifts in the industry structure. It is, of course, the changes that confronted his own company, Intel Corporation, that inspired Andy Grove in this analysis. In the early 1980s Intel was faced with increasing competition from Japanese companies in its traditional DRAM business and had to decide how to respond. It turned out that Intel's earlier successful development of the microchip had the potential to become its future breadwinner. But the company was at an "inflection point" that required a major strategic decision and it was not obvious, at least in the beginning, that the future focus on microchips was the right choice.[34] However, Intel profited from a competitive shift in the industry that took place at the same time as the previously integrated computer industry was fragmented into sub-industries with producers of microcomputers, operating systems, and microprocessors where the *wintel* standard (Microsoft operating systems running on Intel processors) eventually came to dominate the industry.

Hence, the potential for structural shifts in the industry should be an important element of the competitive analysis. The Intel story captures the effects of a particular decision made by a dominant market player (in this case IBM) as it changed its prior strategy of full vertical integration to one of accepting in-sourced components with the purpose of expanding faster into the burgeoning personal computer market where Apple was leading the way in the early 1980s. However, there can be many other sources to structural shifts in the industry, including economic shocks, technological breakthroughs, new product offerings, and different ways of doing things.[35] All of these elements should be on the radar screen as part of an extensive competitive intelligence exercise that also considers exogenous environmental factors.

Complementors comprise those firms that offer complementary goods and services to existing customers. However, as a concept it can be extended to include firms that work closely with incumbents in the industry and deliver essential complementary components, semi-produce, or services that are instrumental for the final market offering to the end-users. This is somewhat different from a conventional view of suppliers as delivering standardized inputs to manufacturing. Instead it emphasizes the importance of close relationships with suppliers and other service providers where the value chain becomes more of a *value network*, with complementary contributions accessing the firm at many different points in the production process. This can have particular significance in competitive analysis because many of these firms are dependent on each other and the collective success of the industry cluster. Firm performance and strategic conduct are then influenced by the relationships maintained with players within the industry network.[36] When firms in the industry cluster operate on the basis of intertwined competencies it may open up a particular competitive dynamic of business transitions, partnerships, alliances, mergers, and acquisitions as the industry evolves. The industry context is not static but changes over time through interrelated actions of competitors, suppliers, wholesale agents, service providers, buyers, retailers, distributors, customers, and complementors as they co-evolve and co-develop the common industry platform. The competitive analysis needs to consider how this co-evolutionary process might take place and what the potential outcomes and consequences are.

A simple way to analyze the value-creation dynamic around an industry would be to slice up the productive activities by the producers, suppliers, competitors, buyers, and customers in Figure 2.4, and consider the relative size (e.g., total revenues) and profitability (e.g., operating margin) of all firms operating within these areas. This can help validate the assessment of relative power positions between these groups, and by monitoring the profit dynamic over time it is possible to identify emerging changes in this power structure. The analysis can be extended further to include more detailed specifications of relevant industry activities. For example, the down-stream activities in the automobile manufacturing industry include things such as new car dealerships, used car dealers, automobile lending, vehicle leasing, auto insurance, services and repairs, automobile parts, and car rentals.[37] Collecting information about revenues and margins among firms in each of these areas will provide a good grasp of where important value-creating activities take place and this can be traced over time. The same idea and approach can be extended to the entire industry network.

As an illustration, the computer industry is comprised of a number of interacting products and services produced by various competitors, suppliers, and complementors, including computer assembly, sales and distribution, microprocessors, operating systems, peripheral products, application software, internet service provisions, etc. This forms an extended network of vertical and complementary activities where suppliers and complementors can be seen as cooperative partners and allies in the business, with competitive activities evolving around interdependent and co-specialized sectors in an industry cluster that forms a common business platform.[38] Hence, the computer industry may be sliced into three major segments: mainframe computers, personal computers, and work stations. These industry segments are serviced by a broad network of suppliers and complementors, including producers of modems, disk drives, displays, software,

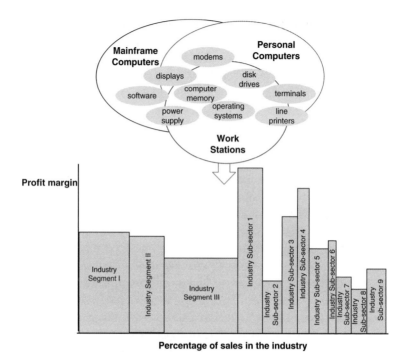

Figure 2.9 Profit pool of industry network

memory, terminals, power supplies, operating systems, line printers, and so forth. Once these industry segments and sub-sectors are identified, their size and profitability can be recorded and analyzed to inform discussions about how value is generated in the industry and how this has changed over time (Figure 2.9). The analysis can reveal where profits are made and real value is created in the industry and how this is modified as new technologies emerge, new players enter, and the competitive dynamic changes.

Clayton Christensen famously analyzed how, in the disk-drive industry, competitive changes evolved from ongoing technological advances during the 1980s and the early 1990s with bursts of disrupted competition.[39] It was generally observed that the innovative product breakthroughs were comprised of known technologies combined and packaged in new, economically feasible ways that could sustain steady improvements in product performance. Christensen also noted that substantially all the firms that were able to develop and adapt these disruptive technologies were new entrants and did not include the dominant incumbents in the industry or the market leaders of yesterday. These insights should sensitize our curiosity to monitor major environmental trends and better understand the competitive developments that take place in the industry and thereby hopefully enable appropriate strategic initiatives in time.

A major critique of five forces analysis is that it takes a relatively static view of the industry because it is focused on the rivalry around close competitors and therefore limits broader considerations about what happens to competition as the future changes. *Hypercompetition* is a conceptualization of such a rapidly changing competitive environment where ongoing innovation makes the industry definition based on a given product market obsolete.[40] Richard D'Aveni distinguishes between four patterns of varying turbulence: equilibrium, fluctuating equilibrium, punctuated equilibrium, and disequilibrium.[41] In *equilibrium* there are few environmental changes and incumbents are in control, so challengers may try to attack market barriers and prevailing power constellations. In *fluctuating equilibrium* the environmental changes are more frequent as incumbents try to sustain their positions by levering existing competencies in new products and challengers try to introduce offerings supported by better core competencies. *Punctuated equilibrium* is characterized by periods of stable dynamics interrupted by bursts of discontinuous change that could be caused by a new revolutionary technology, such as digital imaging in the photographic industry. Here the incumbents are challenged by disruptive technologies where the challengers may see these as a chance to enter the market. Under *disequilibrium* we have reached the true hypercompetitive state, with frequent competence-destroying innovations, product developments, and technology enhancements where both incumbents and challengers try to excel through creativity, speed, and aggressive moves. The distinction between different competitive contexts can be useful in the industry analysis, although it is difficult to determine if and when industries move from one stage to the next, e.g., changing from equilibrium to punctuation or hypercompetitive conditions.

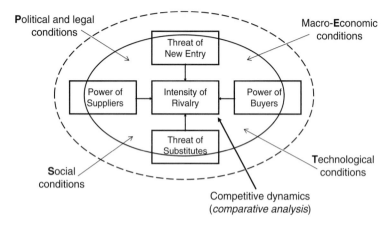

Figure 2.10 The extended environmental model

The changing industry context is influenced by a number of external factors that are beyond the direct control of management and it is exactly the idea behind PEST analysis to try to identify what those factors are, and consider what direct effects they may invoke on the competitive situation, and how they could affect the firm's strategic path. Hence, the analysis of exogenous environmental factors and their potential influences can combine the PEST framework with the five forces industry analysis (Figure 2.10).

That is, we can consider the potential effects of changes in important environmental developments on each of the competitive forces to assess how they might affect profitability in the industry. Some of the exogenous factors to consider could include major economic shocks, regulatory overhauls, new technologies, related product innovation, and advances in management techniques. For example, the economic crisis during 2008 led to spectacular bankruptcies among large global market players, such as Bear Stearns and Lehman Brothers, where new regulatory capital requirements will affect business conduct in the financial industry. A classical example is how digital-imaging technology changed the photographic industry and eroded Kodak's market lead during the 1980s. In a comparable way, the expansion of internet-based services might transform the demand for conventional components such as microchips and hard disks, in the market for personal computers. Similarly, a global switch to light-emitting diodes (LED) may soon challenge the traditional light-bulb industry as regulation drives a push toward more energy-efficient technological solutions.[42] However, it is not clear exactly how and when things will happen that can influence the competitive dynamic and possibly impose a major structural shift in the industry.

One way to deal with the consequences of potentially important but highly uncertain factors in the external environment is to think about possible future scenarios characterized by different development trends in those key factors that reflect relatively extreme but not inconceivable future conditions. That is, the approach is trying to analyze the potential consequences of a competitive setting that is largely unpredictable. For example, the PEST analysis might have uncovered a new trend in consumer behavior partially driven by technological advances that require further development investment as well as the firm being sensitive to the level of global interest rates. These factors may be driven by underlying environmental trends or themes, such as the speed with which the changing demand pattern is adopted among customers and the economic growth prospects as it influences the level of demand, investment intensity, and interest rates. This can be used to describe four scenarios characterized by high–low growth situations and high–low levels of customer adoption that evaluate the firm's ability to deal with each of these situational settings. Hence, it is a methodology to think through possible constellations in a future competitive landscape the firm might be confronted with.[43] It can be a way to challenge groupthink and identify blind spots in the environmental analysis that can avoid future surprises. It is also a way to assess the firm's ability to handle abrupt developments and think about how to deal effectively with possible extreme events and conditions (see Box 2.4 *Scenario analysis*).

The organization builds important external relationships around suppliers, buyers, complementors, and other partners in industry networks that also may include important collaborative contacts to industry organizations, government officials, regulators, and policy makers. Stakeholder analysis provides a framework for considering whether the organization has invested sufficient *social capital* in the important stakeholder relationships.

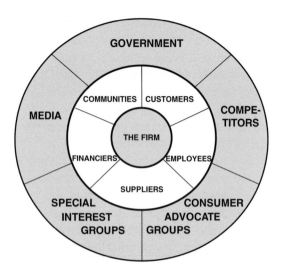

Figure 2.11 Stakeholder considerations. Source: Freeman *et al.* (2010)

The social capital of a firm constitutes the resources it has tied up in its social relationships with other businesses for the purpose of taking collective actions that can bring mutual benefits among all participants in the network.[44] The entities that make up the social network can be uncovered through *stakeholder analysis*, which is a systematic approach to identifying all the groups of people which can exert a significant influence on the business conditions of the firm.[45] In addition to competitive influences from suppliers, customers, and competitors, it includes relationships to the communities where the firm operates and to the firm's financial backers, as well as constituents in the broader society such as government, consumer advocates, special interest groups, and the media that influence how the firm is perceived by the public (Figure 2.11).

A comprehensive and all-inclusive stakeholder analysis helps identify common interests and potential conflicts of interest among important environmental constituents and helps think of ways to manage those relationships for mutual benefits and durable value creation. This will also reduce the potential for managerial neglect of societal obligations and public relations that otherwise could cause serious harm to the corporate reputation. Another approach that can be adopted to extend the horizon of external environmental developments is to consider *social responsibility* and *sustainability* issues.[46] This could imply specific analysis of *social conditions*, e.g., poverty, public health, labor conditions, and human rights, *value contribution*, e.g., life enhancements, individual and societal comforts, *environmental effects*, e.g., reduced pollution and waste, preservation of natural resources, and *cultural context*, e.g., enhancing the community association and heritage.[47] This approach is linked to the stakeholder perspective as it helps the analyst think through potential economic externalities, e.g., pollution, failing product quality, unhealthy working conditions, etc., that can impose damages on key stakeholders and create serious liabilities and future economic claims. It can also help the analyst think through existing operating practices and suggest ways to improve economic efficiencies, e.g., by adopting process technologies that use fewer resources and thus may pollute less, reduce CO_2 emissions, and make production more sustainable. There is mounting evidence that practices with concerns for social and environmental factors are associated with better performance outcomes and thus deserve close attention.[48]

Internal analysis

By conducting an analysis of the external environment that circumscribes the business activities, we try to find out how the firm can achieve higher future returns through re-positioning that takes advantage of environmental developments and trends while fending off the competitive forces in the industry. The next step in the strategy-formulation process is to analyze the internal environmental conditions that determine how future business activities can be carried out (Figure 2.12). This analysis will focus on *firm-specific conditions* that have a significant influence on the organization's ability to create value and execute strategic actions. So, we look inside the firm to understand the various factors that have advanced organizational activities and supported past and current performance outcomes.

The company's current situation can be described by numerous factors, such as the resources and capabilities possessed and mastered by the organization, the productive assets owned by the

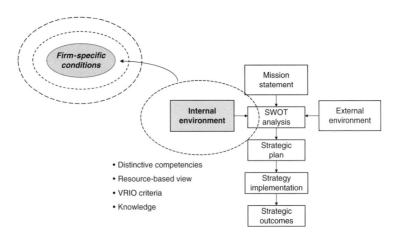

Figure 2.12 Analysis of the internal environment in the strategy model

firm, including related processes and systems, the cost position of internal operations, and the way the firm is organized to carry out its business activities. These elements can be described by separate dimensions of the *social structure* (e.g., distribution of employees per task, number of hierarchical levels, division of labor, rules and procedures, distribution of decision authority, degree of standardization, formalization, and specialization), *technology* (for example, small batch, mass production, or continuous processing), *culture* (comprised of assumptions, values, and artifacts), and *physical structure* (such as geography, layout, design, etc.).[49] This description can be extended through comparisons to stylized organizational models or *typologies*, such as simple structure, machine bureaucracy, professional bureaucracy, divisionalized form, and adhocracy, that depict the characteristics of distinct organizational types.[50] The analysis can be supported by adopting integrative frameworks considering the important elements of an organizational structure. This can include, for example, the McKinsey 7S framework based on the seven dimensions of strategy, structure, skills, systems, shared values, style, and staff, or the concept model for organization design developed by Galbraith, considering task, people, compensation, processes, and structure (Figure 2.13).[51] Collecting the relevant information for internal analysis can be rather

Galbraith's organizing model

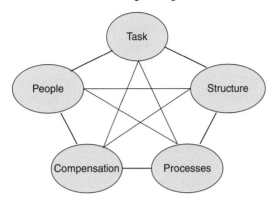

McKinsey's 7S framework

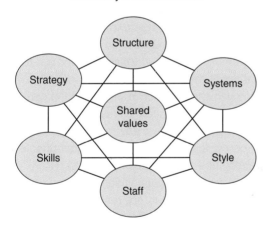

Figure 2.13 Organizational structure – two analytical frameworks

challenging. The real insights are frequently hidden deep within the firm, which is one reason why this part of the strategy analysis is often downplayed in classroom settings. The information is simply difficult to find and obtain. It often requires on-site knowledge and hands-on insights into the organizational peculiarities, although some of it can be teased out of publicly accessible sources. Other things like corporate culture, however, must be sensed directly from inside probing at the firm. So, a combination of archival descriptive material from the firm itself and field studies and interviews with key members of the organization is a must, possibly garnered with industry experts' insights and people's personal experiences from the business network.

While the analytical frameworks may help line up the important internal elements and dimensions of the organization, the *resource-based view* of the firm can help explain why some of the uncovered features are potential contributors to the value-creating potential of the firm. The underlying rationale is fairly straightforward, i.e., that firm-specific value-creating features that are unique to the organization provide the basis for it to maintain or develop durable returns from its business.[52] These internal conditions are essentially built by firm resources that may take a variety of forms, reflecting different types of financial, physical, human, and organizational capital invested in business activities. We sometimes argue that the firm's ability to do things is shaped by capabilities and competencies, or by core capabilities and core competencies. Thus we run the risk here of engaging in a general "terminology soup," which isn't foreign to the strategy field. The thing is that the internal processes, practices, systems, and even the cultures of organizations can all be conceived as firm-specific resources. Hence, to simplify things we argue that resources can take many forms, capabilities and competencies can be comprised of a number of identifiable resources, and core capabilities and core competencies are higher-order constructs formed by capabilities and/or competencies. As a consequence, we do not really distinguish between resources, capabilities, and competencies, although we might do so in special cases, where the capabilities and/or competencies are identified as being comprised of specified complementary resources.

$$\text{capabilities} = \text{competencies} = \text{resources} \quad \text{or} \quad f_1(\text{resources})$$

$$\text{core-competencies} = f_2(\text{competencies}) \quad \text{and}$$
$$\text{core-capabilities} = f_3(\text{capabilities})$$

Due to the many possible resource combinations, firms can have unique features even though they operate in the same industry, belong to the same strategic group, and appear to have similar business processes. If the industry has just some important and unique resources that are scattered heterogeneously among the firms and those resources are relatively immobile, i.e., are not easily transferred from one firm to the other, then there is a basis for differentiability. Some of these resources may be very subtle and could relate to social skills, interconnectedness between individual functional experts, interrelationships between production processes, etc. So, many small activities, actions, and decisions that are hard to emulate can create collective firm value over time and may, in fact, be a less risky approach than engaging in large resource-committing decisions made at headquarters. That is, the firm's resource base can lead to sustainable competitive advantages, reflected in longer-term excess performance outcomes, if the resources that support the business activities have value, are rare, are hard to imitate, and can be organized for exploitation. The value of resources derives from their ability to support unique efficiency measures or product features that improve cost economies or enhance market position. The rarity of resources determines how durable the value effects are, i.e., if the resources are accessible and available to everyone there can be no specific values attached to them. The concern about inimitability relates to whether the resources can be easily copied or imitated by competitors where they only represent sustainable advantages, if they are hard to replicate. The organizing criterion is important to effectively exploit the embedded advantages of unique firm-specific resources by integrating them into complementary and interacting resources in the organization. These are the so-called VRIO criteria (see Box 2.5 *Resource-based economics (VRIO)*).

Analyzing the firm's value chain is one approach that tries to determine where the sources of a firm's competitive advantage might be located and thereby identify specific resources that support this value enhancement. The ability to create competitive advantage with above-average returns can stem from many discrete activities the firm performs throughout its operating processes. The *value chain* is a collection of activities performed to develop, produce, sell, and support the firm's products and services.[53] The generic form of the value chain relates to the many internal processes pursued by a single business or product

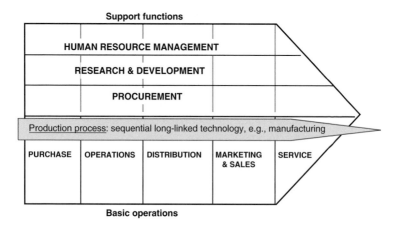

Figure 2.14 Analyzing the value chain for competitive advantage. Source: adapted from Porter (1985)

market firm. The value chain consists of basic or primary activities and a number of support functions (Figure 2.14). Hence, the *basic operations* start with purchase activities where the firm acquires the necessary inputs for the production process, sometimes referred to as inbound logistics. The next sequence of activities is operations where the inputs are integrated into the final product in the production process. Then the final goods are brought to the distributor or directly to the end-users in a process often referred to as outbound logistics. Marketing and sales maintain the contacts to the customers and advertise values the firm can deliver, and may engage in direct negotiations with the customers. Finally, the after-sale service activities ensure that product qualities and values are properly revealed and deal with replacements, repairs, and complaints. The *support functions* do not handle any of the physical activities that transform the inputs to final outputs but conduct administrative and coordinative tasks that enable the basic operations. This may include areas such as human resource management, research and development, and procurement of various external services. These value activities within the value chain can be seen as potential sources of competitive advantage. Since it constitutes a cohesive system of interdependent activities the very structure and coordination of the system may also be a source of competitive advantage.

Each of the discrete processes, technologies, and activities identified in the value chain analysis may need to be further disaggregated into smaller, meaningful components. The linkages between supplier order-entry systems and purchase functions in inbound logistics are also integral to the value chain, as are links between distribution and the procurement systems of major distributors. For example, the use of automated inventory-replenishment systems or vendor-managed inventory programs, where inventory restocking is triggered electronically by actual sales registered by the distributor, has provided a competitive advantage for some manufacturing firms, e.g., in the clothing and consumer goods industries. Hence, the basic idea behind the value chain analysis is to look for distinct value activities, interacting processes, or linked processing systems that create a strong value position as a source of differentiation or cost efficiency.

The conventional value chain captures the sequential steps in the production process of a manufacturing company and essentially describes what may be referred to as a *sequential long-linked technology*.[54] Manufacturing remains a central element of our economic apparatus, but the value-creating components of the economy have steadily moved from manufacturing industries to services-related industries, with value processes moving from conventional production toward professional services and broader service networks that represent significantly different value chain constructs.[55] (See Box 2.6 *Alternative value chain concepts.*)

SWOT analysis

The activities associated with the in-depth analyses of external and internal environmental conditions of the firm based on information from decision makers within the organization as well as outside expert evidence provide the ground for the next step in the strategy-formulation process. Basically, the *SWOT analysis* uses the gathered insights to address a number of central issues: (1) given our existing resources, competencies, and skills, what can we do to improve our resource endowment? (2) In view of trends and developments in the business environment, what can

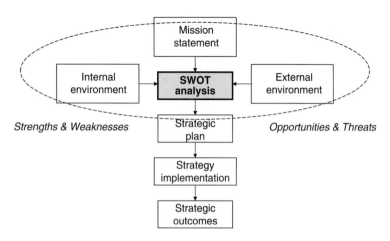

Figure 2.15 Conducting the SWOT analysis in the strategy model

we do to improve our current market offerings? (3) With our purpose, long-term goals, and values, what do we want to do to improve our strategic position? These fundamental issues build both on the inside-out perspective identifying internal strengths and weaknesses and on the outside-in perspective identifying the external opportunities and threats that make up the SWOT analysis (Figure 2.15). The underlying tenet of the SWOT analysis, then, is to analyze the strategic situation of the firm as a basic foundation for the ensuing formulation of the strategy. This analysis is used to pinpoint areas for improvement and development of viable alternatives for strategic actions in line with the corporate mission.

The SWOT analysis provides a framework for systematic analysis and for thinking about strategic alternatives. It does not necessarily require a lot of financial and computational backing but may serve as a frame for qualitative assessments that provide a setting for involved discussions among the management team and important decision makers. The SWOT analysis can become rather descriptive as it lists internal strengths and weaknesses as well as external opportunities and threats (Figure 2.16).

Strengths refer to internal factors that make the firm more competitive and improve its market position. *Weaknesses* refer to faults, shortcomings, and limitations that make the firm less competitive and prevent it from achieving key goals. *Opportunities* refer to new types of demand, market niches, technology

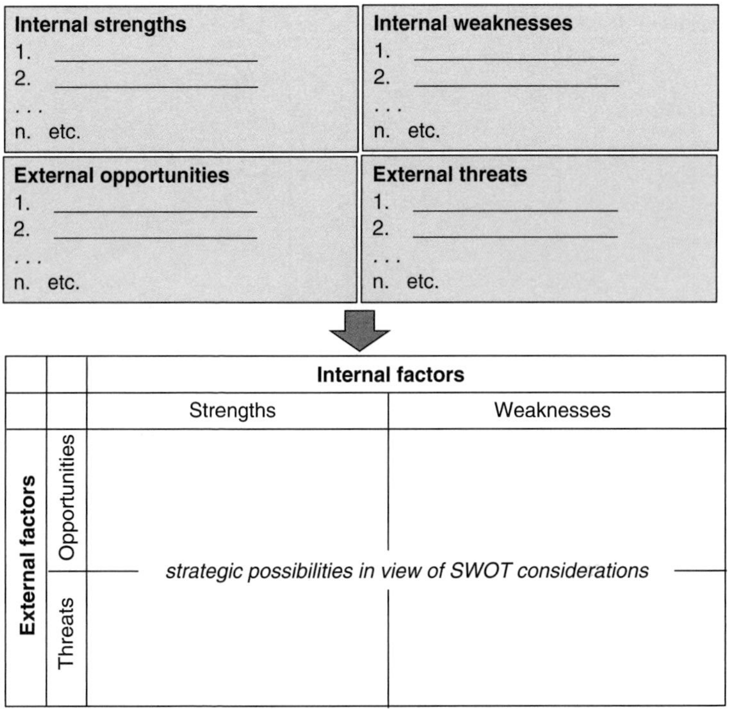

Internal strengths	Internal weaknesses
1. _____	1. _____
2. _____	2. _____
. . .	. . .
n. etc.	n. etc.
External opportunities	**External threats**
1. _____	1. _____
2. _____	2. _____
. . .	. . .
n. etc.	n. etc.

		Internal factors	
		Strengths	Weaknesses
External factors	Opportunities		
	Threats	*strategic possibilities in view of SWOT considerations*	

Figure 2.16 Conducting the SWOT analysis

applications, etc. that can improve the firm's competitive situation. *Threats* refer to new inventions, regulatory requirements, product introductions, etc. that may jeopardize the firm's competitive position. In principle, the internal strengths and weaknesses are more closely linked to managerial controls whereas external opportunities and threats typically are risk factors imposed from the outside. Under all circumstances, the firm needs to do something active to circumvent the adverse effects of internal weaknesses and external threats and to gain the potential benefits from internal strengths and external opportunities. A possible downside to the SWOT analysis is that it may lead to "feel-good" conversations with little practical effect. Therefore, to move from the descriptive nature of the framework to potential solutions and actions, we can sketch possible actions and strategic moves associated with use of "internal strengths against

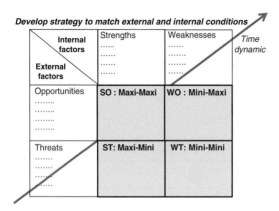

Figure 2.17 Adopting a TOWS analytical approach. Source: adapted from Weihrich (1982)

external opportunities," "internal weaknesses against external opportunities," "internal strengths against external threats," and "internal weaknesses against external threats" in four quadrants (Figure 2.16). This serves to outline possible strategic interventions with a view to the outlined SWOT considerations. The TOWS matrix provides a compressed and accessible format for the listed strengths, weaknesses, opportunities, and threats set up against each other in an interaction matrix that frames four policy quadrants (Figure 2.17).[56]

Internal strengths against external opportunities is the "maxi–maxi" quadrant where ways are found to protect and enhance the strengths and engage them in a manner that will exploit the identified opportunities. The internal weaknesses against external opportunities is the "mini–maxi" quadrant where the focus is to reduce the weaknesses and possibly turn them into strengths so they enhance, or at least do not jeopardize, the ability to exploit the opportunities. The internal strengths against external threats represent the "maxi–mini" quadrant where the concern is to maneuver in ways that can reduce the threat and possibly turn it into an opportunity by levering some of the existing strengths. The internal weaknesses against external threats is the "mini–mini" quadrant where the situation is potentially critical and where one might think of (demanding) ways of simultaneously changing weaknesses into strengths and threats into opportunities, or alternatively find options to move away from this position and go toward some of the more viable quadrants.

The analysis identifies strategic alternatives and opens for evaluation and eventual choice of a preferred strategic path going forward and strategic actions that must be taken to reach this development trajectory. The TOWS matrix can also provide a practical way to sketch and think through the time-dynamic aspects of proposed solutions in view of changes in the internal and external environments. So, the content of the matrix can be monitored backward, say 3–5 years back, to see how the environmental context presented solutions then and how they may have changed. Similarly, by trying to look forward, say 3–5 years ahead, one may consider how environmental conditions can change and what effects these changes would have on the alternative solutions before making final choices. The SWOT analysis pinpoints and narrows down the key factors in the internal and external environments that are expected to have the greatest impact on future strategic outcomes and that will influence the major strategic issues the firm is going to face. It is worth noting again that these strategic issues do not necessarily present themselves to executive management but must be uncovered through this kind of active and engaged analysis.[57]

Many of the central issues uncovered in the SWOT analysis may have strategic repercussions down the road as the firm tries to implement and enact a chosen strategic path, which is the case when the issues can exert a significant influence on future performance outcomes. This may serve as a useful basis to conduct *strategic issue analyses* to help the management team think through how to deal with a major strategic challenge and consider how such a challenge can be dealt with effectively if conditions change unfavorably. This type of analysis can also be conducted in conjunction with decisions to engage in a major strategic initiative and then becomes a way to assess successful execution in spite of exposures to major environmental risks. The analysis can use the SWOT framework to identify major risks and opportunities based on an evaluation of their significance and then monitor them as the strategic initiative proceeds. However, it requires a valid and robust identification of the underlying issue and environmental factors that can influence it. A common

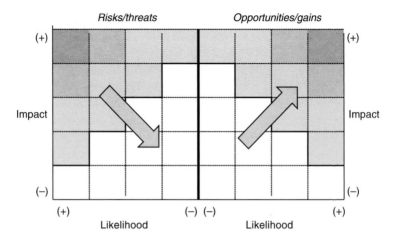

Figure 2.18 Identifying, prioritizing, and monitoring strategic issues

analytical approach is to first identify and prioritize the risk factors that can influence the issue by assessing their potential impact on performance and the likelihood of occurrence. This should consider both possible downside losses and upside gains. Various remedies to avoid and address the issues if they intensify are then evaluated and developments are monitored on an ongoing basis (Figure 2.18).

The term *strategic business model* has become a normal part of the business vocabulary and in effect is a construct that integrates all the different aspects of strategy discussed so far. Its origin is not that clear but has a strong resemblance to the concept of business design introduced in the mid 1990s. The *business design* is determined by assumptions about customer priorities, the customers the firm caters to, the scope of products and services it offers, the product/service features, the way inputs are sourced, how production is organized, and how outputs are sold and distributed, etc. In short, it is everything that defines the strategy. In the words of Adrian Slyvotsky: "A business design is the totality of how a company selects its customers, defines and differentiates its offerings, defines the tasks it will perform itself and those it will outsource, configures its resources, goes to market, creates utility for customers, and captures profit ... It is

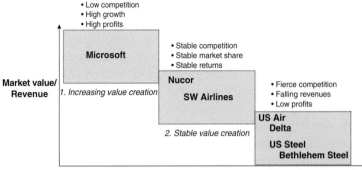

Figure 2.19 Value migration between business models. Source: adapted from Slyvotsky and Morrison (1997)

the entire system for delivering utility to customers and earning a profit from that activity."[58] The ability to create economic value derives from those business designs that provide more value to the customers and capture more value for the producers. However, business designs change all the time as firms invent new ways of doing things. That is, the way firms address customers in an industry goes through different cycles as old designs become obsolete and new ones take over and begin to dominate the value creation. A simple comparative metric such as a firm's market value divided by its total revenues can record how competing firms with different business designs represent value inflows or outflows to the industry or remain steady (Figure 2.19). Hence, for example, Nucor has been a long-term value provider in the US steel industry compared with the large incumbents.[59] Similarly, Southwest Airlines has been a steady performer in the US airline industry compared with other recognized market players.

Understanding how the value-creation potential migrates among different players in the industry is arguably an important concern for top management. Assuming a position of value inflow – the first phase – where firms with successful business models absorb value from other industry participants, is obviously preferred, although the second phase of stability probably is fine, too, whereas value outflow – the third phase – is a losing position. So, it is important to identify when an inflection point between stability and value outflow is eminent, but it is difficult to determine with any precision. However, uncovering the value profile of different business models in the industry reflecting the value migration between representative companies can be a useful analytical exercise and provides new insights. It can also be a useful way to study changes in value creation between interrelated industries and sub-industries and may reveal important trends that need more attention.

Business model renewal and business concept innovation have been touted as important ways to gain competitive advantage.[60] Yet, some of the most robust and successful business models, such as Nucor and Southwest Airlines, have remained largely unchanged since their inception decades ago. Nonetheless, the conscious focus on the business model and its various elements can be useful in strategy analysis as a way to better understand "how an organization creates, delivers, and captures value."[61] Alexander Osterwalder and Yves Pigneur characterize the business model by nine elements that determine who the customers are, what they offer, how the organizational infrastructure is set up, and how the business is financially viable. These elements comprise the customers, the value delivered, the channels for delivery, the types of relationships, what the customers will pay for, what resources are needed to provide value to the customer, the key activities of the firm, who the key partners are, and the cost structure of the very set-up. This is one of several frameworks, but they all provide a basis to consider the essential "building blocks" of a successful strategy, although this obviously does not constitute a foolproof recipe for success. The future is uncertain, which is why it holds promise, but good environmental analyses can help the strategist take more informed and better decisions. The best future strategy is one that hasn't been invented yet and it must be tried out before we know whether it truly works.

The concept of *strategic fit* is a close cousin to the idea of a business model formed by a consistent set of building blocks. We recognize the concept of fit from organization theory where structural elements should be adapted so they are internally consistent. This is extended to strategy where high performance is driven by alignment between the strategic offering, the organizational set-up formed to deliver it, and the current market conditions.[62] According to Michael Porter, fit can drive both competitive advantage and sustainability, and he identifies three types of fit. First-order fit corresponds to "simple consistency" between the functional activities in the firm and its overall strategy. Second-order fit arises when the effects of different activities are "reinforcing" each other, and third-order fit "optimizes the efforts" as the activities create incremental value.[63] While this classification into "degrees of fit" can be difficult to discern in practice, it does reflect the underlying belief that well-designed market offerings supported by a thoughtful organization design can feed competitive advantage in ways that resemble the efficacies deriving from a well-orchestrated business model.

A possible complementary analytical approach is expressed in *blue ocean* strategy where the idea is to enhance value by creating "uncontested market space" that captures new demand and discards irrelevant product features.[64] It suggests that systematic analyses of markets, customers, and competitive responses can help identify new favorable strategic market spots for future pursuit. By mapping competitive offers against perceived customer needs we may uncover the paths followed by specific strategy groups, and by considering the true values customers want and are willing to pay for, it might be possible to find better ways to address those customers. Enhancing key product features and discarding superfluous trimmings should then capture new sales and also cut off excessive operational costs. Conversely, a *red ocean* approach would argue for an alternative way to gain competitive advantage in hypercompetitive markets by consistently adhering to "discount strategies" where the market is captured by being the cheapest producer of basic customer needs.[65] So, the reality is that there is more than one way to skin the cat, and herein lies the beauty.

The *balanced scorecard* (BS) is often used by executives to understand and explain their strategy. The BS approach considers a mix of financial and non-financial measures, often reported in a concise format that focuses on essential qualities key customers would like to receive, adherence to targeted operational efficiencies, and the firm's financial performance. It articulates how essential resources in the firm (human, physical, and process related) drive expected performance outcomes and thereby provides a sort of "blueprint" for managing the firm's strategic priorities.[66] The scorecards by themselves are not really part of the strategy-formulation process but mapping the implied performance relationships can be useful for analytical purposes. The scorecards typically serve a strategic control function that we will revert to in the ensuing chapters. Discussions around the balanced scorecard may help create new insights and form a better understanding of the firm's strategic situation and value-creating process. It is intricately linked to the search for relevant key performance indicators (KPIs) that go beyond conventional financial ratios. Here one should be aware of the potential advantages as well as the pitfalls of strategic *benchmarking* efforts.[67] By focusing rigidly on the ability to optimize the current strategy, management can become too focused on existing competencies at the expense of searching for new competencies and technologies needed to compete under tomorrow's environmental conditions. That is, the firm can gradually enter into a *competency trap* and may eventually suffer from the so-called *Icarus syndrome*.[68] So, rather than using simplifying benchmarks, management should rely on the insights gathered from their informed strategy analysis. In the words of Jeffrey Pfeffer and Robert Sutton: "The fundamental problem is that few companies, in their urge to copy … ever ask the basic question of *why* something might enhance performance."[69] In other words, stick to the evidence and meaningful propositions extracted from a critical strategy analysis and don't just rely on what seems to have worked for others. What really matters is what will work for you.

Strategic plan

The completed strategy formulation process comprising mission statement, external analysis, internal analysis, and SWOT analysis has helped management outline viable strategic alternatives that can lead to executive decisions about strategic initiatives to be pursued in the future. To the extent this happens, the formal strategic management model suggests that a strategic plan should be developed by listing the major activities that need to be carried out, including who is taking action and when. In other words, the preparation of this document serves to enable thinking through all the things that need to be done to work successfully toward fulfillment of the intended strategy. Therefore, it also makes sense to involve all parties implicated by its execution in the completion of the document, and particularly in the discussions around it, both to gain multiple perspectives and to motivate. This can help in identifying potential challenges and obstacles to be addressed as well as gaining buy-in from important internal stakeholders in the subsequent implementation phase.

The strategic initiatives derived from the strategy formulation process can be seen as business projects that require detailed implementation plans, i.e., a strategic plan, to ensure effective execution. This plan should consider what it takes to reach the intended outcomes. It defines the most important issues that can challenge the project completion, many of which were uncovered in the prior analysis of strengths, weaknesses, opportunities, and threats. To the extent there are shortcomings, the implied *capability gaps* should be addressed appropriately. Similarly, potential impediments, such as internal resistance and cultural barriers, should be considered as well. These factors can often have a major influence on success and overall performance. The needs for specific professional competencies, training programs, research and development activities, etc. should be included in the planning.

The strategic plan should address all the key issues identified in the preceding analyses to outline ways to deal with them effectively. There should be a timetable for necessary tasks considering time-bound interdependencies between activities and completion of specific tasks. Task completion should be specified along an action-oriented time line with measurable outcome targets. The necessary resources must be made available to complete the tasks in an effective and timely manner. The plan should identify key performance indicators (KPIs) that can help monitor progress and identify needed adjustments and task updates. Defining appropriate measures and milestones for the process will be helpful in working toward the final objectives.

The strategic plan will identify appropriate performance measures that define successful completion of the projects, including defined hurdles along the way to evaluate progression. This implies that investments made over the duration of the projects are held against original projections where effects from ongoing adjustments are assessed against the plan. The planning process should think about environmental factors that might affect the fulfillment of tasks and lead to underperformance. It can be useful to develop contingency plans that outline responses to potential risk events based on general what-if analysis. This may reveal new possibilities and limitations in the projects that need precautions. Despite the planning process, unexpected things can and will still happen. However, these events can represent opportunities as much as threats for the underlying projects.[70] For example, new technologies and increasing demand can improve the economics of strategic initiatives whereas resource-demanding problems can have the opposite effect. Hence, it is important to build flexibility into the projected strategic initiatives to make room for adaptive responses that take advantage from updated information and new knowledge obtained along the way.

Once the strategic initiatives are planned, the next step in the process is to execute the projects in the strategy and implement them in line with the firm's overarching mission.

Conclusion

In this chapter, we have outlined the *rational analytical approach* to strategy making that corresponds to the conventional strategic management model. To many people in many places this is what strategy is. Here we have tried to provide a comprehensive overview of the process and a variety of analytical techniques that can be applied in this effort while realizing that new theories and models will continue to update and refine the analyses. One essential premise of this strategy-making approach is that we must be as well informed as possible in our strategic deliberations. Indeed, this was an essential insight promoted in the early beginnings of the strategy field. That is, the increasing complexity and speed of change require more thorough analyses to tackle the strategic challenges.[71] This is the foundation for *facts-based management* as a way to make more sound and unbiased strategic decisions.[72] By using informed assessments of the competitive landscape and the firm's position in it, there is less chance that strategic decisions will be dominated by devastating *cognitive biases* that we know influence humans, and powerful executives in particular.[73] This means that corporate decision makers should be in a better position to avoid committing *type-three errors*, i.e., solving the wrong problem precisely.[74] Providing an informed basis for taking strategic actions can, therefore, help reduce the likelihood that we will commit type-one, -two, and -three errors. However, it does not safeguard against *type-four errors*, defined as deliberate attempts to commit type-three errors.[75] To avoid these situations, we have to turn to the softer issues such as corporate values and culture, which is why considerations about mission statements should not be underestimated at the outset of the strategy formulation process.

By now we have a complete overview of the strategy formulation process, including suggestions for informed strategy analysis. But is this how strategy really happens in organizations? We will turn to this question and related issues in the next chapter.

Box 2.1 Corporate value statements – three examples

1. A. P. Moller – Maersk

Together with policies and programs, the new "Maersk Principles of Conduct" are designed to help business units and employees make the right choices in their daily engagement with colleagues, customers, suppliers, investors, and the community.

Our values are:

- **Constant Care** – Take care of today, actively prepare for tomorrow.
- **Humbleness** – Listen, learn, share, and give space to others.
- **Uprightness** – Our word is our bond.
- **Our Employees** – The right environment for the right people.

- **Our Name** – The sum of our values: passionately striving higher.

[www.maersk.com/aboutmaersk/whoweare/pages/values.aspx]

2. Mars Incorporated – the Five Principles of Mars

Quality – The consumer is our boss, quality is our work and value for money is our goal.
Responsibility – As individuals, we demand total responsibility from ourselves; as Associates, we support the responsibilities of others.
Mutuality – A mutual benefit is a shared benefit; a shared benefit will endure.
Efficiency – We use resources to the full, waste nothing and do only what we can do best.
Freedom – We need freedom to shape our future; we need profit to remain free.

[www.mars.com/global/about-mars/the-five-principles-of-mars.aspx]

3. Bayer – Science for a better life

The mission statement underscores Bayer's willingness as an inventor company to help shape the future and our determination to come up with innovations that benefit humankind. Of special importance are new products emerging from Bayer's active substance research, the consumer health business, the growth markets of Asia and new areas such as biotechnology and nanotechnology.

Our values:

- A will to succeed.
- A passion for our stakeholders.
- Integrity, openness and honesty.
- Respect for people and nature.
- Sustainability of our actions.

[www.bayer.com/en/mission-statement.aspx]

Box 2.2 A mission statement – an example

Our vision, values, policies, and ambition

"Touch the World" gives us a general direction, explaining what we stand for and where we are heading.

A vision alone is not enough for Novozymes to make our mark on the world and get closer to our vision of balance between better business, cleaner environment and better lives. For this reason we have brought together the fundamental guidelines for our day-to-day work in Touch the World. Touch the World is a simple guide consisting of four elements: our vision, company idea, commitment, and values.

Our vision:

We are heading for a future where our biological solutions create the necessary balance between better business, cleaner environment, and better lives.

Our company idea:

Rethink Tomorrow! *Novozymes* is committed to nothing less than changing the very foundations of our industrial system for the better. *We believe that through bioinnovation we can potentially re-engineer thousands of everyday products to deliver enhanced performance on a sustainable basis at no extra cost.*

Our company commitment:

We will do business by continuously improving our financial, environmental, and social performance to drive the world toward sustainability.

Our values:

1. Dare to lead – *because the future is created by you* (strive to be the best, never settle for what we have today, set brave goals and follow through, take initiative and volunteer yourself, develop yourself and your team).

2. Trust and earn trust – *because nothing beats a circle of trust* (clarify expectations and keep your promises, demonstrate professionalism, empower others, be open and honest, take care of others).
3. Connect to create – *because the world is full of ideas* (seek to understand the bigger picture, embrace diversity, learn from the outside, challenge conventions, take pride in finding solutions with others).
4. Unlock passion – *because passion makes dreams come alive* (inspire and excite others, love what you do, seek simple solutions fast, focus on opportunities rather than barriers, do not fear mistakes – learn from them).

Our ambition: Changing the world together with our customers.

[www.novozymes.com]

Box 2.3 Failing corporate conduct – three examples

1. Enron Corporation

As officers and employees of Enron Corp, its subsidiaries, and its affiliated companies ("Enron" or collectively the "Company"), we are responsible for conducting the business affairs of the Company in accordance with all applicable laws and in a moral and honest manner. To make certain that we understand what is expected of us, Enron has adopted certain policies, with the approval of the board of directors, all of which are set forth in the enclosed booklet, revised July 2000.

[Memorandum from Kenneth Lay, Chairman, July 1, 2000]

Enron's Code of Ethics – Values
Respect – we treat others as we would like to be treated ourselves.
Integrity – we work with customers and prospects openly, honestly, and sincerely.

Communication – we have an obligation to communicate.
Excellence – we are satisfied with nothing less than the very best in everything we do.

2. British Petroleum

The incident – On April 20, 2010 the Deepwater Horizon oil rig operated by Transocean Ltd. and commissioned by BP Plc. (the biggest oil producer in the Gulf of Mexico) exploded and sank while the search went on for 11 missing workers and efforts were undertaken to contain a large oil spill.

Our *code of conduct* is the cornerstone of our commitment to integrity. As Tony Hayward, our former group chief executive, affirmed: "Our reputation, and therefore our future as a business, depends on each of us, everywhere, every day, taking personal responsibility for the conduct of BP's business."

What does the code cover? The code covers five key areas of our business operations:
Health, safety, security and the environment – fundamental rules and guidance to help us protect the natural environment, the safety of the communities in which we operate, and the health, safety and security of our people.

[Official BP website]

3. LM Wind Power

Providing a safe, diverse and inspiring working environment
"A safe working environment is the prerequisite for our people to be able to deliver high quality products, efficient production processes and continuous improvement. LM Wind Power seeks to provide the best possible processes and facilities for all employees, from incorporating ergonomic improvements to make building our products more comfortable to technology research and investments that make our workplaces safer."

[Official LMWP website]

LM Wind Power signs the UN Global Compact – When is a green company, green enough? LM Wind Power, the world's largest wind turbine blade, brakes and service supplier to the wind industry, announced today that it has signed the *United Nations Global Compact.*

[Press release, February 1, 2011]

Poison Scandal at Green Danish Pioneer – Thousands of mainly unskilled workers made the Danish wind miracle happen at LM Wind Power factories, supplying seven out of ten of the world's largest wind turbine manufacturers. But, many were sick of the yellow poison. Thousands of employees at LM Wind Power have for years been exposed to the poison styrene.

[*Berlingske Sunday* – front-page article, February 20, 2011]

Box 2.4 Scenario analysis

A *scenario* is a consistent description of the future business environment that can be used as a common basis for strategic thinking particularly for companies operating in rapidly changing and highly uncertain industries where influential environmental factors are beyond simple statistical analysis. As a starting point the firm should identify the important exogenous environmental factors that may exert a significant influence on the competitive dynamics in the industry and hence affect future strategy. This process can adopt a variety of frameworks, e.g., PEST, industry, competitor, and stakeholder analysis involving internal and external experts, Delphi techniques, etc. The factors can be arranged according to potential impact and level of uncertainty (see figure below). Factors 1, 2, 3, and 4 are then candidates for setting up scenarios for further analysis.

Further considerations specifying what causes the uncertainties around these influential factors may help uncover major themes capturing trends, developments, and

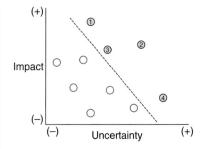

events that fuel those uncertainties. This can be used to set up a number of consistent base scenarios and express those in extensive descriptions that incorporate the identified uncertainty themes. The themes might, for example, relate to the future growth rate in the global economy ranging from low "decline" to high "growth" and by the speed of innovation in the product market ranging from gradual "evolution" to dramatic "revolution" (see figure below). This classification of themes develops into four scenarios of "more of the same", "extreme competition", "surprises", and "brave new world". These scenarios can be characterized and described in more detail to form a basis for internal discussions and strategic thinking exercises trying to assess what the likely effects will be and whether and how the firm can/should respond to these representative situations. While this establishes a somewhat generic framework for scenario analysis it can obviously take many different forms depending on the industry and its circumstances.

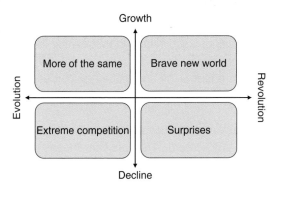

Box 2.5 Resource-based economics (VRIO)

The resource-based view explains how firm resources and capabilities can create value, form competitive advantage, and drive sustainable competitive advantage. By analyzing the firm's resources, it is possible to assess the potential for sustainable competitive advantage.

First, we identify important resources and competencies in the firm that can take the form of: (1) financial capital, (2) physical capital, (3) human capital, and (4) organizational capital. *Financial capital* includes things like cash in hand, equity and capital reserves, organizational slack, etc. This constitutes the resources that can enhance development of business activities and implementation of strategic initiatives and actions. *Physical capital* is comprised of buildings, plant and equipment, market access, retail outlets, warehouses, computers, software, production technologies, automated warehousing, etc. These resources support current business activities and may be used as the basis for future product and process innovation. *Human capital* consists of educated and trained people, intelligence, knowledge and experiential insights, social relationships, and entrepreneurial abilities. Many of these resources are intangible human-based constructs that can help the organization think, innovate, and act in new entrepreneurial ways. *Organizational capital* includes things like organizational structure, incentives, planning processes, control systems, communication channels, knowledge storage, and information systems used to manage current business activities and that can be levered into new strategic ventures.

Second, we should prioritize the indentified resources and capabilities in order of importance, distinctiveness, and economic influence.

Third, the listed resources and capabilities are assessed in accordance with the VRIO criteria. This basically means that it is determined whether they are valuable, rare, inimitable, and organizable for the firm, or not. To the extent a resource or capability fulfills all four criteria there is a basis for driving sustainable competitive advantage from this source (see framework below).

Is a resource or capability …				Sustainable competitive advantage
Valuable?	Rare?	Inimitable?	Organizable?	
1. Yes/No	Yes/No	Yes/No	Yes/No	**Yes/No**
2. Yes/No	Yes/No	Yes/No	Yes/No	**Yes/No**
3. Yes/No	Yes/No	Yes/No	Yes/No	**Yes/No**
4. Yes/No	Yes/No	Yes/No	Yes/No	**Yes/No**
5. Yes/No	Yes/No	Yes/No	Yes/No	**Yes/No**
6. Yes/No	Yes/No	Yes/No	Yes/No	**Yes/No**

All four criteria must be fulfilled!

Adopting a business model perspective we might, for example, identify unique resources at *Southwest Airlines* attached to their point-to-point system (as opposed to conventional hub-and-spoke), using an all Boing-737 fleet, and maintaining a strong service culture. The competition has tried to emulate this but with mixed results.

Using a value chain perspective we can identify unique resources at *Dell Computer* related to their internet-based personal ordering system, a mass-customization technology, and direct distribution combined with online service centers. These elements of their value chain are well described (see the Dell website) but have not been easy for competitors to copy successfully.

Box 2.6 Alternative value chain concepts

The conventional value chain refers to the long-linked technologies of production processes with serial inter-dependencies as observed in various manufacturing industries.

1. Value shops

The value shop refers to so-called *intensive technologies* including processes related to advisory and diagnostic services. It applies to firms that make a business from solving problems for their customers. These organizations include professional services firms in fields such as medicine, law, architecture, engineering, oil exploration, construction, investment banking, consulting, etc. The primary activities comprise problem acquisition (origination), problem solving, choice, execution, control, and evaluation that take place sequentially across large pools of clients (see figure below).

The quality of solutions as perceived by the customers and the associated reputation is an important value driver and the ability to integrate knowledge developed from prior consultations can improve production effectiveness.

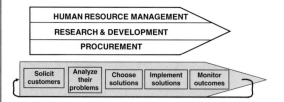

Source: adapted from Stabell and Fjeldstad (1998)

2. Service networks

The service network refers to so-called *mediating technologies* where processes link the customers together in large interacting pools. It applies to firms that conduct business by linking customers in large interacting networks. This includes industries such as telecommunications, internet provision, energy distribution, retailing, insurance, banking, postal services, transportation, etc. The primary activities comprise network promotion and contract management (to hook up individual clients), service provisioning, and infrastructure operations to ensure effective execution (see figure below).

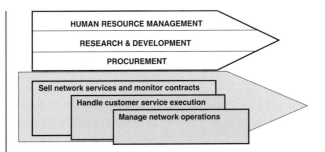

Source: adapted from Stabell and Fjeldstad (1998)

The scale of the network enhances the value to the customers, improves capacity utilization and creates scale economies. Effective customer handling and the reliability of the network infrastructure are essential competitive parameters.

Notes

1 This rational approach to decision making can be found in many earlier management writings, for example P. F. Drucker, The effective decision, *Harvard Business Review* 45(1): 92–98, 1967; H. Simon *et al.*, Decision making and problem solving, *Interfaces* 17(5): 11–31, 1987.
2 For variations on this theme see a number of strategy textbooks, e.g., G. G. Dess *et al.*, *Strategic Management: Creating Competitive Advantages*, McGraw-Hill: Boston, MA (p. 24), 2008; R. de Wit, R. Meyer, *Strategy – Process, Content, Context*, Thomson: London (p. 590), 2004; J. S. Harrison, *Strategic Management of Resources and Relationships*, Wiley: New York (p. 122), 2003; G. Johnson *et al.*, *Exploring Corporate Strategy,* FT Prentice Hall: Harlow (p. 207), 2006; J. McGee *et al.*, *Strategy: Analysis & Practice*, McGraw-Hill: London (p. 14), 2005; C. W. Hill, G. R. Jones, *Strategic Management Theory: An Integrated Approach*, Houghton Mifflin: Boston, MA (p. 45), 2001; D. L. Rainey, *Enterprise-Wide Strategic Management*, Cambridge University Press (p. 332), 2010; G. Saloner *et al.*, *Strategic Management*, Wiley: New York (p. 24), 2001; A. A. Thompson *et al.*, *Crafting and Executing Strategy: The Quest for Competitive Advantage*, McGraw-Hill Irwin: New York, 2005 (p. 20).
3 See, for example, C. Anderson, Values-based management, *Academy of Management Executive* 11(4): 25–46, 1997.
4 R. E. Freeman, *Strategic Management: A Stakeholder Approach*, Cambridge University Press, 1984.

5 R. E. Freeman *et al.*, *Stakeholder Theory: The State of the Art*, Cambridge University Press, 2010.

6 See, for example G. Owen, *The Rise and Fall of Great Companies: Courtaulds and the Reshaping of the Man-Made Fibers Industry*, Oxford University Press: New York, 2010; J. Collins, J. Porras, *Built to Last: Successful Habits of Visionary Companies*, Random House: London, 1994.

7 T. J. Andersen, Corporate relationship management as driver of socially responsible behavior, *Nordic Symposium for Corporate Social Responsibility*, Copenhagen Business School, June 2011.

8 Official news release: "The Maersk Principles of Conduct in place," February 6, 2010.

9 See the company website: www.maersk.com/AboutMaersk/WhoWeAre/Pages/Values.aspx.

10 C. H. House, R. L. Price, *The HP Phenomenon: Innovation and Business Transformation*, Stanford University Press, 2009.

11 D. Packard, *The HP Way: How Bill Hewlett and I Built Our Company*, HarperCollins: New York, 1995.

12 J. Collins, *Good to Great: Why Some Companies Make the Leap … and Others Don't*, Random House Business Books: London, 2001 (p. 195).

13 J. B. Quinn, Strategic change: "logical incrementalism," *Sloan Management Review* 20(1): 7–21, 1978; J. B. Quinn *Strategies for Change: Logical Incrementalism*, Irwin: Homewood, IL, 1980.

14 N. Ejler *et al.*, *Managing the Knowledge-Intensive Firm*, Routledge: London, 2011.

15 In this context, it is interesting to note that a number of contemporary strategy texts emphasizing innovation and dynamic adaptation make no explicit references to corporate mission and values, for example C. Bilton, S. Cummings, *Creative Strategy: Reconnecting Business and Innovation*, Wiley: Chichester, 2010; T. H. Davenport *et al.*, *Strategic Management in the Innovation Economy: Strategy Approaches and Tools for Dynamic Innovation Capabilities*, Publicis Corporate Publishing and Wiley-VCH Verlag: Erlangen, Germany, 2006; D. J. Teece, *Dynamic Capabilities and Strategic Management: Organizing for Innovation and Growth*, Oxford University Press: New York, 2009.

16 E. H. Schein, *Organizational Culture and Leadership*, Jossey-Bass: San Francisco, 2004.

17 See, for example, classics such as W. Dill, Environment as an influence on managerial autonomy, *Administrative Science Quarterly* 2(2): 409–443, 1958; J. Thompson, *Organizations in Action*, McGraw-Hill: New York, 1967; L. Fahey *et al.*, Environmental scanning and forecasting in strategic planning – the state of the art, *Long Range Planning* 14(1): 32–39, 1981.

18 A social responsibility perspective considering relationships to stakeholders in civil society can extend the analysis of the external environment to include broader concerns for important social factors that otherwise might be overlooked. See, for example, B. Kytle, J. G. Ruggie, Corporate social responsibility as risk management: A model for multinationals,

Working Paper No. 10, John F. Kennedy School of Government, Harvard University, 2005.

19 Once the important external environmental factors are identified they can be assessed further by applying Delphi techniques where the "experts" evaluate potential impacts and a facilitator mediates discussions around reported means and deviations to reach a common view. See, for example, H. A. Linstone, M. Turoff, *The Delphi Method: Techniques and Applications*, Addison-Wesley: Reading, MA, 1975; H. A. Linstone, *Multiple Perspectives for Decision Making: Bridging the Gap between Analysis and Action*, Elsevier: New York, 1984 (p. 327); G. Bojadziev, M. Bojadziev, *Fuzzy Logic for Business, Finance, and Management* (second edn.), World Scientific Publishing: Singapore, 2007 (p. 71).

20 The term "Black Swan" refers to unusual conditions and unlikely events that are beyond normal statistical analysis. N. N. Taleb, *The Black Swan: The Impact of the Highly Improbable*, Random House: New York, 2007.

21 See, for example, M. H. Bazerman, M. D. Watkins, *Predictable Surprises: The Disasters You Should Have Seen Coming, and How to Prevent Them*, Harvard Business Press: Boston, MA, 2008.

22 For example, D. Besnako *et al.*, *Economics of Strategy* (fifth edn.), Wiley: Hoboken, NJ, 2010.

23 J. S. Bain, *Barriers to New Competition*, Harvard University Press: Cambridge, MA, 1956.

24 M. E. Porter, *Competitive Strategy: Techniques for Analyzing Industries and Competitors,* Collier Macmillan: London, 1980.

25 M. E. Porter, The five competitive forces that shape strategy, *Harvard Business Review* 86(1): 78–93, 2008.

26 See, for example, M. H. Bazerman, D. A. Moore, *Judgment in Managerial Decision Making* (seventh edn.), Wiley: Hoboken, NJ, 2009.

27 Adapted from M. E. Porter, *Competitive Strategy: Techniques for Analyzing Industries and Competitors,* Collier Macmillan: London, 1980.

28 See, for example, B. Gilad, *Early Warning: Using Competitive Intelligence to Anticipate Market Shifts, Control Risk, and Create Powerful Strategies*, American Management Association (AMACOM): New York, 2004; S. Sharp, *Competitive Intelligence Advantage: How to Minimize Risk, Avoid Surprises, and Grow Your Business in a Changing World*, Wiley: Hoboken, NJ, 2009.

29 See, for example, A. K. Dixit, B. J. Nalebuff, *The Art of Strategy: A Game Theorist's Guide to Success in Business and Life*, Norton: New York, 2008; P. K. Dutta, *Strategies and Games: Theory and Practice*, MIT Press: Cambridge, MA, 1999; J. Miller, *Game Theory at Work: How to Use Game Theory to Outthink and Outmaneuver Your Competition*, McGraw-Hill: New York, 2003; L. Fisher, *Rock, Paper, Scissors: Game Theory in Everyday Life*, Hay House: London, 2008.

30 See, for example, E. F. Harrison, *The Managerial Decision-Making Process*, Houghton Mifflin: Boston, MA, 1999 (p. 374).

31 R. M. Grant, *Contemporary Strategy Analysis* (fourth edn.), Blackwell Publishing: Malden, MA, 2002 (p. 111).

32 A. M. Brandenburger, B. J. Nalebuff, *Co-opetition*, Currency Doubleday: New York, 1996.

33 A. S. Grove, *Only the Paranoid Survive: How to Exploit the Crisis Points that Challenge Every Company and Career*, HarperCollins Business: London, 1997.

34 The term "strategic inflection point" was coined by R. A. Burgelman and A. S. Grove: Strategic dissonance, *California Management Review* 38(2): 8–28, 1996; *Strategy Is Destiny: How Strategy-Making Shapes a Company's Future*, Free Press: New York, 2002.

35 For example discussed in C. H. Fine, *Clock Speed: Winning Industry Control in the Age of Temporary Advantage*, Basic Books: New York, 1998.

36 See, for example, R. Gulati *et al.*, Strategic networks, *Strategic Management Journal* Special Issue 21(3): 203–215, 2000.

37 See, for example, G. G. Dess *et al.*, *Strategic Management: Creating Competitive Advantage* (second edn.), McGraw-Hill Irwin: Boston, MA, 2005 (p. 172); R. M. Grant *Contemporary Strategy Analysis* (sixth edn.), Blackwell Publishing: Malden, MA, 2008 (p. 116).

38 D. J. Teece, *Dynamic Capabilities and Strategic Management*, Oxford University Press: New York, 2009.

39 C. M. Christensen, *The Innovator's Dilemma: When New Technologies Cause Great Firms to Fail*, Harvard Business School Press: Boston, MA, 1997.

40 R. A. D'Aveni, *Hypercompetition: Managing the Dynamics of Strategic Maneuvering*, Free Press: New York, 1994.

41 R. A. D'Aveni, Strategic supremacy through disruption and dominance, *Sloan Management Review* Spring: 127–135, 1999.

42 Light bulbs: Charge of the LED brigade, *The Economist*, August 20, 2011.

43 See, for example, L. Fahey, How corporations learn from scenarios, *Strategy & Leadership* 31(2): 5–15, 2003; P. J. H. Schoemaker, Scenario planning: A tool for strategic thinking, *Sloan Management Review*, Winter: 25–40, 2003; R. Ramirez *et al.*, *Business Planning for Turbulent Tines: New Methods for Applying Scenarios*, Earthscan: London, 2008; B. Ralston, I. Wilson, *The Scenario Planning Handbook*. Thomson/South-Western: Mason, OH, 2006.

44 See, for example, M. S. Granovetter, The strength of weak ties, *American Journal of Sociology* 78(6): 1360–1380, 1973; J. Nahapiet, S. Ghoshal, Social capital, intellectual capital, and the organizational advantage, *Academy of Management Review* 23(2): 242, 1998.

45 R. E. Freeman *et al.*, *Stakeholder Theory: The State of the Art*, Cambridge University Press, 2010.

46 A. Werbach, *Strategy for Sustainability: A Business Manifesto*, Harvard Business School Press: Boston, MA, 2009.

47 These considerations have been stimulated further by the official launch of the UN Compact in 2000.

48 See, for example, S. Ambec, P. Lanoie, Does it pay to be green? A systematic overview, *Academy of Management Perspectives* 22(4): 45–62, 2008; M. P. Sharfman, C. S. Fernando, Environmental risk management and the cost of capital, *Strategic Management Journal* 29: 569–592, 2008.

49 See M. J. Hatch, *Organization Theory* (second edn.), Oxford University Press, 2006.

50 H. Mintzberg, *The Structuring of Organizations*, Prentice Hall: Englewood Cliffs, NJ, 1979; H. Mintzberg, *Structures in Fives: Designing Effective Organizations*, Prentice Hall: Englewood Cliffs, NJ, 1983.

51 J. R. Galbraith, *Organization Design*, Addison-Wesley: Reading, MA, 1977; R. H. Waterman, The seven elements of strategic fit, *Journal of Business Strategy* 2(3): 69–73, 1982.

52 J. B. Barney, *Gaining and Sustaining Competitive Advantage* (second edn.), Prentice Hall: Upper Saddle River, NJ, 2002.

53 M. E. Porter, *Competitive Advantage: Creating and Sustaining Superior Performance*, Free Press: New York, 1985.

54 This terminology was coined by Thompson who distinguished between *sequential long-linked technologies* with serial interdependencies (e.g., companies that manufacture products), *intensive technologies* for customized solutions, change and therapeutic activities (e.g., advisory shops), and *mediating technologies* linking interdependent customers (e.g., network firms). J. Thompson, *Organizations in Action*, McGraw-Hill: New York, 1967.

55 C. B. Stabell, Ø. D. Fjeldstad Configuring value for competitive advantage, *Strategic Management Journal* 19(5): 413–437, 1998.

56 H. Weihrich, The TOWS matrix – A tool for situational analysis, *Long Range Planning* 15(2): 54–66, 1982.

57 A point made earlier by Igor Ansoff. See I. Ansoff, *Corporate Strategy*, McGraw-Hill: New York, 1965.

58 A. J. Slywotsky, *Value Migration: How to Think Several Moves Ahead of the Competition*, Harvard Business School Press: Boston, MA, 1996; A. J. Slywotsky, D. J. Morrison, *The Profit Zone: How Strategic Business Design Will Lead You to Tomorrow's Profits*, Wiley: Chichester, 1997.

59 Bethlehem Steel, once the second largest US steel company, was bought in 2003 by International Steel, which later merged with the European Mittal Steel Group.

60 See, for example, G. Hamel, *Leading the Revolution*, Harvard Business School Press: Boston, MA, 2000.

61 A. Osterwalder, Y. Pigneur, *Business Model Generation*, Wiley: Hoboken, NJ, 2010.

62 See, for example, A. Fiegenbaum *et al.*, Strategic reference point theory, *Strategic Management Journal* 17(2): 219–235, 1996.

63 M. E. Porter, What is strategy? *Harvard Business Review*, November–December: 61–78, 1996; R. S. Kaplan, D. P. Norton, *Alignment: Using the Balanced Scorecard to Create Corporate Synergies*. Harvard Business School Press: Boston, MA, 2006.

64 W. C. Kim, R. Mauborgne, *Blue Ocean Strategy: How to Create Uncontested Market Space and Make the Competition Irrelevant*, Harvard Business School Press: Boston, MA, 2005.

65 M. M. Andersen, F. Poulfelt, *Discount Business Strategies: How the New Market Leaders are Redefining Business Strategy*, Wiley: Chichester, 2006.

66 See R. S. Kaplan, D. P. Norton, *The Strategy-Focused Organization: How Balanced Scorecard Companies Thrive in the New Business Environment*, Harvard

Business School Press: Boston, MA, 2001. R. S. Kaplan, D. P. Norton, *Strategy Maps: Converting Intangible Assets into Tangible Outcomes*, Harvard Business School Press: Boston, MA, 2004.

67 See, for example, J. Denrell, Selection bias and the perils of benchmarking, *Harvard Business Review* 83(4): 114–119, 2005.

68 A. D. Levinthal, J. G. March, The myopia of learning, *Strategic Management Journal* Special Issue 14: 95–112, 1993; D. Miller, *The Icarus Paradox: How Exceptional Companies Bring About Their Own Downfall*, Harper Business: New York, 1990.

69 J. Pfeffer, R. I. Sutton, *Hard Facts, Dangerous Half-Truths and Total Nonsense: Profiting from Evidence-Based Management*, Harvard Business School Press: Boston, MA, 2006 (p. 7).

70 Contemporary project planning notes the potential negative consequences of rigid plans that cannot be modified to accommodate new important information during the implementation period. See, for example, C. Chapman, S. Ward, *Project Risk Management: Processes, Techniques and Insights*, Wiley: Chichester, 2004; P. S. Royer, *Project Risk Management: A Proactive Approach*, Management Concepts: Vienna, VA, 2002.

71 D. Schendel, C. Hofer, *Strategic Management: A New View of Business Policy and Planning*, Little, Brown: Boston, MA, 1979.

72 J. Pfeffer, R. I. Sutton, *Hard Facts, Dangerous Half-Truths and Total Nonsense: Profiting from Evidence-Based Management*, Harvard Business School Press: Boston, MA, 2006.

73 See, for example, S. Finkelstein, *Why Smart Executives Fail – and What You Can Learn from Their Mistakes*, Portfolio: New York, 2003.

74 H. Raiffa, *Decision Analysis: Introductory Lectures on Choices under Uncertainty*, Addison-Wesley: Reading, MA, 1968.

75 I. I. Mitroff, A. Silvers, *Dirty Rotten Strategies: How We Trick Ourselves and Others into Solving the Wrong Problems Precisely*, Stanford Business Books: Stanford, CA, 2010.

3 Strategy execution

Learning points

- Discuss how strategy happens
- See strategy as managing a portfolio of projects
- Strategy formed through a pattern of decisions and actions
- Link strategy formation to corporate entrepreneurship
- Form the background for an integrative model

Once the future strategic path has been staked out in the strategy formulation process, the next logical step in a rational analytical approach to strategy making is to ensure that the necessary actions are carried out to make the intended strategic aims come true. In accordance with this prescriptive view of strategy making, top management drives the strategic thinking process and forms the overarching plans for the necessary actions to be taken. Then the organization's line and middle managers step in to ensure that the stipulated actions are executed in accordance with the strategic plan. By *strategy execution* we typically mean successful implementation to accomplish the strategic plan. So, if the strategy fails, it is often ascribed to poor implementation, thus implying that the underlying strategy signed off by the board was alright – top management was just not able to make things happen and ensure that the intended aims came true. Hence, successful implementation may hinge upon the acceptance of middle management because when managers find their self-interest compromised, they may delay, obstruct, or even sabotage implementation.[1] In addition to assessing the potential obstacles and aligning resources and reward structures, it is often considered important to "sell" the strategy to organizational members.[2] Hence, the strategy textbooks frequently argue that communication is essential for effective execution of the strategy to gain support and clarify to managers throughout the organization what it is they are supposed to do. Similarly, an underlying tenet in much of the change management literature is to prevent employee resistance and achieve buy-in, commitment, and consensus around planned actions.[3] This reflects a view that as long as top management clearly explains the intended strategy and aligns people in the organization accordingly, then things are supposed to happen as planned.

Conversely, some argue that the competitive context might change before the planned actions can be carried out and that the underlying assumptions, therefore, are outdated by the time the strategy is implemented.[4] Instead the organization should rely on business initiatives taken at the bottom of the organization as managers learn from changes in the environment and see the need for new products, services, and practices in a rapidly changing market place. So, there are arguments for a designed *top-down*-driven strategy as well as for *bottom-up* approaches where strategic outcomes emerge from initiatives taken by managers within the organization. However, the reality is probably not as simple as either of these alternative views suggests but is in all likelihood comprised of more complicated back and forth processes that interweave top-down and bottom-up processes over time. In fact, strategy formulation and implementation do not necessarily constitute distinctive stages enacted in a linear manner but are interconnected phenomena that intermingle over time.[5] Hence, the path to strategy execution where concrete organizational actions are taken derives from a mix of formally structured activities that interact with unstructured initiatives and improvised interventions that often play out in intriguing and complex ways (Figure 3.1).

There are few formal definitions of strategy implementation but it is generally seen as something that is supposed to take place after the strategic plan has been conceived. The views adopted to describe implementation activities range from the operationalization of an articulated plan to the interpersonal dynamics that surround ensuing organizational actions.[6] So, the particular meanings of implementation and execution differ across more nuanced understandings of how organizations come to realize their strategic outcomes. The formal *strategy-making process* discussed in the previous chapter is commonly perceived as a regular and recurring phenomenon where the organization

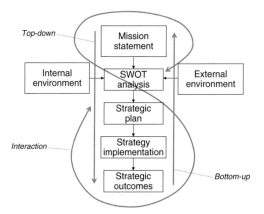

Figure 3.1 How does strategy really shape up?

formulates its strategy, outlines a strategic plan for forward actions, and then implements the actions stipulated in the plan.[7] The *planning horizon* indicates the time period management looks into the future as it extrapolates strategic aims and actions. Many organizations adopt three-, five-, or ten-year time windows to develop their strategic goals but at the same time develop short-term action plans to outline efforts for interim strategy execution. The chosen time window is important as it frames the expectations for future resource allocation and brings managerial attention to interim needs for coordination of organizational actions.[8] While the strategic thinking should look several years ahead, strategy-making processes commonly coincide with the annual budget cycles. This may sound rather mundane and driven by convenience, but it has the potential advantage of matching the planning intervals with conventions for monthly and quarterly reporting periods and budget follow-up meetings. So, in practice the planning process is typically an annual recurring event.

In many organizations the strategy-making process starts off by top management some time around mid-year communicating their strategic ambitions setting performance targets for the next accounting period.[9] This often signals the development of more detailed strategic plans in business units and functional entities submitted to head office for further scrutiny and discussions before entering a formal corporate plan with expense budgets and capital allocations for the coming year.[10] Strategy textbooks rarely promote one particular process as being more effective, possibly in realization that there are as many process variations as there are organizations around. The fact is that there are multiple ways to pursue the planning exercise and it is often discussed in rather generic terms. In practice, strategy making does not merely follow a simple planning process but has many intertwined elements to it (see Box 3.1 *Corporate strategy development*).

Hence, strategies somehow take form through intended actions shaped by interpretations of the competitive context and ongoing adaptations to changing environmental conditions. This has inspired the concept of *strategy formation* where a view of strategy as "a pattern in a stream of decisions" has provided the basis for descriptive studies of how strategies actually come about in organizations.[11] For example, Mintzberg and Waters traced the strategic development of the Montreal-based retailer Steinberg over sixty years and indentified six strategic shifts during this period as the firm responded to changing economic, socio-political, and technological conditions.[12]

Different strategy-making modes

The broader views on strategy formation have inspired a number of representative categorizations of how firms conduct their strategy process that present distinct *strategy-making modes*.[13] Mintzberg identified three modes of planning, entrepreneurial, and adaptive strategy making. The *planning* mode corresponds to the conventional strategic management model that arguably applies to large organizations operating in relatively stable and predictable industries where analytical forecasts can be useful. The *entrepreneurial* mode reflects organizations where the vision of a dominant owner, e.g., in a start-up company, imposes a particular strategic purpose and behavioral conduct on the entire organization. The *adaptive* mode supposedly captures organizations that operate in dynamic environments where strategic actions are modified and adapted in accordance with emerging changes in the environment.[14] Here, the planned activities correspond to the firm's *intended* strategy whereas the ad hoc adaptive activities correspond to the *emergent* strategy (Figure 3.2). These strategy-making modes span from autocratic

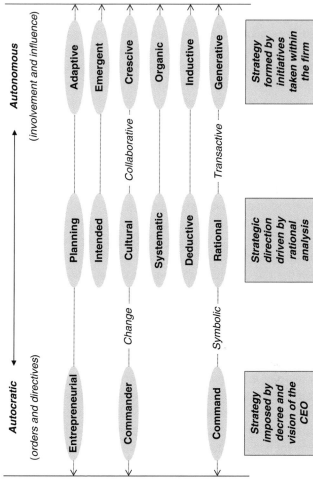

Figure 3.2 Some typologies for the strategy-making process. Source: adapted from Andersen (2004)

processes driven by orders and directives from top management to more autonomous processes driven by the involvement and influences exerted by managers at the lower hierarchical levels in the organization.

There have been many other attempts to describe different approaches to strategy making. Bourgeois and Brodwin outlined five typologies ranging from a highly autocratic top-down process referred to as *commander* via intermediate *change*, *cultural* and *collaborative* forms to an autonomous and interactive *crescive* bottom-up process.[15] Ansoff referred to planning as a *systematic* approach and recognized a role for *reactive* and *organic* strategic activities where the organization responds to unexpected changes.[16] Nonaka distinguished between analytics-based *deductive* modes and *inductive* modes influenced by initiatives taken among employees.[17] Based on studies of large Japanese firms he suggested a particular *middle-up-down* approach where dynamic interaction between top-down and bottom-up processes is at play. Here, middle managers assume the important role of transmitting top management's vision to lower-level managers while capturing the employees' realistic sense of how things are and what should be done. Thereby they facilitate a bridging process between the top and the bottom of the organization. Stuart Hart integrated themes of rationality, vision, and involvement around five modes (*command*, *symbolic*, *rational*, *transactive*, *generative*), ranging from a command mode with strong centralized controls to a generative mode driven by autonomous actions among organizational members.[18] Assuming that firms are able to pursue one or more of these modes simultaneously may suggest that organizations that master multiple strategy modes are more successful.[19] For example, tight competition makes it necessary to impose centralized cost efficiencies whereas a high-growth environment calls for decentralized development of business opportunities. Hence, it might be opportune to pursue both aspects at the same time with the possibility of switching emphasis between approaches as the competitive conditions change.

Given the complexity of the many tasks organizations must perform, the strategic focus of different business units varies from trying to optimize existing processes to dealing with ad hoc issues. Hence, strategy formation can be affected simultaneously by a variety of factors that make it difficult and less meaningful to ascribe a single pattern to strategy making across the entire organization, even though some patterns can be more predominant than others. The need to employ different strategy approaches can differ across functional areas, where operations may be preoccupied with process optimization whereas sales is more focused on product and service innovation. Furthermore, there may be differences across geographical boundaries as particular competitive and socio-political conditions require different strategic responses. The call for specific strategy-making approaches can also vary over time as new competing inventions and industry shifts occur in abrupt bursts and economic activity evolves along unpredictable business cycles.

This seems to suggest that it is advantageous to remain flexible and allow for possible strategic redirection while maintaining a certain repertoire of strategy-making modes that can support future strategic needs. One approach is to establish a capability for flexible responses, as captured in Quinn's concept of *logical incrementalism*.[20] Here, the chief executive establishes fairly general long-term goals and aspirations to guide organizational activities but at the same time avoids making them detailed and concrete so they become a straitjacket for future adaptation to business activities. This way the organization retains the flexibility to act, modify business activities, and change strategic direction when it is needed while at the same time being consistent toward an overarching purpose. In terms of Hart's terminology, this approach can be interpreted as a combination of symbolic and generative strategy-making modes. Hence, the senior executives set the general aims and goals but involve key managers in the decision-making process to assess alternative responses when new strategic challenges arise. This means that formulation and implementation activities are intertwined and constitute interacting phenomena rather than two distinct activities separated by time. As Quinn argues: "Constantly integrating the simultaneous incremental process of strategy formulation and implementation is the central art of effective strategic management." So, logical incrementalism can be interpreted as a longitudinal process where business development takes place as a consequence of many small and often unplanned incremental responses as opposed to one large or a few extensively planned initiatives. In a comparison between *deterministic planning* and *incremental adaptive* strategy making, Bourgeois proposes that "goals and means interact and adjust in light of what is currently feasible and politically acceptable."[21]

Seen in this context, maybe one of the most important benefits of the formal planning process is to involve key decision makers across the organization in assessments of the firm's competitive conditions derived from rational analyses and supported by updated information. Even though the associated discussions may not lead to complete agreement about the environmental context, the process has the potential to create a common understanding of the strategic challenges the organization is confronted with and a shared analytical framework for dealing with strategic issues when they emerge.[22] This may facilitate more open discussions based on a common corporate language as environmental developments are interpreted and alternative strategic initiatives are evaluated. The diversity of views can help in this process whereas achieving complete consensus has the potential of forming a basis for "groupthink" and inability to see new developments.[23] Strong consensus can reduce divergent views and thereby possibly speed up the decision-making process, but it does not necessarily lead to better solutions and decision outcomes.

Kathleen Eisenhardt studied fast decision making among firms in turbulent industries and found that comprehensive analyses of the underlying issues and the development and consideration of more alternative options are all part of a good and timely strategic decision-making process.[24] At the same time, she found that the use of real-time information speeds up the decision process so embedded risks and opportunities are spotted faster where the interpretation of updated information sharpens the intuition of the executive decision makers. The involvement of key managers in the decision process, and engaging experienced advisors to assess alternatives, support the evaluative discussions, although active conflict resolution by the senior executive can be required. Eventually the senior executive might have to cut through once discussions have reached a certain point to get at a final decision that will resolve potential disagreements and conflicts of opinion. Hence, we are introduced to a comprehensive analytical process with direct involvement and online information updating that has some of the hallmarks of both top-down and bottom-up processes.

Strategy implementation

The prescriptive rational analytical approach to strategy, referred to as strategy formulation, or strategic planning, takes a sequential linear view of the strategy-making process that for a good reason precludes advance treatment of unforeseeable and hence unexpected events. Yet, it holds the promise of establishing useful insights about the competitive environment and potential challenges associated with its dynamic evolution while establishing common ground for strategic discussions among key decision makers in the organization. Hence, the reality is that most companies somehow think about strategy and use it to plan for the future. Accordingly, Kaplan and Norton claim that "despite the many criticisms and complaints levied against it, strategic planning remains senior executives' favorite management tool."[25] According to the *traditional planning* approach, the strategic objectives from the formulation process should feed into concrete plans for strategic actions to be carried out with (at least) one initiative per stated objective. A planning review will scrutinize the proposed operations in more detail to refine the process and gain additional rationalizations. The ability to overcome inertia and resistance among people in the organization is considered a high priority in this process. Once the initiatives are rolled out, their progress could be discussed at regular operational and strategy review meetings including relevant members from the business units involved in the planned activities. The meetings would typically be conducted on a quarterly or monthly basis, although no real consensus exists with regards to the best frequency. The development of corporate activities and strategic outcomes is compared with planned results, as prescribed by the strategic control loop, and may help identify adaptations necessary to the general strategy annually or possibly each quarter. This approach combines the strategic and operational activities and assigns discretionary projects and programs to achieve specific strategic objectives. The related ability to link general strategic aims to operational initiatives in recurring planning, control, and feedback loops defines the tasks to be accomplished by staff in a central office of strategic management.

However, one can question the efficacy of this approach and its ability to ascertain new developments with sufficient speed and opportunism and its ability to identify related changes in the contemporary risk and opportunity landscape. The comfort associated with regular and recurring planning and budget reviews around planned targets may divert attention from the many small things that occur around the edges of the organization and that are observed by people engaged in the daily operational tasks. It is often through the ongoing interaction with important internal and external stakeholders that organizational members identify subtle changes in demand patterns, business practices, and technological applications. Hence, drawing on Hrebiniak, one can claim that "strategic success demands a 'simultaneous' view of planning and doing."[26] This is not so just because plans have to be enacted to make a difference, it is more because there is a need for ongoing updating from the current activities in many parts of the organization as various plans, projects, and programs are carried out. That is, the planning process will influence subsequent actions but the continuous learning from ongoing execution efforts will uncover necessary changes to the strategy. In other words, the execution of planned strategic actions is shaped by a series of integrated decisions over time informed by ongoing controls and interactive feedback interventions. Hence, the involvement of people is vital to successful execution because politics, inertia, and resistance may get in the way, but even more importantly because the ability to share essential information and knowledge is central to the development of good adaptive solutions along the way.

It seems pretty safe to assume that when a planned strategy is implemented it never pans out in accordance with the original plan, so the strategy most likely has to be amended several times during implementation. From this perspective the analytical efforts in the planning phase can be overdone with excessive details to the detriment of effective execution. Since we cannot know everything in advance and can gain incremental insights through experiments with trial-and-error learning, it is arguably important to "start doing" once there is agreement that a certain initiative will move the organization in the right direction.[27] However, if the execution of strategic initiatives is delegated and falls outside the view of senior management, there could be a problem because then the executives are out of tune and it might be difficult to make subsequent changes in the strategic direction. Since it is people in the organization that execute concrete operations and thereby implement the strategy, the executives should remain involved and not dissociate themselves once the strategy is formulated. Their direct engagement can accommodate timely strategic adaptations as things evolve. Whereas general acceptance of corporate aims and aspirations may be important to encourage organizational actions, some argue that people generally do not resist change. Instead most problems with strategy implementation are caused by a lack of leadership attention, interest, and support.[28] In this context, the establishment of a strategic project office (SPO) or office of strategic management (OSM) may help facilitate ongoing interaction between senior management and the many doers throughout the organization as a way to ensure more effective execution.

The preceding discussion suggests that the strategy-making process is complex and consists of interacting elements of formulation and implementation activities where the enactment of concrete strategic activities can be described in different ways and interpreted through different lenses. This points to at least five partially complementary ways to interpret the making or execution of strategy: (1) strategy developed from investment in business projects, (2) strategy evolving from a portfolio of "real options," (3) strategy formed by decisions that lead to particular actions, (4) strategy driven by entrepreneurial initiatives taken throughout the organization, and (5) strategy shaped by habitual and learned organizational practices. In the following sections, we take a closer look at these perspectives.

Strategy as project management

If you ask an executive how he or she will ensure that a decision to move the organization in a certain direction is executed, a likely response is that it is done by establishing a number of projects for concrete business activities to accomplish these key objectives. The projects can take many different forms, including product development, restructuring the supply chain, geographical expansion of sales, building internal communication and information systems, etc. Each of these projects may try to accomplish one or more of the strategic goals, such as grow revenues, improve customer satisfaction, reduce production costs, increase operating effectiveness, and so forth. Collectively the portfolio of business projects should satisfy the overarching strategic aims set by the corporate leadership where concrete project activities constitute areas that change the way things are done. That is, the project activities reflect a move away from the present where the expected consequences from the underlying changes should correspond to a new and hopefully better strategic position. Hence it is argued that "what a company is doing – its de facto strategy – can be summed up by identifying the group of projects in which it invests."[29]

From this perspective strategy is executed when the organization engages in ongoing project investments that commit resources to carry out specific organizational activities. Managing a portfolio of resource-committing projects requires management focus and prioritization of resource utilization. This exercise is partially accomplished through the support of the corporate finance function in the capital budgeting process employed by the firm. This is an area where the stringency of financial analysis can support the strategic assessments of the future cash flows from planned project activities. That is, major projects are presumably set in motion only if the internal evaluations can provide convincing scenarios of expected future net benefits.[30]

Hence, the execution of strategy is accomplished as the outcome of a series of projected actions over time where gradual shifts in the firm's strategic position require ongoing investment commitments. The proposed project investments should be inspired by the overarching organizational purpose aimed at accomplishing stated strategic goals, with specific intentions translated into concrete outcomes and performance metrics. The major project activities should be scrutinized and assessed for economic viability before investment resources are committed, and analyses made of risk factors that could have significant downside and upside effects

Figure 3.3 Managing risk and opportunities in major projects. Adapted from LEGO Systems A/S

during the project life. That is, a certain element of control is appropriate during the commissioning and project start-up phase. The initial project plan will outline required activities and stipulate their expected cash flow effects, including assigned dates for task accomplishment. For major projects, it can make sense to conduct a project risk analysis to identify and assess major events that could derail the project or create opportunistic conditions that might turn the project into a blockbuster (Figure 3.3).[31] These events and their preconditions should obviously be monitored throughout the life of each project until it is completed.

The interpretation of project investments as enactment of strategic initiatives emphasizes that the way the organization governs the individual projects and manages the project portfolio determines whether the strategy execution will be associated with success or failure. The ability of executives to sponsor, monitor, and engage in an effective project-governance process is essential, but also difficult to orchestrate. It comprises regular efforts to review the progression of major projects while retaining sufficient flexibility to revise projected activities and realign the projects as things evolve. This adaptive capacity is particularly important for organizations operating under turbulent conditions and might be accommodated by a *project risk management* process aimed at identifying essential risk factors and thinking through ways to avoid downside losses and realize upside gains. In turbulent environments characterized by frequent changes and high complexity it is difficult to predict or even foresee future conditions and, therefore, it is important to retain flexibility. This includes the ability to learn from experimentation and modify activities throughout the life of the projects. As argued by Chapman and Ward: "Excessive planning detail in a deterministic framework can be a serious handicap. A simply defined, deterministic base plan embedded in a simple understanding of the uncertainties involved can be much more effective."[32]

Firms operating in information-technology industries are often considered among the prime exponents to turbulent business conditions where project development efforts are exposed to continuous changes in demand combined with new developments in technological capabilities. So, there is great uncertainty regarding the particular needs the products and systems are supposed to fulfill even within a relatively short time horizon, as well as the appropriate choice of related technologies to achieve the best solutions. This double whammy creates a highly complex set of circumstances and increases the uncertainties around the best way to proceed with strategic projects that are exposed to turbulent conditions. As stated by Schwaber: "The more complex the system, the more likely it is that central control systems will break down."[33] That is, we need a more flexible approach to the project-planning process under these circumstances.

Given the conditions in the information-technology and software industries, actors in this environment have developed alternative project management processes to deal more effectively with the uncertain conditions. The adaptive project-development process referred to as *scrum* might serve as an inspirational source for effective execution of strategic project-planning activities (see Box 3.2 *Agile project management*). Scrum works by moving away from reliance on a central authority in the planning process to building adaptive activities into the organization through the involvement and initiatives taken by teams of individuals engaged in the actual project work. That is, it reflects a form of execution that combines central coordination with decentralized authority to dispatch project resources in the face of ongoing developments.

Hence, the project management perspective shows that top management needs to be continuously involved in the execution of important strategic projects and to engage in discussions on updated competitive information. The projects should be flexible and offer opportunities for modifications that adapt activities along the way. Hence, there are diminishing returns to detailed planning, particularly around projects executed in turbulent environments.

Strategy as managing real options

All business opportunities and potential actions are in effect strategic options in the sense that they can affect the future business activities of the firm. Formally, a *real option* is a right (or opportunity), but not an obligation, to carry out a particular action, or set of actions, at some point in the future. It captures the essence of flexibility and has value because the firm can use, or exercise, it if conditions turn favorable or leave it altogether if conditions are unfavorable.[34] That is, it holds the promise of realizing an upside gain while avoiding commitments that cause downside losses. Real options can take many forms. For example, a business project ready for implementation is a typical option because the holder has the flexibility to decide when, and whether, to set activities in motion (see Box 3.3 *A typical real option*). It is generally noted that options create a portfolio of choice "designed to secure the big payoffs of the best-case scenarios while minimizing losses in the worst-case scenarios" and this is useful under environmental uncertainty.[35]

In a development project the firm can skip advancement of the project altogether at different stages in the future if the interim steps indicate that conditions are unfavorable. Other flexibilities include the ability to expand and contract production capacity or to switch the use of productive assets for different purposes and thereby increase the adaptive capacity of the firm. Options can also take the form of buy-out clauses in joint ventures that allow the holder to expand the business. Hence, the strategic alliance between Samsung Electronics Corporation (SEC) and Sony Corporation around production of LCD monitors paved the way for SEC's subsequent move into LED flat screens as a market leader.[36] In short, there are different kinds of real options that can improve the maneuverability of the firm. However, we have to recognize the inherent flexibilities first. That is, we can conceive of resources and productive assets the organization controls as having *latent options* embedded that loom under the surface waiting to be recognized.[37] Being conscious about these flexibilities can be very helpful and it makes sense to consider them when the organization invests resources in real assets and sets up its operating structure. For example, when Southwest Airlines was rejected at short notice from the flight-reservation system managed by two competitors it was faced with an unexpected strategic dilemma of not being able to sell tickets. However, the airline quickly realized through internal scrutiny that people in the booking department had experimented with a ticketless booking system where the tickets could be sold online via the company website.[38]

In view of the rational analytical strategy-making process, the real options perspective can enter as part of the SWOT analysis in the formulation phase to help identify flexibilities embedded in existing assets and resources that identify alternative actions available to the firm (Figure 3.4). So, new viable solutions can be developed by reconfiguring existing resources and competencies in ways that respond better to the current business conditions. It seems similarly pertinent to adopt a real options perspective

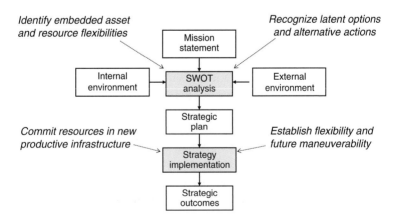

Figure 3.4 Recognizing and building real options in the strategy-making process

during implementation where the organization sets up the new operating facilities and processes and tries to build in flexibilities that can extend the room to maneuver. The ability to identify inherent flexibilities and map alternative actions available to the firm can be an important way to assess corporate maneuverability in view of major events or competitive changes.

The real options perspective presents two distinct aspects that can help set up appropriate resource-committing decisions. One aspect relates to the development of new products, processes, and technologies that may become future business propositions but where there are lots of uncertainties about the workability of these exploratory activities. We want to establish a prudent way to conduct these exploratory investments by expanding commitments gradually as some of the fundamental uncertainties are cleared along the way. Prudence suggests that development investments progress only if the conditions around the project continue to show promise. The ability to abandon the investment commitments at certain threshold points creates such flexibility so we can adopt an *abandonment option* approach to assess the staging of different investment programs (Figure 3.5).[39] Another aspect relates to the exercise of the business propositions as strategic options once they are fully developed. That is, once the exploratory activities have come to fruition and are developed into full-fledged business projects, then the investment decision is different – it has changed from being an exploratory exercise to a major irreversible strategic investment opportunity. Here prudence prescribes that one should enter into the business venture only if there is reasonable certainty that it will provide a satisfactory return. The embedded flexibility is that we can postpone, or defer, the investment decision until we feel reasonably sure about the outcome. However, we can still skip the whole thing if the favorable conditions fail to materialize. Hence, we use a *deferral option* approach to assess the appropriate timing of these strategic implementation decisions. For example, Infineon Technologies, the German semiconductor company, used the options framework to assess the best way to introduce new SOI (silicon on insulator) technology in place of conventional bulk CMOS (complementary metal-oxide-semiconductor) processing. The analysis could

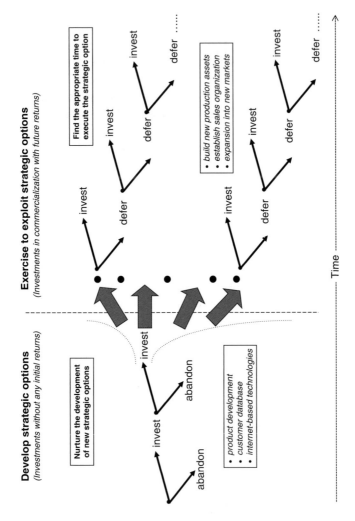

Figure 3.5 Two aspects of the real options perspective – development and exercise. Source: Andersen (2000)

determine a staging structure of deferral options that was superior to both a full technology switch and a deferral of the decision.[40]

The combination of abandonment and deferral option decisions is an attempt to see real options development and the execution of options in a dynamic perspective. It is important to consider how the organization can establish a setting where real options are created in an effective and relatively costless manner. It is equally important to be able to exercise the real options at the opportune moments where the upside potential is the highest, or to decide to leave them. From a strategy perspective the success criteria are to develop, create, and acquire real options as cheaply as possible to form a portfolio of flexibilities that gives the firm sufficient maneuverability and then to manage and exercise the real options in the portfolio in an optimal manner.[41] The ability to create real options efficiently has to do with an organizational setting that is aware and creative and gives sufficient leeway to take initiatives and innovate. Similarly, the ability to exercise real options effectively depends on decision processes supported by informed analyses and inputs from relevant stakeholders with diverse views on the environmental conditions.

We may also look at the real options available to the firm as a collection of business opportunities where some need further development while others are more mature and ready for implementation. That is, some options may need further nursing before they become ripe, while some are ready to harvest, whereas other options may wither and thus need to be weeded out. However, you never know the precise outcome of these efforts because it depends on how business conditions evolve over time. In Leuhrman's words: "Managing a portfolio of strategic options is like growing a garden of tomatoes in an unpredictable climate."[42] So, once the real options have been identified as part of the portfolio, management can try to assess them in terms of their immediate value to the firm if they are exercised (the *intrinsic* value) and the potential future value they may represent (the *time* value). A high intrinsic value argues for immediate exercise of the option whereas a high time value encourages postponement of exercise. The higher the net present value (NPV) of future cash flows from the business proposition compared with the up-front investment, the higher the intrinsic value. The longer the remaining

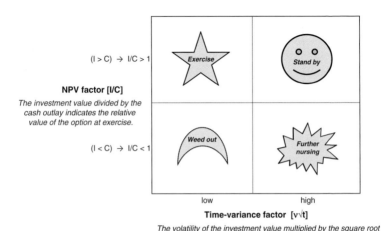

$(I > C) \rightarrow I/C > 1$

NPV factor [I/C]

The investment value divided by the cash outlay indicates the relative value of the option at exercise.

$(I < C) \rightarrow I/C < 1$

low   high

Time-variance factor [v√t]

The volatility of the investment value multiplied by the square root of time to expiry indicates the future value potential of the option.

Figure 3.6 A framework to assess and manage real options

time and the higher the volatility of expected cash flows, the higher is the time value.[43] Hence, we can use related measures as decision parameters to manage the portfolio.

We can plot the identified real options into a two-by-two framework ordered by (1) an *NPV factor* and (2) a *time-variance factor* (Figure 3.6). The NPV factor is the investment value (I) of the business (the net present value of the future cash flows) divided by the cash investment (C) needed to start the business proposition. If this ratio is above 1, it means that the intrinsic value is positive (I > C), whereas a value below 1 corresponds to a negative intrinsic value (I < C). So, an NPV factor above 1 indicates that it pays off to exercise now. The time-variance factor is calculated as the volatility of the investment value, i.e., the standard deviation in the expected annual cash flows from the business proposition during its lifetime, multiplied by the square root of the time (number of years) remaining of the option. A high time-variance factor indicates a potential payoff if the option is kept. Therefore, we can read the map in the following way. Options in the lower left quadrant with NPV factor below 1 and low time-variance factor have little immediate value and little potential, so they are candidates for *weeding out*. Options in the lower right-hand quadrant, with NPV factor below 1 and high time-variance factor, have little immediate value but show potential and, therefore, need *nursing* to seek out the potential. Options in the upper right-hand quadrant with NPV factor above 1 and high time-variance factor have immediate value but also future potential and thus should be on *stand-by*, ready to go. Options in the upper left quadrant with NPV factor above 1 and low time-variance factor have immediate value and no additional potential, so they are ready for *exercise* if it coincides with the strategic aims of the firm.

This discussion suggests at least two possible ways of adopting real options reasoning into the strategy-making process. One way is to think about the dynamic life cycle of real options as first being developed and subsequently utilized. The application of abandonment option models can help set up different staging structures as new investments are made to develop real options and deferral option models can help set the decision criteria to exercise fully developed options. A complementary way to analyze the portfolio of real options is in terms of their immediate value from exercise and the remaining time value as essential decision criteria for weeding out, nursing, stand-by, and exercise.[44]

Hence, the real options perspective provides a way to analyze development and exploitation of business opportunities that can shape future growth and adapt the firm's strategic position in view of changing business conditions. The analytical frameworks deal with "official" recognized options and can guide the timing of resource allocations into these activities. In addition there are presumed to be a number of "latent" unrecognized options embedded in the resource bundles available to the firm that can be uncovered in critical situations.

Strategy as managerial decision making

The view of strategy making as outcomes arising from decisions made by managers throughout the organization and ensuing action outcomes has always been an engrained element of the strategy concept. Andrews argued that "corporate strategy is the pattern of decisions in a company that determines and reveals its objectives, purposes, or goals."[45] This strategy view implies that the way organizational decision makers act over time will display a discernible pattern of actions that shapes strategic outcomes and eventually reflects the underlying aims that drive the corporation. In a seminal study, Joseph Bower analyzed the capital budgeting decisions conducted in a major corporation and uncovered how many resource-committing investments are made by managers dispersed throughout the organization.[46] In large organizations it is not possible for the executives to process all investment decisions, so formal decision authority is allocated to managers within the organization, typically structured by the importance of the decision as determined by the absolute size of the investment. Below certain investment amounts the decision to make the investment is, therefore, allocated to lower managerial levels. Penrose already observed that "progressive decentralization of authority and of subordinate responsibility which leaves untouched the cumulation of ultimate responsibility is a necessary condition for continued growth beyond a relatively small size firm."[47] However, Noda and Bower further demonstrated how lower-level managers make investment proposals to accommodate what they see as strategic shortcomings and that these proposals need the backing of divisional managers to progress into corporate strategy initiatives. Hence, even though it seems obvious that top management is unable to handle all capital-allocation decisions, the study uncovered how important the effect of many small investment decisions can be for the strategic evolution of the firm. The agglomeration of many small decisions may turn out to be quite significant for the corporate strategy as the committed resources develop competencies in path-dependent ways and thereby eventually influence the types of business activities the organization is able to handle.[48]

Noda and Bower compared the development of the wireless communications businesses in the telecom companies BellSouth and US West after the breakup of the US Bell system in 1983. The diverse strategic directions with an emphasis on familiar telecommunication businesses in BellSouth versus the perception of being a diversified telecom holding company in US West affected the way managers in the two companies acted in the emerging markets for wireless services. Hence, BellSouth experienced broad development of regional and international wireless businesses reinforced by ongoing success that eventually made it an official part of the corporate strategic focus (the company was acquired by AT&T in 2006). In contrast, due to lack of initial success in wireless initiatives, US West gradually diverged toward unrelated activities such as real estate and financial services, but eventually switched back to a focus on network services in multimedia and broadband. This required other competencies than could be extracted from the existing wireless business, so the company was unable to expand into these related telecom activities (US West merged with Qwest Communications International in 2000, which in turn merged with CenturyLink in 2011).

The fact that many resource-committing decisions are dispersed among managers scattered throughout the organization at all hierarchical levels and with different functional responsibilities invites a focus on the managerial decision-making process. Many subtle aspects affect the decision outcomes, where the process more often than not is characterized by unstructured procedures, high uncertainty, and ambiguous decision criteria.[49] Organizational decision makers use competitive and environmental information and draw on technical expertise and their own managerial experience when dealing with decisions.[50] However, they are typically short on complete, updated, and valid information, act under time pressure with limited resources available, and use cognitive simplifications to deal with the complexities of the underlying reality (Figure 3.7).

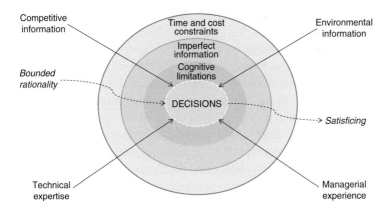

Figure 3.7 Influences on managerial decision making. Source: adapted from Harrison (1995)

This goes back to Simon's assertions about lack of common preferences among decision makers and the limitations in human mental capacity that create conditions of *bounded rationality* and principles of *satisficing* as opposed to optimization of decision outcomes.[51] In these situations the process may be influenced by the power of individual decision makers as well as dominant coalitions of managers that can form prevailing perceptions and opinions.[52] The debacle around Porsche's attempt to take over Volkswagen AG (VW) during 2005–2009 is a prime example of how internal power struggles garnered with executive biases can affect high-level executive decisions.[53] The decision outcomes can be affected by a variety of cognitive biases ascribed to individuals acting in all phases of the process, from problem identification and alternative generation, to final evaluation and selection.[54] For example, the demise of Arthur Andersen LLP (once one of the "Big Five" accounting firms) while auditing the books of Enron Corporation is widely ascribed to human flaws of greed and negligence. However, there were many advance warnings about the potential conflicts between due diligence and individual rewards that management simply ignored because business was good.[55]

So, the potential biases of key managers in the organization are important for the ability to execute decisions successfully. However, careful planning to implement major decisions does not provide a blank guarantee that successful outcomes will ensue. A recent study found that managerial experience and readiness of organizational members are important to execute strategic decisions effectively.[56] Managers gain their *experience* from prior development activities and form competences that can be used to accomplish comparable implementation tasks more effectively. Organizational members obtain *readiness* when the implementation tasks they are supposed to execute are prioritized by management and they are given authority to carry out the necessary tasks. That is, managers should have relevant experiences and be properly empowered. Hence, the effectiveness of actions taken by managers and their people within the organization matter, and senior management is instrumental in forming the organizational setting that makes it possible.

The view of strategy as managerial decisions reflected in a pattern of corporate actions over time has provided the backdrop for detailed longitudinal studies of how strategies took shape in specific company settings.[57] Some of these studies revealed that strategies were rather stable over long periods of time and show major shifts only with certain time intervals typically spurred by changes in the competitive environment.[58] These longer periods of stability with short bursts of change reflect what is referred to as *punctuated equilibrium*. So, there may be a need for periods of stability after major organizational changes to reconcile and streamline internal processes. Other interpretations relate to inertial forces that may hamper organizations from making the necessary changes until things become critical and there is a need for intervention by external change agent to break the mold.[59] Others see these outcomes as influenced by the characteristics of the competitive environment. That is, if we are dealing with dramatic changes that can destroy the existing competences of incumbents, then occasional changes can lead to punctuated equilibrium whereas continuous and ongoing changes are associated with hypercompetitive conditions of disequilibrium (Figure 3.8).[60] Hence, Intel's switch from leading producer of memory chips to a focus on microprocessors as the computer industry changed from vertical integration to a horizontal structure in the early 1980s is an example of a one-time competence-destroying change.[61] The subsequent influences of the internet have gradually changed this competitive environment in the computer products industry toward conditions of hypercompetitive disequilibrium.

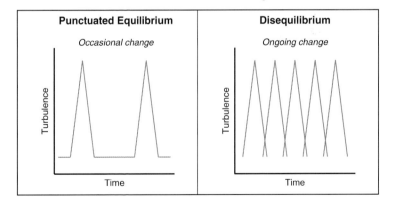

Figure 3.8 Patterns of strategic turbulence. Source: adapted from D'Aveni (1999)

Based on ideas of emerging strategic responses and dispersed decision power, Mintzberg argues: "Strategies can develop inadvertently, without the conscious intention of senior management."[62] This can happen, for example, if a sales manager observes a new customer need and convinces the production department to amend the product specs to accommodate this sales opportunity. Subsequently, other customers may try a similar product version where other managers in the sales team follow suit toward their customers and suddenly the firm could be in an entirely new product market that may offer the firm a successful route to future expansion.[63] This sounds like a somewhat anarchistic unconscious way of forming strategy, but if the responsive initiatives taken by managers in the organization are in line with the overarching aims and ambitions of the firm, it may constitute a viable adaptive strategy-making process. The ultimate example of "organized anarchy" is the classical depiction of managerial choices as a *garbage can* (see Box 3.4 *A garbage can model of choice*).[64] It is interesting to note that the garbage can model can be quite effective in dealing with turbulent environmental conditions characterized by high uncertainty where deterministic planning approaches fall short. Hence, a certain amount of "irrational" experimentation may in fact be associated with more optimal adaptive responses.[65]

Without adopting any extreme views one can safely assume that important resource-committing decisions are made by managers at multiple hierarchical levels throughout the organization. Hence, Bower and Gilbert claim that "senior executives, divisional managers, and operational managers all play a role in deciding which opportunities a company will pursue and which it will pass by."[66] Taken together, all of these decisions commit resources, instigate concrete actions, and build competencies along the way that eventually drive the execution of strategic initiatives and determine organizational outcomes. In the words of Blenko et al.: "A company's value is no more or less than the sum of the decisions it makes and executes."[67] While there may be a tendency in strategic management to primarily focus on the seemingly important decisions made in the executive suites, it is equally important to attend to the day-to-day decisions made by middle managers and frontline employees.[68]

Many decisions made at lower hierarchical levels, e.g., among sales, procurement, and production managers, can be very important to the way in which the organization observes new business opportunities, responds to them, and thereby ensures ongoing adaptation to competitive changes.

Hence, the decision-making perspective indicates that strategic actions are taken by many individuals scattered throughout the organization, which underscores the importance of a common direction and an organizational context that facilitates effective decision making. This includes forming an appropriate decision structure and imposing practices and management systems that give access to updated information and facilitate interactive communication.

Strategy as entrepreneurial initiatives

The role of entrepreneurship has been recognized as an essential element of effective strategy making in organizations since the inception of the field. It is captured in Schumpeter's concept of *creative destruction* according to which growth in economic value is inherently associated with the ability of entrepreneurs to come up with new ways to do things that outdate incumbent firms and make old products and processes obsolete. Schumpeter fundamentally saw the capitalistic model as a dynamic system of ongoing change toward new and better ways to compete and perform. In his words: "Capitalism, then, is by nature a form or method of economic change and not only never is but never can be stationary."[69] What keeps economic development going, then, is the introduction of new products and services, new methods of production and distribution, and new market structures and forms of industrial organization. Andrews adopted this focus on entrepreneurship and talked about strategy as "putting market opportunity and corporate capability together into a suitably entrepreneurial combination."[70] Hence, it takes a certain entrepreneurial mindset to gauge how the competitive environment is changing and where new promising business opportunities arise. The ability to encourage and foster new entrepreneurial initiatives within the organization can have important repercussions for the strategy-making process, and understanding where they come from and knowing how they can be enhanced is therefore an essential part of strategy making.

Entrepreneurs are important as creators of new firms that can rejuvenate the competitive dynamic and build new industries, but the entrepreneurial activities inside already established firms are equally important as a way to retain competitiveness, create strategic renewal, and prolong corporate survival. Hence, the term *corporate entrepreneurship* refers to the entrepreneurial behavior that takes place within the large and mid-sized firms in established industries.[71] In this context, a simple definition of entrepreneurship is "the process of creating value by bringing together a unique combination of resources to exploit an opportunity."[72] This implies that people in the organization can uncover new business opportunities through formal strategy discussions supported by analyses and observations from unfolding events in day-to-day business activities. It also identifies alternative responses to capture emerging opportunities using resources and competencies available to the firm and that can be assembled to accomplish the necessary tasks.

This entrepreneurship approach can assume a specific strategic role as "a vision-directed, organization-wide reliance on entrepreneurial behavior that purposefully and continuously rejuvenates the organization."[73] This suggests that executives can build entrepreneurship into strategy execution through conscious choice. The challenge for top management, then, becomes how to create an organizational setting that is conducive to effective entrepreneurial behavior among managerial decision makers. Vijay Sathe suggests that corporate entrepreneurship is encouraged by a corporate culture that "permits rule-bending and limits what is considered irresponsible behavior to violations of personal integrity and business ethics."[74] He further suggests that business creation is encouraged better by pursuing a *small-is-beautiful* philosophy characterized by high performance expectations and where local managers have a great deal of autonomy to find appropriate ways of accomplishing things. Here the executive role is more to challenge the strategic thinking as opposed to deciding the best strategies and telling everybody what to do. In contrast, pursuing a *bigger-is-better* philosophy emphasizing large one-off

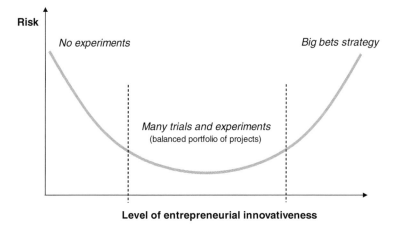

Figure 3.9 Entrepreneurial initiatives for experimentation and innovation. Source: adapted from Kuratko *et al.* (2011)

opportunities is risky and stands a lower chance of being successfully executed. That is, a more broad-based entrepreneurial engagement among operating managers in the organization is a way to allow for many but smaller trials and low-risk experiments with a better chance of achieving favorable risk–return outcomes (Figure 3.9).[75] Hence, entrepreneurial firms engage employees in open thinking about the external environment and challenge existing perceptions in ways that allow them to act as agents of change, creating new types of customer value while rewriting the rules rather than monitoring competitors and reacting to competitive moves.

In a study of strategic initiatives, Lechner and Floyd identified two firms representing a success story and a failure.[76] The successful initiatives derived from ideas among a group of involved managers who saw a potential for an effective internet-based marketing approach. The initial process was characterized by a search for a good solution through experimentation and open discussions to reach a solid proposal for top management approval and where subsequent development entailed repeated tests and product iterations discussed at frequent meetings. The failed initiative arose from a senior executive who saw a need to develop a web-based sales channel to preempt observed competitive moves. The process responsibility was imposed on another manager to head a project group, and when divergent opinions among members created doubts about the viability of the initiative, the senior executive forced it through. It eventually failed to be implemented due to key people resigning and failure to coordinate a viable solution. Apart from illustrating different origins of strategic initiatives from lower-level managers as well as top managers, this highlights the importance of small, iterative experiments and open communication about results as opposed to a directive approach to develop entrepreneurial initiatives.

In another noteworthy study, Sarasvathy investigated how successful entrepreneurs actually behave and develop their business ventures.[77] She used the term *effectuation* to denote the prudent search process adopted by successful entrepreneurs where they develop business initiatives through networks of engaged stakeholders. She said: "Effectual logic provides useful design principles for transforming extant environments into new futures in the face of ambiguous goals." The entrepreneurial expertise uncovered in this analysis identifies five basic principles. The *bird-in-the-hand* principle reflects that successful entrepreneurs pursue means-driven actions with current competencies as the starting point for the search, rather than setting long-term goals that require many new competencies. The *affordable-loss* principle illustrates that successful entrepreneurs commit only resources they are willing to lose, i.e., they do not base investment decisions on return calculations from extensive business plans. The *crazy-quilt* principle shows that commitments are made through negotiations with stakeholders that show genuine interest and willingness to contribute to the business idea. The *lemonade* principle reflects that entrepreneurs acknowledge the uncertainty of new ventures and mix and mingle available possibilities with little risk avoidance and in ways that use surprises to pursue new opportunities. Finally, the *pilot-in-the-plane* principle indicates that successful entrepreneurs use personal relations and possibilities as they emerge in the opportunity-development process.

The logic of entrepreneurial expertise interprets the world as open and *in-the-making* where new opportunities are *fabricated* as much as they are observed, recognized, and discovered in the competitive environment. New products, services, and processes evolve through gradual developmental efforts rather than being revealed as grand inventions. The development process is driven by an urge to exploit opportunities rather than avoid failure. These characteristics of successful entrepreneurial behavior seem well suited to a corporate entrepreneurship approach as well where many actors within the same organization can engage in incremental trial-and-error learning in their efforts to develop better solutions.

Hence, the entrepreneurship view argues that new ideas and experimentation happen throughout the organization in the form of smaller ventures conducted by engaged specialists and supportive managers. It is possible to conduct prudent entrepreneurial activities as individuals develop ventures in small-stakes probes with interested stakeholders. This kind of entrepreneurial behavior thrives on a particular organizational setting honed by top management.

Strategy as practice

The strategy-making perspectives discussed so far are all focused on different aspects of how strategies are accomplished and executed within an organizational setting. The *strategy as practice* perspective is no different in this regard as Johnson *et al.* "are calling for an emphasis on the detailed processes and practices which constitute the day-to-day activities of organizational life *and* which relate to strategic outcomes."[78] This promotes an *activity-based view* of strategy making, i.e., strategic outcomes are seen to derive from the varied activities that are carried out by many people in different parts of the organization. Hence, they argue that "strategy is something that *people do*. Strategy is an activity."[79] In this context, it is claimed that strategies rarely come about as the result of large path-breaking, one-off decisions made by top management but in most cases are the consequence of a quite complex set of activities and organizational processes where people act and respond. Therefore, strategy making cannot be seen as only concerned with decisions taken in executive suites and conceived for implementation by line managers and lower-ranking operating managers, even though this is assumed in much of the strategy literature. So, according to these scholars, the strategy of practice is "a concern with what people do in relation to strategy and how this is influenced by and influences their organizational and institutional contexts."

The challenge with this particular approach to strategy making and execution is that all firms are different and conduct strategic activities in their own unique ways, partially influenced by engrained values and experiences derived from past practices. Hence, new insights about strategy-making processes must be obtained from detailed case studies rich on firm-specific information that generate many and diverse observations, to the possible detriment of obtaining generalizable findings on the key characteristics of effective strategy execution. When we look at strategy practices they are often initiated by top management ideas about the company's strategic aims where more concrete corporate actions are developed from the involved engagement of managers with business and operational responsibilities who interact with members of top management and other operating managers. The related planning activities may be tightly linked to the periodic financial and budgetary exercises in the firm as well as timetables for existing operating procedures, including rituals for off-site strategy brainstorming sessions, capital budgeting exercises, operational planning meetings, etc.

These practices may constitute approaches to exchange ideas, views, and perspectives in strategic thinking between management levels and integrate strategic themes across functional areas and responsibilities. This can lead to common ideas about strategic aims as well as outlining concrete strategic initiatives to move forward, including stipulations for implied investment needs and their expected outcomes. However, the actual execution of intended initiatives is still subsumed in these practices. Here empirical studies provide us with interesting insights that illustrate situations where formal planning deliberations can become detached from the things that actually happen within the organization. At the same time they illustrate how subdued development activities unknown to top management may actually constitute initiatives with significant strategic consequences.

Robert Burgelman's studies of internal corporate ventures show how initiatives developed and promoted by individuals and decision practices conducted deep within the organization eventually can drive these activities into significant strategic business activities long before they are part of the official corporate strategy.[80] Hence, many of these venture activities are not initiated by top management or even discussed at board meetings – they come about because the organization contains a number of astute, able, and engaged people who see new opportunities and take the liberty to pursue them.[81] This obviously raises the relevant question of who innovates and develops the new corporate business ideas. Based on the various views on strategy making it seems that some initiatives derive from intended top-driven decisions whereas other initiatives develop and evolve as small bottom-up venture decisions. Now, even large resource-committing decisions need adaptive changes along the way where ad hoc decisions respond to emerging needs and where the actual execution, therefore, is affected by the responsive initiatives taken by operating managers. At the same time, small business ventures can be initiated by individuals or groups of operating managers and may become so successful that they grow to a substantive size. In this case they will need more formal management attention as further expansion requires corporate resources, which eventually make them a recognized part of the official strategy condoned by top management.

Hence, we can conceive of two different types of initiatives with potential strategic effects: (1) initiatives imposed by top management in accordance with the firm's official strategy, and (2) venture initiatives started by operating managers to pursue new business ideas outside the scope of the official strategy. The initiatives taken by top management typically constitute large-stake resource commitments based on assumptions about expected developments in the competitive environment. However, substantial uncertainties remain about the way things are going to change and what the effects of planned actions will actually be. Hence, a certain level of adaptability in the execution of the proposed solutions is required. The decisions made by the operating specialists are typically small-stake resource commitments taken beneath the limits for executive decisions. These investments can be promising, but are obviously not guaranteed, and may gain middle management attention if they

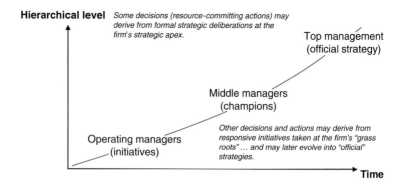

Figure 3.10 Top-driven and entrepreneurial bottom-up initiatives

succeed and expand in earnings volume over time (Figure 3.10). If this happens, middle managers can support or "champion" their ongoing development and promote their candidacy to top management as an official corporate business strategy. Hence, the dispersed business ventures initially pursued at lower hierarchical levels in the organization can be a promising source of low-risk probing for future business opportunities.

Some of the low-stakes business ventures developed from the organizational grass roots can become vital in situations where the firm tries to change its strategic direction, for example as a consequence of major overhauls in the industry structure. This is exactly what happened when Intel Corporation changed its strategy in the early 1980s from being a major producer of memory chips (DRAMs) to become a dominant player in the new market for microprocessors.[82] Intel was feeling increasing pressure from Japanese companies due to their competitive advantage in mass production and favorable financing position, which undercut Intel's ability to compete on price. Andy Grove, then CEO of Intel, noted the challenging competitive situation but did not find it easy to determine the appropriate strategic response. A continuation of these business conditions made it clear that unless something was done, the prior climb to the top of the industry would be followed by a dramatic decline due to increasing competitive pressures (Figure 3.11) – Intel had to make a move that could change this business trajectory. The company had truly reached a *strategic inflection point* where status quo would mean gradual

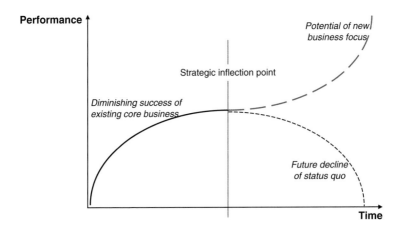

Figure 3.11 Inflection points in the strategy-making process. Source: adapted from Burgelman and Grove (1996)

elimination of business and eventual closure of the company. A new initiative was required to turn things around. Intel had actually designed its leading microprocessor into the original IBM PC in 1981 and this business took off but still without figuring as a core business of the firm. According to Grove, Intel "continued to spend heavily on R&D. Most of it was spent on memory chips. But at the same time a smaller team worked on technology for another device we had invented in 1970 or so: microprocessors."[83] It was not until mid 1986 that the firm eventually changed its focus from DRAMs to become a prime producer of microprocessors. Hence, it took a long period of soul searching before top management decided that the microprocessor business had developed to become the next strategic product market for the firm. The most interesting part maybe is that Andy Grove realized how important these lower-level initiatives were as they pretty much happened below the radar screen of the top management team: "Men and women lower in the organization, unbeknownst to us, got us ready to execute the strategic turn that saved our necks and gave us a great future."

This was an eye opener to corporate management and inspired a highly relevant discussion about how organizations can see strategic inflection points when they occur and handle them more effectively once they are identified. Part of the solution seems to be a certain balance between internal venture developments that probe potential future business activities. The new ventures may become the business areas that can respond to new competitive challenges. This shows the importance of a top management team that imposes an organizational setting to facilitate internal venturing activities and communicates effectively to stay informed about new initiatives. The tricky thing is that new ventures must be explored some time before they are needed to change the strategic course – it is too late to set them in motion when the competitive situation has changed. These organizational practices seemed instrumental in the case of Intel. Grove argued that the business development occurred "not as a result of any specific strategic direction by senior management but as a result of daily decisions by middle managers: the production planners and the finance people who sat around the table at endless production allocation meetings."

The discussions of project, real options, decision making, and entrepreneurial strategy perspectives pinpoint the need for ongoing interaction and communication between managers at different hierarchical levels over time. Projects must be initiated and adapted, options recognized and developed, decisions made and enacted, and entrepreneurial ventures turned into future business activities as time goes by and ongoing monitoring of events and open communication to assess environmental conditions and the need to modify actions is required.[84] Hence, the mission statement and the creation of a common understanding about the competitive situation developed through the planning process provide necessary aspirations for managers throughout the organization as they pursue initiatives and ventures to accommodate, utilize, and exploit new opportunities (Figure 3.12a). The periodic strategy discussions conducted among involved managers as part of strategy formulation based on rational analytical inputs should give aspirations and direction to middle and operating managers as they take on new initiatives in response to changing market conditions, or develop promising business opportunities that seem to emerge. This directive influence can also help facilitate use of rational decision criteria in the evaluation of dispersed initiatives.

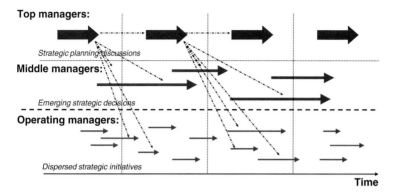

Figure 3.12a Strategic aspirations induced by the top managers

Conversely, the various initiatives taken by middle and operating managers at lower levels will generate outcomes and experiences that give hints about the viability of these ventures as future strategic opportunities for the company. These experiences can be useful as input in the future planning discussions where successful ventures are prime candidates for corporate businesses expansion. Negative experiences serve as learning points that give useful information in the forward-looking planning considerations. Hence, these grass-roots initiatives are a source of inspiration for the strategy discussions conducted in subsequent planning activities (Figure 3.12b). This illustrates conjoint top-down and bottom-up processes that interact across management hierarchies and operate dynamically over time.

The discussion proposes a different strategy-making process where many important strategic initiatives derive from lower-level operating managers and functional specialists where the role of top management is to enable and facilitate the process. It represents the so-called *Bower–Burgelman model* (Figure 3.13).[85] This model distinguishes between three layers of managers: top managers, middle managers, and operating managers. Top management sets the *structural context* of the organization, including general direction, policies, structure, incentives, and management systems. This forms the organizational setting that affects the way managers throughout the organization act and

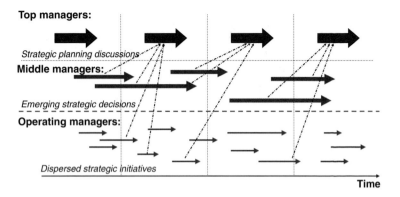

Top managers:

Strategic planning discussions

Middle managers:

Emerging strategic decisions

Operating managers:

Dispersed strategic initiatives

Time

Figure 3.12b Strategic inspiration derived from operating managers. Source: adapted from Andersen (2002)

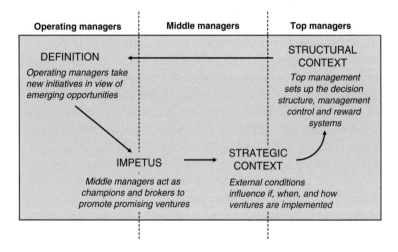

Figure 3.13 The Bower–Burgelman strategy-making model. Source: adapted from Burgelman (1996)

operate. New strategic initiatives are taken by operating managers that are close to customers, collaborators, and colleagues, and therefore observe new needs and opportunities that arise from changing competitive conditions. These activities eventually create the future strategic actions and thus are referred to as *definition*. If the internal ventures fare well and develop into promising business propositions, it is noted by the middle managers, who in turn will seek to gain support for further expansion of these activities and thereby create a certain *impetus*. If the success continues, the organization is likely to consider these activities as part of the official business portfolio, which will include it in the official *strategy context* of the firm. The model suggests an entirely different dynamic to the strategy-making process where important exploratory initiatives originate from managers at the bottom of the organization and where top management assumes the role of enablers and facilitators.

This strategy model captures an *evolutionary* perspective to strategy development building on the principles of variation, selection, and retention as the variety of strategic initiatives taken by actors within the organization are the source for new business development. The middle managers play the role of brokers between top management and managers in the operating entities and they seek out successful business initiatives to develop further and champion for eventual buy-in as part of the official corporate strategy. According to Burgelman, the "intra-organizational variation comes about as the result of individuals pursuing strategic initiatives" where "selection works through administrative and cultural mechanisms regulating the allocation of resources." That is, business opportunities evolve from entrepreneurial experiments initiated at lower hierarchical levels and top management later gets to choose from them. In other words, "strategic action at higher levels in the management hierarchy benefits from interpretation of the outcomes of strategic action at lower levels."[86]

However, this is a somewhat one-sided interpretation of the implied strategy-making process because top management obviously influences the structural context of the organization that in turn affects the conditions under which the dispersed initiatives can be taken at lower management levels. Furthermore, top management also make resource-committing decisions as a consequence of the planning discussions around the official corporate strategy. For example, top management can decide to expand, contract, or switch the level of activity between different business activities as part of the formal capital budgeting exercise. They also devote resources to specific

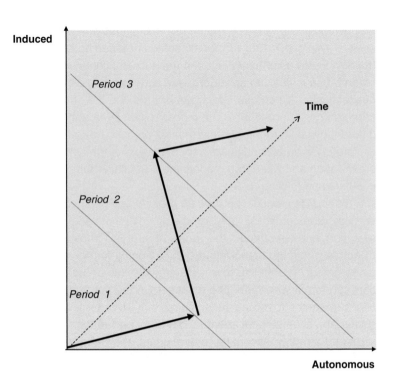

Figure 3.14 Induced and autonomous resource commitments. Source: adapted from Burgelman (2005)

research and development activities with the aim of restructuring and redirecting the emphasis of different business activities. That is, some investment decisions are driven by the official strategic aims of top management and other investment decisions are made further down the organization as operating managers take initiatives to try new business opportunities. The centrally determined investments are referred to as *induced* strategy initiatives whereas the investments taken at the operating level are referred to as *autonomous* strategy initiatives (Figure 3.14).

Reverting to the example of strategic changes in Intel, a different emphasis on these two types of investment commitments was observed over different time periods. In the time before Intel reached the inflection point in the early 1980s (*period 1*), a relatively large portion of investment resources was devoted to autonomous initiatives, which saved the company because the microprocessor business was developed that allowed a switch from memory to computer chips. In the subsequent period (*period 2*), the company purposely focused corporate investments on expansion of the microprocessor business. However, later in time (*period 3*), when the internet required new solutions, there were no ready answers, and more leeway was given to autonomous initiatives to try out new alternatives. Hence, the emphasis on induced and autonomous strategy initiatives can change over time.[87]

Conclusion

The preceding discussion of strategy execution argues that strategy comes about as the consequence of an amalgam of resource-committing initiatives decided by executive management at the organization's strategic apex and dispersed initiatives taken by operating managers scattered throughout the organization as they try out new business opportunities. Top management needs a certain number of exploratory investment initiatives to test the viability of new business ideas identified by local managers that are closer to actual events and uncover challenges and opportunities. Conversely, the lower-level managers benefit from the contributions provided by the process of rational strategy analyses as the means to give general direction and create a common understanding of the competitive situation. So, managers try to make sense of developments in the surrounding environment and allow for ongoing fine tuning of current business activities as well as initiating innovative business propositions from within the organization. Hence, the potential of an internal garbage can process may be to generate a certain level of random search for new business activities needed to create strategic options and provide a basis to navigate safely through turbulent and uncertain environments.

A central rational analytical planning approach can be seen as a way to create a common understanding of the competitive rules that apply to the corporate business activities as a guide to the incremental steps taken to realize intended strategic aims. Conversely, a decentralized structure gives room to experiment with new business initiatives that respond to current developments guided by the collective strategic understanding. This suggests that an integrative strategy-making process can combine advantages of central planning activities and dispersed exploratory initiatives as an effective way to handle changing conditions. We will pursue this further in the following chapter.

Box 3.1 Corporate strategy development

This outlines various activities that affect the formation of strategy in a corporation and therefore constitute some of the central elements in the complex strategy-making process as observed in representative (western) firms operating in global knowledge-intensive industries.

Annual strategy plan

The annual planning process is started by general strategic aims and goals expressed by top management with aspiring growth targets and profit margins per business segment and region for the coming years. This guides comprehensive planning and budget discussions among business unit managers that are condensed into unit plans and budgets forwarded to the finance department. The submitted information is presented to top management in an aggregated corporate strategy and budget report. This is followed by interactive meetings between top managers and business unit managers to decide on necessary adjustments and reach an agreed action plan with stipulated outcomes. The adjusted results are incorporated into an overarching corporate strategy plan and projected into next year's budget. Major actions included in the strategy plan are considered in the central capital budgeting process to reserve investment resources for implementation by involved project teams.

Interim strategic exploration

Initiatives can arise in between the annual planning and budget cycle and can be triggered by different things. They may result from executive discussions at the monthly budget and quarterly strategy follow-up meetings. They could be inspired by concerns raised in ongoing exchanges within the top management team, possibly involving finance executives, or informal discussions with business unit heads and operating officers. These encounters might flag concerns or pinpoint opportunities that must be analyzed on an ad hoc basis to explore possible initiatives that may or may not lead to new interim projects and updated action plans. Any updated activities that require new resources are then coordinated with the central capital budgeting plan. There is typically some flexibility to engage in new formal investments outside the annual resource-allocation process.

Grass-roots initiatives

New business ideas continuously arise in the business units and regional sales offices that are close to operations and local customers, which enable them to observe technological changes and new emerging consumer needs. Other ideas derive from research activities where ongoing development projects may uncover new capabilities that can be used in enhanced product offerings. These ideas and potential business initiatives are entered into a central log and assessed by designated cross-functional evaluation teams. They have regular meetings to discuss the viability of identified links between new capabilities and products. The initial conceptualization and ongoing evaluations of these business opportunities (options) are catalogued and reviewed regularly.

Integration and interaction

The CEO makes it a point to travel to as many business and regional offices as possible every year to present and discuss the overarching purpose and business ideas that drive the company. This is intended to create an inclusive and committed corporate culture. It also allows the CEO and top management to get direct responses and new insights from all parts of the firm and its people. It intermingles with regular budget follow-up reports and strategy review discussions conducted monthly and quarterly. At lower management levels there are regular project follow-up meetings in project teams and among cross-functional groups. There are formal communication and reporting links as well as communication and information technologies enabling informal ad hoc exchange of knowledge, insights, and updated business observations.

Hence, it is clear that strategy formation is influenced by many factors where the complex internal processes and communication patterns play a role. However, this cannot be read off the annual reports or official documents on company websites, it has to be observed within the firms themselves.

Box 3.2 Agile project management

The main principles of scrum

Scrum is used in complex projects where it is impossible to predict all the things that will occur during the project. The approach opens for experimentation and adaptations along the way as the project unfolds and replaces a deterministic approach based on detailed plans and work schedules. The scrum process is set up to develop project activities in incremental adaptive steps. A team of individuals with relevant competencies and experiences is assembled and takes a look at the project requirements and considers the need for skills and capabilities. It then collectively determines how to build the functionality of the project, modifying the approach daily as new complexities, difficulties, and surprises emerge.

The process follows an iterative structure where work is done in *sprints*. Each sprint is an iteration of thirty calendar days. It starts with a four-hour planning meeting where the *product owner* provides a status of the *project backlog* to all the team members against the overall project aims and they agree how much of the backlog they can commit to produce over the sprint. Then the team sets a tentative plan for the coming sprint activities. The team is collectively responsible for the project results. They hold *daily scrum* meetings for fifteen minutes every morning where each team member deals with three issues: what was done the previous day, what will be done today, and what are the impediments to achieve the sprint goals. The meeting synchronizes the work, coordinates individual activities, and provides a collegial forum to raise issues and quickly learn from other team members. At the end of the sprint there is a four-hour informal meeting where team members present what they achieved in terms of fulfilling the targeted backlog. All interested stakeholders can attend the meeting (see figure).

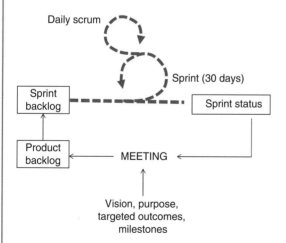

The product owner is responsible for the product backlog and a *burn-down chart* indicating the amount of work needed to complete the project. The product owner is also responsible for the economics of the project. The work proceeds in accordance with the *pigs and chicken* principle. The *pigs* are committed to the project because they have their own skin on the line. The *chicken* are spectators with vested interests but no direct contributions. The team members make up their own management. All other managers are chicken, with no say in the process. The team members are responsible for their own management development. Everything is visible in the reporting and available for all stakeholders.

Box 3.3 A typical real option

A typical real option is made up by a business proposition that promises a certain future return. This is an option because the holder can decide whether or not to invest in the business, i.e., it represents decision flexibility. It constitutes a so-called call option because the holder can decide to set the business in motion and be "long" in the underlying asset. This will be considered only when the expected net present value from the venture exceeds the initial investment required to effectuate the business opportunity. The total value of this option is made up by the sum of the *intrinsic value*, i.e., the net value of the project cash flows minus the initial investment, and the *time value*, which reflects the incremental gain from an optimal exercise in the future (see figure).

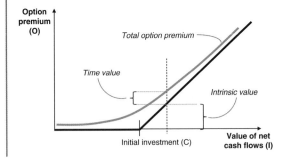

Assuming no transaction costs, that the net value of cash flows follows a lognormal distribution, the volatility of cash flows and interest rates remain unchanged, and the option premium is valued on a continuous basis, we may use the Black–Scholes formula to make a rough estimate of the option premium (O):

$$O = I[N(d_1)] - C[N(d_2)]e^{-rt}$$

$$d_1 = \left[\ln(I/C) + \left(\frac{r + v^2}{2}\right)\right] / v\sqrt{t}$$

$$d_2 = d_1 - v\sqrt{t}$$

O – option premium (total)

I – investment value (net present value of cash flows from business opportunity)

C – cash outflow (the initial investment needed to start the business venture)

N() – cumulative normal density function

t – time remaining to exercise the business venture [days/ 365]

v – volatility (annualized standard deviation) of cash flows from the venture

r – the interest rate

I/C expresses the so-called NPV factor and indicates the significance of the intrinsic value (I – C). A positive intrinsic value corresponds to an NPV factor above 1 ([I-C] > 0 → I/C > 1). $v\sqrt{t}$ expresses the time-value factor and indicates the amount of time value left in the real option over the remaining time it can be exercised.

This real option should be exercised only when the intrinsic value at least exceeds the time value because the immediate gain then compensates for any expected incremental value that remains due to the underlying uncertainty of the expected cash flows generated by the business opportunity.

If the strategic outcomes are substantially different from the planned aims due to fundamental changes in assumptions and expectations, it may lead to rethinking of the entire strategy. This way the organization can learn from potential discrepancies between realized and expected outcomes to adjust the strategic path.

Box 3.4 A garbage can model of choice

The principles of the "garbage can" in organizational decision making may arise when there are no clear strategic preferences, technologies are not clearly specified, and involvement varies according to effort and circumstance. Hence, the managers engage with their own favored solutions to deal with problems they encounter. Problems arise on an ongoing basis throughout the organization as time goes by. The *garbage can* depicts the stochastic meetings between managers with favored solutions and problems that emerge within the organization. The pairing of solutions to problems can depend on structural features such as cueing, ordering, power, and energy, and are influenced by chance and happenstance. The particular match between solutions and problems may be good or poor and thus can lead to both positive or negative outcomes, depending on the match. There is no rational order to the process or attempts to "optimize" the allocation of solutions to deal with particular types of problems. In principle, people are self-obsessed, biased by their prior experiences, and try to promote their own solutions to any problem that arises.

Choice opportunities where decisions can be made appear on an ongoing basis and the particular match of available solutions to emerging problems is determined by the eligibility of participants and the energy each of them displays in the process, e.g., affected by decision structure and incentives. So, we can illustrate the process as a lot of problems and solutions that are thrown into a large can. When we shake the can the solutions will somehow hit into a problem partially influenced by the density of participants and problems as well as the energy expended in shaking the can (see figure). The eventual match between solutions and problems will determine the organizational performance outcomes.

The garbage can model provides a framework to analyze decision-making processes when the ideal assumptions of rational choice no longer prevail, which may be the case at

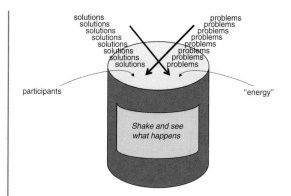

solutions
solutions
solutions
solutions
solutions
solutions
solutions
solutions

problems
problems
problems
problems
problems
problems
problems
problems

participants

"energy"

*Shake and see
what happens*

times of high turbulence and uncertainty. In many cases we
do not know what the real problem is and how it is going
to evolve over time while the organization may have no agreed
preferences. This can be the case when the future is unknown
and it is impossible to foresee what will happen.

Notes

1 W. D. Guth, I. C. Macmillan, Strategy implementation versus middle management self-interest, *Strategic Management Journal* 7(4): 313–327, 1986.
2 D. C. Hambrick, A. A. Canella, Strategy implementation as substance and selling, *Academy of Management Executive* 3: 278–285, 1989.
3 For a good overview of this topical focus see, for example, J. Hayes, *The Theory and Practice of Change Management* (second edn.), Palgrave Macmillan: Hampshire, 2007.
4 See, for example, H. Mintzberg, *The Rise and Fall of Strategic Planning*, Prentice Hall: Upper Saddle River, NJ, 1994.
5 S. Wally, R. Baum, Personal and structural determinants of the pace of strategic decision-making, *Academy of Management Journal* 37(4): 932–956, 1994.
6 C. H. Noble, The eclectic roots of strategy implementation research, *Journal of Business Research* 45(2): 119–134, 1999.
7 L. J. Bourgeois, Strategy and environment: A conceptual integration, *Academy of Management Review* 5(1): 25–39, 1980.
8 T. K. Das, Strategic planning and individual temporal orientation, *Strategic Management Journal* 8(2): 203–209, 1987.
9 In some companies the annual strategic planning exercise is launched earlier, e.g., during the second quarter of the year, and may culminate with detailed forecasts for the coming years completed during the fourth quarter before the end

of the current accounting year. This planning process can be combined with quarterly strategy review meetings where quarterly results are compared with prior plans and updated budgeting figures.

10 R. M. Grant, Strategic planning in a turbulent environment: evidence from the oil majors, *Strategic Management Journal* 24(6): 491–517, 2003.

11 H. Mintzberg, Patterns in strategy formation, *Management Science* 24(9): 934–948, 1978; H. Mintzberg, A. McHugh, Strategy formation in an adhocracy, *Administrative Science Quarterly* 30(2): 160–197, 1985.

12 H. Mintzberg, J. A. Waters, Tracking strategy in an entrepreneurial firm, *Academy of Management Journal* 25(3): 465–499, 1982.

13 T. J. Andersen, Integrating decentralized strategy making and strategic planning processes in dynamic environments, *Journal of Management Studies* 41(8): 1271–1299, 2004.

14 H. Mintzberg, Strategy making in three modes, *California Management Review* 16(2): 44–54, 1973; H. Mintzberg, Patterns in strategy formation, *Management Science* 24(9): 934–948, 1978.

15 L. Bourgeois, D. Brodwin, Strategic implementation: Five approaches to an elusive phenomenon, *Strategic Management Journal* 5(3): 241–264, 1986.

16 H. I. Ansoff, The emerging paradigm of strategic behavior, *Strategic Management Journal* 8(6): 501–515, 1987.

17 I. Nonaka, Toward middle-up-down management: accelerating information creation, *Sloan Management Review* 29(3): 9–18, 1988.

18 S. L. Hart, An integrative framework for strategy making processes, *Academy of Management Review* 17: 327–351, 1992.

19 A related empirical study tested this mixed-mode hypothesis and found some support for it. S. L. Hart, C. Banbury, How different strategy-making processes can make a difference, *Strategic Management Journal* 15: 251–269, 1994.

20 J. B. Quinn, *Strategies for Change: Logical Incrementalism*, Irwin: Homewood, IL, 1980.

21 L. J. Bourgeois, Performance and consensus, *Strategic Management Journal* 1(3): 227–248, 1980.

22 J. Hendry, Strategic decision making, discourse and strategy as a social practice, *Journal of Management Studies* 37(7): 955–977, 2000.

23 I. L. Janis, Groupthink, *Psychology Today* 5(6): 43–46, 1971.

24 K. M. Eisenhardt, Making fast strategic decisions in high-velocity environments, *Academy of Management Journal* 32(3): 543–576, 1989.

25 R. S. Kaplan, D. P. Norton, *The Execution Premium: Linking Strategy to Operations for Competitive Advantage*, Harvard Business School Publishing: Boston, MA, 2008.

26 L. G. Hrebiniak, *Making Strategy Work: Leading Effective Execution and Change*, Wharton School Publishing, Pearson Education: Upper Saddle River, NJ, 2005.

27 L. A. Schlesinger, C. F. Kiefer, *Just Start: Take Action, Embrace Uncertainty, Create the Future*, Harvard Business Review Press: Boston, MA, 2012.

28 R. Spekuland, *Beyond Strategy: The Leader's Role in Successful Implementation*, Jossey-Bass: San Francisco, CA, 2009.

29 M. Morgan, R. E. Levitt, W. Malek, *Executing Your Strategy: How to Break It Down and Get It Done*, Harvard Business School Press: Boston, MA, 2007.

30 The conventional approach applied for this purpose is the discounted cash flow (DCF) methodology where financial evaluations and decisions about future business engagements are made based on the net present value (NPV) rules. For a good overview of these approaches see, for example, R. A. Brealey, S. C. Myers, *Principles of Corporate Finance* (sixth edn.), Irwin McGraw-Hill: Boston, MA, 2000; A. Damodaran, *Corporate Finance*, Wiley: New York, 2001.

31 The analytical process focused on risks and opportunities depicted in Figure 3.3 illustrates the so-called Active Risk and Opportunity Planning (AROP) approach developed by LEGO Systems A/S for application in its project management efforts (reprinted with permission).

32 C. Chapman, S. Ward, *Project Risk Management: Processes, Techniques and Insights* (second edn.), Wiley: Chichester, 2003.

33 K. Schwaber, *Agile Project Management with Scrum*, Microsoft Press: Redmond, WA, 2004.

34 See T. J. Andersen, Strategic exposures and real options, Chapter 10 in *Global Derivatives: A Strategic Risk Management Perspective*, FT Prentice Hall: Harlow, 2006.

35 H. Courtney, J. Kirkland, P. Viguerie, Strategy under uncertainty, *Harvard Business Review* 75(6): 67–79, 1997.

36 T. J. Andersen, Case: Samsung Electronics Corporation, Copenhagen Business School, 2010.

37 E. H. Bowman, D. Hurry, Strategy through the options lens: An integrated view of resource investments and the incremental-choice process, *Academy of Management Review* 18(4): 760–782, 1993.

38 See Y. Sheffi, *The Resilient Enterprise: Overcoming Vulnerability for Competitive Advantage*, MIT Press: Cambridge, MA, 2007.

39 T. J. Andersen, Real options analysis in strategic decision making: An applied approach in a dual options framework, *Journal of Applied Management Studies* 9(2): 235–255, 2000.

40 T. J. Andersen, A real options approach to strategy making: Applications in the global semiconductor, pharmaceutical, and astronautics industries, *Strategic Management Society Annual International Conference*, San Francisco, 2001.

41 Finance theory does not tell us much about low-cost creation of options or about the optimal exercise of real options. The theoretical option premium is based on assumptions about market equilibrium where the options are traded at fair prices that reflect the options' future potential value under prevailing market conditions. In contrast, strategy analysts realize that valuable real options are firm-specific and often based on unique organizational resources. Hence, the ways to develop costless real options and exercise them in an optimal manner also depends on firm-specific processes.

42 T. Leuhrman, Strategy as a portfolio of real options, *Harvard Business Review* 76(5): 89–99, 1998.

43 The volatility measure (v) corresponds to an annualized standard deviation. Hence, the volatility can be derived directly from the standard deviation of annual observations whereas data with other frequencies must be transformed. For example, a standard deviation of monthly observations (ms) is annualized by multiplying by the square root of 12 ($v = ms \sqrt{12}$) and a standard deviation of quarterly observations (qs) is annualized by multiplying by the square root of 4 ($v = qs \sqrt{4}$).

44 The portfolio approach can be combined with scenario analysis where future scenarios question the firm's ability to respond to challenges imposed by extreme but not unlikely future business situations. The identification of latent options can be useful here. See K. D. Miller, H.G. Waller, Scenarios, real options, and integrated risk management, *Long Range Planning* 36: 93–107, 2003.

45 K. R. Andrews, *The Concept of Corporate Strategy*, Dow-Jones Irwin: Homewood, IL, 1971.

46 J. Bower, *Managing the Resource Allocation Process*, Harvard Business School Press: Boston, MA, 1970, 1986.

47 E. Penrose, *The Theory of the Growth of the Firm* (fourth edn.), Oxford University Press (first published in 1959), 2009.

48 T. Noda, J. Bower, Strategy making as integrated processes of resource allocation, Strategic Management Journal 17 (special issue): 159–192, 1996.

49 H. Mintzberg *et al.*, The structure of "unstructured" decision processes, *Adminstrative Science Quarterly* 21(2): 246–274, 1976.

50 E. F. Harrison, *The Managerial Decision-Making Process,* Houghton Mifflin: Boston, MA, 1995.

51 H. A. Simon, *Administrative Behavior: A Study of Decision-Making Processes in Administrative Organizations* (fourth edn.), Free Press: New York (first published in 1945), 1997.

52 V. K. Narayanan, L. Fahey, The micro-politics of strategy formulation, *Strategic Management Journal* 7(1): 25–34, 1982; G. R. Salancik, J. Pfeffer, Who gets power – and how they hold on to it: A strategic contingency model of power, *Organizational Dynamics* 5(3): 3–21, 1977.

53 See T. J. Andersen, Case: Porsche (D), Copenhagen Business School (available through the European Case Clearing Corporation – ECCH), 2010.

54 C. R. Schwenk, Cognitive simplification processes in strategic decision-making, *Strategic Management Journal* 5(2): 111–128, 1984.

55 See, for example, M. H. Bazerman, M. D. Watkins, *Predictable Surprises: The Disasters You Should Have Seen Coming, and How to Prevent Them*, Harvard Business School Press: Boston, MA, 2008.

56 S. Miller *et al.*, Beyond planning strategies for successfully implementing strategic decisions, *Long Range Planning* 37: 201–218, 2004.

57 D. Miller, P. Friesen, *Organizations: A Quantum View,* Prentice Hall: Englewood Cliffs, NJ, 1984.

58 See, for example, H. Mintzberg, J. A. Waters, Tracking strategy in an entrepreneurial firm, *Academy of Management Journal* 25(3): 465–499, 1982.

59 E. Romanelli, M. L. Tushman, Organizational transformation as punctuated equilibrium, *Academy of Management Journal* 37(5): 1141–1166, 1986.

60 R. D'Aveni, Strategic supremacy through disruption and dominance, *Sloan Management Review* Spring: 127–135, 1999.

61 R. D'Aveni, *Strategic Supremacy: How Industry Leaders Create Growth, Wealth, and Power through Spheres of Influence,* Free Press: New York, 1999.

62 H. Mintzberg, The fall and rise of strategic planning, *Harvard Business Review* 72(1): 107–114, 1994.

63 See, for example, T. J. Andersen, A. H. Segars, The impact of IT on decision structure and firm performance: Evidence from the textile and apparel industry, *Information & Management* 39(2): 85–100, 2001.

64 M. D. Cohen *et al.*, A garbage can model of organizational choice, *Administrative Science Quarterly* 17(1): 1–25, 1972.

65 R. S. Sutton, A. Barto, *Reinforcement Learning,* MIT Press: Cambridge, MA, 1998.

66 J. L. Bower, C. G. Gilbert, How managers' everyday decisions create or destroy your company's strategy, *Harvard Business Review* 82(5): 72–79, 2007.

67 M. W. Blenko, M. C. Mankins, P. Rogers, The decision-driven organization, *Harvard Business Review* 88(6): 54–62, 2010.

68 M. W. Blenko *et al.*, *Decide & Deliver: 5 Steps to Breakthrough Performance in Your Organization*, Harvard Business School Press: Boston, MA, 2010.

69 J. A. Schumpeter, *Capitalism, Socialism and Democracy*, Harper & Row: New York (originally published in 1942), 1975.

70 K. R. Andrews, *The Concept of Corporate Strategy*. Dow-Jones Irwin: Homewood, IL, 1971.

71 D. F. Kuratko *et al.*, *Corporate Innovation & Entrepreneurship: Entrepreneurial Development within Organizations* (third edn.), South-Western: International edn., Nashville, TN, 2011.

72 H. H. Stevenson, J. C. Jarillo-Mossi, Preserving entrepreneurship as companies grow, *Journal of Business Strategy* 10: 76–89, 1986.

73 R. G. Ireland *et al.*, Conceptualizing corporate entrepreneurship strategy, *Entrepreneurship Theory and Practice* 33(1): 19–46, 2009.

74 V. Sathe, *Corporate Entrepreneurship: Top Managers and New Business Creation*, Cambridge University Press, 2003.

75 D. F. Kuratko *et al.*, *Corporate Innovation & Entrepreneurship*, International edn., South-Western: Nashville, TN, 2011.

76 C. Lechner, S. W. Floyd, Searching, processing and practicing – key learning activities in exploratory initiatives, *Long Range Planning* 40(1): 9–29, 2007.

77 S. Sarasvathy, *Effectuation: Elements of Entrepreneurial Expertise*, Edward Elgar: Cheltenham, 2008.

78 G. Johnson *et al.*, Micro strategy and strategizing: Towards an activity-based view, *Journal of Management Studies* 40(1): 3–22, 2003.

79 G. Johnson *et al.*, *Strategy as Practice,* Cambridge University Press, 2007.

80 R. A. Burgelman, A process model of internal corporate venturing in the diversified major firm, *Administrative Science Quarterly* 28(2): 223–244, 1983; R. A. Burgelman, A model of the interaction of strategic behavior, corporate context, and the concept of strategy, *Academy of Management Review* 8(1): 61–70, 1983.

81 A notable example of this is the "Medal of Defiance" awarded at Hewlett-Packard "in recognition of extraordinary contempt and defiance beyond the normal call of engineering duty." C. H. House, R. L. Price, *The HP Phenomenon: Innovation and Business Transformation*. Stanford Business Books: Stanford, CA, 2009.

82 R. A. Burgelman, A. S. Grove, Strategic dissonance, *California Management Review* 38(2): 8–28, 1996.

83 A. S. Grove, *Only the Paranoid Survive: How to Exploit the Crisis Points that Challenge Every Company and Career*, HarperCollins Business: London, 1997.

84 T. J. Andersen, How to reconcile the strategy dilemma? *European Business Forum* 9(1): 32–35, 2002.

85 R. A. Burgelman, A process model of strategic business exit: Implications for an evolutionary perspective on strategy, *Strategic Management Journal* 17(S1): 193–214, 1996.

86 R. A. Burgelman, The role of strategy making in organizational evolution, Chapter 3 in Bower and Gilbert (eds.), *From Resource Allocation to Strategy*, Oxford University Press: New York, 2005.

87 A recent study reports that the distribution between induced and autonomous investments in Intel varied from 35:65 in 1984 to 15:85 in 1991 and 50:50 by 2005, i.e., substantial investment resources were committed in the form of autonomous venture initiatives. See R. A. Burgelman, A. S. Grove, Let chaos reign, then rein in chaos – repeatedly: Managing strategic dynamics for corporate longevity, *Strategic Management Journal* 28(10): 965–979, 2007.

4 Integrative strategy

Learning points

- Introduce the integrative strategy-making approach
- Explicate the dynamic of central and decentralized processes
- Outline the premises for strategic response capabilities and adaptation
- Link interactive control systems to strategy making

The strategic path pursued by a firm over time is the consequence of decisions and initiatives taken by managers at all levels with different functional responsibilities in various parts of the organization. Based on a general mission and overarching aims, top management typically induces an annual planning exercise where the intended developments in the official strategy are analyzed and discussed, which serves as a yardstick for ongoing business activities within the firm. In some cases this will stimulate concrete resource-committing proposals that are handled together with other investment projects included as part of the formal capital budgeting procedures. At the same time, organizations provide some leeway, although to different degrees, for individuals to pursue entrepreneurial initiatives related to operational conditions within their functional areas, such as pursuing new market opportunities, improving internal processes, inventing new technologies, etc. Some of these initiatives may eventually become successful ventures in their own right that will require significant investments as they expand to become general business activities for the firm. This way the strategic business portfolio evolves as the outcome of resource-committing investments made throughout the organization, influenced by a general mission, corporate values, a common understanding of the competitive situation, the decision structure, information systems, communication processes, the organizational setting, and individual behaviors. Hence, by *integrative strategy making* we mean the amalgam of all these activities and structural elements in the organization that leads to strategic outcomes over time. More specifically, we refer to the interaction dynamic between the central planning activities and decentralized responsive initiatives taken by many individuals throughout the organization.

The integrative strategy view looks upon strategic management as a process where organizational activities eventually shape and form the realized strategies as time goes by. The strategy-formation process is comprised of formal planning exercises conducted in accordance with structured cyclical patterns of activities as well as informal development of ideas, insights, and initiatives that emerge among individuals in the operating entities as environmental conditions change. The ability to gain value from interacting planning discussions and experiences from dispersed strategic initiatives is very much a function of the organizational structure, information flows, communication channels, management control systems, etc. It is also affected by the relative power of organizational decision makers and potential political plays among dominant groups or coalitions of people as well as the social conditions that frame the cognitive dynamic between influential individuals.[1] Hence, it is a central corporate management focus to establish an organizational setting that is conducive to an effective integrative strategy-making process.

However, the *process perspective* does not provide a clear-cut delineation of an optimal way to develop future strategy because organizational strategy making is comprised of a highly complex and intriguing mixture of formal and informal activities. Retrospective empirical investigations of the strategy-formation process often rely on somewhat murky recollections of seemingly deliberate actions garnered with confusion about the associated involvement of individuals located at different management levels. Hence, the integrative strategy-making approach tries to explore how important strategic activities are conducted by people at multiple levels in the organization across a diversity of functional specializations over time. In this context, it seems apparent that part of the strategy-formation process is based on deliberations and discussions about intended outcomes pursued in conjunction with adaptive initiatives taken along the way as organizational members try to execute and mold their daily business activities.

As Markides argues: "The truth of the matter is that the process of developing a superior strategy is part planning, part gut feeling, and part trial and error until you hit upon something that works."[2]

The fact that the real world in which we act is complex and continues to change often in unpredictable ways makes it difficult and indeed superfluous to plan strategic projects in nitty-gritty detail. There must be room to maneuver in accordance with the changing context and improvise with new solutions that can make things work better. Or, in the words of Napoleon: "Get your principles straight. The rest is a matter of detail." It is told that Napoleon included his officers in the strategy deliberations to ensure that key areas would be adequately addressed and to form common understanding, build trust, and gain proper buy-in to the overarching intentions. Napoleon's teams were then empowered to take actions in battle as required by circumstance based on the up-front clarification of purpose and in line with the principles and broad directives established in advance.[3] Hence, the combination of participative planning and authority to take decisions in the field around empowered teams can form the basis for responsive initiatives that drive adaptive actions and flexible execution of organizational activities.

The process perspective invites a stronger focus on responsive behaviors that facilitate the organization's ability to adapt to changing environmental conditions. In contrast, the positioning perspective argues that a firm should take advantage of prevailing market powers and enhance its bargaining position to gain higher returns. In his initial analysis, Michael Porter suggested two viable strategic paradigms based on competitive advantage driven by cost efficiencies and product differentiation. While a number of research contributions seem to indicate that firms often choose a strategic posture based on principles of cost competition and differentiated offerings, there are different sources of competitive advantage and the identified strategy typologies do not fall stringently within the simple generic strategy framework.[4] What is more, "there is no clear evidence here that no-distinctive-emphasis designs are any more or any less capable of above-average performance than other archetypes."[5] In other words, there is no significant difference found in performance between firms that adhere to one of the generic strategies compared with those that do both at the same time and that in principle should be *stuck in the middle*. The arguments for the generic strategy hypothesis were that a firm had to choose between scale economic gains associated with standardized mass production or creating differentiated products to satisfy specific customer needs in more expensive, customized production set-ups. So, one had to choose between competitive advantage in the form of standardized low-cost production or costly differentiated craft production. No middle ground seemed possible. However, there are (at least) five reasons why the surrounding business reality has changed the competitive odds where the choice between generic low-cost and differentiation strategies no longer prevails.

1. *New technologies*: information technology supports *flexible manufacturing* capabilities that enable production of diverse outputs economically allowing for mixed parts and variations in assembly, process sequence, volume and the design of products. *Agile production* processes allow manufacturing firms to respond quickly to customer needs and market changes while controlling both cost and quality by employing technologies that allow the marketing, design, and production functions to share common data. Furthermore, computer-aided manufacturing systems provide *mass-customization* techniques to produce custom outputs efficiently.[6] Dell Computer is the prime example of this technology-driven strategic flexibility.

2. *New production practices*: the principles of *continuous improvement* involve human intervention both to enhance process efficiencies and to gain qualitative improvements in output. Incremental processing adaptations out-compete the economic gains to be achieved from learning curve effects. This relates to the *kaizen* philosophy adopted in Japanese firms to improve manufacturing, engineering, and business practices. It is derived from principles of *quality control* to ensure that processing and output are consistent with little waste of resources and *lean* processes that discard resource expenditures for anything but the creation of customer value.[7] Toyota Motor Corporation (TMC) has been the role model for studies of the continuous improvement methodology.

3. *New market pressures*: large dominant market intermediaries exert competitive forces that require both competitive prices and high-quality products. Large retailing distributers with a dominant market position push for the best-quality products at the lowest possible prices and make it difficult to differentiate across market segments as enormous stores offer everything from "milk to Matchbox toys" at extremely low prices.[8] This puts pressure on producers to pursue simultaneous improvements in product features and production cost. Wal-Mart Stores exemplifies the pressure to offer quality products at low prices.

4. *New strategic ideas*: the aim of *blue-ocean* strategy is to create new demand in uncontested market space as opposed to competing for known customers in an existing industry. It suggests that a superior market position can be achieved by heeding new, previously unnoticed and differentiating product features while eliminating conventional features no longer in demand to save production cost. Southwest Airlines downplayed conventional perks in flight, such as meals, lounges, and choice seating, and emphasized speed and friendly service instead. That is, *red-ocean* strategies, where firms compete in conventional industries on reliable standardized products and services, can also be successful.[9]

5. *New business models*: there has been an increasing focus on the service aspects of products to expand the revenue base and induce corporate growth that enhances differentiating service features. The service features emphasize the role of different parts of the *business model* to enhance both customer value and processing efficiencies. This can be achieved through a superior *fit* between different product features, complementary service elements, sourcing and distribution channels, etc.[10] For example, Gap, the American clothing and accessories retailer, combines fast restocking of stores with short model cycles and automatic replenishment from suppliers in a cohesive system that suits its core customers.

Instead, competitive advantage is accomplished by an ability to manage existing offerings efficiently with multiple value-creating features and at the same time innovate, respond, and adapt with new features that enable the firm to retain its competitive edge. For example, Apple Inc. (formerly Apple Computer) has been extremely successful in recent years, with new innovative product offerings, such as iPod, iTunes, iPhone, and iPad, that extend initial successes and build unique customer experiences. Hence, the contemporary strategic challenge is more related to optimizing current practices and simultaneously engaging in innovative changes in products and processes that can create a value-enhancing potential for the future. This captures the essential discussion about balancing *exploitation* of current practices and *exploration* for better practices, where the former increases the efficiencies of status quo and the latter incurs costs to induce necessary change for the future.[11] Integrative strategy making can give a valuable perspective on this conundrum as it constitutes a combination of *forward-looking*, integrating and coordinating analysis and *backward-looking* experiential learning from enactment of business activities and responsive actions. The forward-looking planning process considers the need to organize activities across functions, levels, and time for existing business as well as new projects. The backward-looking experiences gained from execution of current activities provide an immediate sense of the effectiveness of existing processes as well as giving pointers to new initiatives that can improve existing conduct.

Long- and short-cycled activities

Integrative strategy making can be seen as the outcome of resource-committing decisions and responsive actions taken at different levels of the organization across different time horizons. At the *strategic level*, top management engages in a forward-looking process with a *long cycle time* that typically comprises a multiple-year planning horizon where a general mission and rational analytical deductions outline proposed future investment needs and strategic activities. At the *tactical level*, the strategic considerations are confined to planned activities and their expected effects over the next accounting year as the appropriate planning horizon. This is often tied to quarterly or monthly budget follow-up reviews that monitor outcomes against long-term

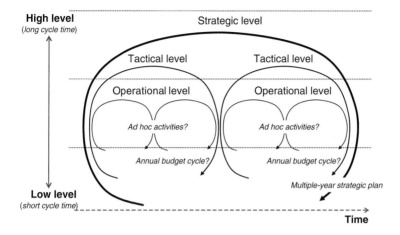

High level
(*long cycle time*)

Strategic level

Tactical level

Tactical level

Operational level

Operational level

Ad hoc activities?

Ad hoc activities?

Annual budget cycle?

Annual budget cycle?

Multiple-year strategic plan

Low level
(*short cycle time*)

Time

Figure 4.1 Cycles in the integrative strategy-making process. Source: Andersen and Schrøder (2010)

intentions and update planned activities with short-term action plans. At the *operational level*, managers with functional responsibilities may take a variety of responsive initiatives where the effects can be observed within a *short cycle time* that can be counted in weeks, months, and quarters. These experiments with modified approaches and new ways to do things provide frequent learning points that can enhance the insights about effective and ineffective actions.[12] This string of organizational process activities convoluted across level and time is shown graphically in Figure 4.1. The many short-cycled actions taken at lower operational levels constitute experimental probing activities where the immediate responses to new local situations provide the basis for generating environmental knowledge that can inform future strategy deliberations. The insights generated among operational and functionally focused managers can feed into the discussions about longer-cycled initiatives taken at the tactical and strategic levels.

The interpretation of the strategy-making process as a combination of long-cycled planning activities and short-cycled initiatives that respond to emerging events can be compared to the dynamic process of human thinking. The human brain seems to operate through complementary processes embedded in slow reflective and fast responsive systems.[13] The *slow system* is an effortful conscious activity that interprets outcomes from interactions with the environmental context and considers forward moves through reasoning based on observed relationships. The *fast system* operates with little effort and observes outcomes from ongoing interactions between the body and the surrounding environment (see Box 4.1 *The "new" brain metaphor*). The interplay between brain, body, and environment resembles an organizational setting where a central analytical process deals with future things to do and a decentralized process that acts on immediate influences from the surrounding business environment. Hence, the world presents itself through the fast system, whereas the slow system interprets and reasons about what the fast system is experiencing.[14]

The logical linear processing that has been associated with the brain's left hemisphere can be seen as an attempt at analytical planning, whereas the holistic sensations of the brain's right hemisphere resemble the emotional and social aspects of management. To emphasize this distinction, it was even suggested that we plan on the left side and manage on the right side of the brain.[15] The conventional view on strategic management is often perceived as a central process of planning, execution, and monitoring. The implied control loop updates management on organizational outcomes that can help pinpoint the needs for corrective actions. However, these decisions are typically confined to top management and may, therefore, preclude updated inputs from experiences gained in short-cycled actions taken by lower-level managers. In a decentralized structure, decision authority is moved to lower hierarchical levels where operating managers can voice opinions and take initiatives within their areas of responsibility. This gives more influence to people located closer to relevant situational information and operational expertise.[16] These local reactions to emerging events can generate experiential insights about different aspects of the competitive environment that can be forwarded for consideration in the central planning process.

Hence, it is important to combine slow, forward-looking control features at the corporate center with an ability to learn from fast actions taken in response to observed changes in the

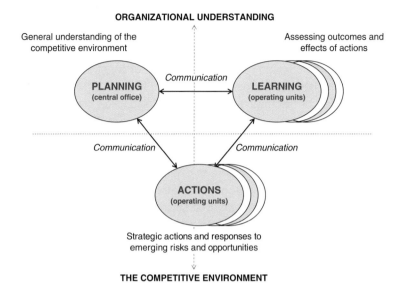

ORGANIZATIONAL UNDERSTANDING

General understanding of the competitive environment

Assessing outcomes and effects of actions

PLANNING
(central office)

Communication

LEARNING
(operating units)

Communication

Communication

ACTIONS
(operating units)

Strategic actions and responses to emerging risks and opportunities

THE COMPETITIVE ENVIRONMENT

Figure 4.2 Central planning and learning from operating actions. Source: Andersen and Fredens (2011)

local environments (Figure 4.2). The reality of the competitive conditions is observed from the effects derived from the many fast actions taken by local managers in response to risks and opportunities observed in different parts of the organization. Communicating these decentralized experiences to the corporate center makes it possible to assess how different actions work (or not) and thereby to update interpretations of the environmental context.[17] When these response effects are held against the assumptions adopted in the planning process, the understanding of the firm's strategic situation is updated, and the new insights can inform the strategic discussions between managers at different organizational levels. Therefore, it is the dynamic interaction between experiential insights gained from responsive actions and the slow, forward-looking planning considerations that forms a more realistic view of the competitive environment.

The slow, or long-cycled, planning activities and associated control processes can help develop a shared cognitive understanding of the firm's competitive environment by engaging key people in the discussions. Involving decision makers from different parts of the organization in the planning deliberations can form a shared cognition across a broad set of constituents with different insights and experiences. Hence, the strategic planning process can be seen as a discourse that reconciles diverse insights and forms a common understanding of strategic developments in the firm as a guide to ongoing decisions.[18] The fast local decisions where empowered managers in the operating units engage with stakeholders to explore alternative solutions in view of changes in the local context can generate new business propositions. For example, an able functional manager at TDC, the Danish telecommunications company, developed an online music service (PLAY) entirely on his own, but when it was offered as part of the mobile telephone package, it gave the company a strategic edge.[19] That is, autonomous responsive initiatives that allow local experimentation are the means to uncover new opportunities that can inform the strategy discussions in the central planning process. Hence, strategic management and control processes can conduct updated, forward-looking evaluations of opportunities uncovered by decentralized responsive actions.

These combined fast and slow processes can stimulate an underlying *dynamic* that depicts an organizational ability to take actions, interact, and adapt. This dynamic based on fast and slow processes creates a system that modifies organizational activities in nonlinear ways where future outcomes are difficult to predict.[20] In other words, individual responses are taken in conjunction with other actions pursued by individuals in different parts of the firm that together with ongoing events in the environment can have unpredictable effects. Such an integrative structure comprised of a planning process driven by rational deduction and linear computations circumscribed by dispersed autonomous actions can be construed as a cohesive dynamic system that makes up the organization's ability to respond and adapt. The ongoing actions derived from managerial decisions throughout the organization are affected by many individuals inside and outside the organization and the outcomes from them constitute nonlinear processes.

Central and peripheral processes

The common strategy view sees top management as the central instigator of strategic initiatives where different cognitive capabilities among executives across competing firms can explain why some organizations develop better strategies than others.[21] This is also reflected in a broad literature around the role of top managers in strategy making, with particular focus on the effects of individual executive characteristics and the composition of top management teams on strategic outcomes.[22] However, since the complex strategy-making process in reality involves an amalgam of central and dispersed activities, the cognitive perspective should be extended to include managerial decision makers at all organizational levels.[23] So, the ability to invoke adaptive change in the organization is likely to require individual cognitive capabilities among top managers as well as middle and operating managers throughout the organization who are responsible for the handling of the daily activities. Accordingly, we claim that the organization's ability to respond effectively relies on the combined efforts of central and peripheral agents, where top managers confront their evolving cognitive understanding of the strategic context with the experiential insights gained by lower-level managers in regular interactive processes. This ongoing updating of the strategic knowledge at top management with current events in different parts of the organization is a key to understanding adaptive organizations.

This is consistent with empirical evidence indicating that firms pursuing multiple strategy modes at the same time, for example by combining central planning and decentralized strategy making, are associated with superior performance.[24] These findings point to the superiority of complementary central and peripheral processes where central and peripheral actors interact and stimulate an underlying dynamic to interpret, act, learn, and adapt (Figure 4.3). The dynamic interaction between central and peripheral actors is the fundamental mechanism behind adaptive organizational change under turbulent conditions.

We can infer this dynamic perspective to integrative strategy making comprised of central intended activities and decentralized

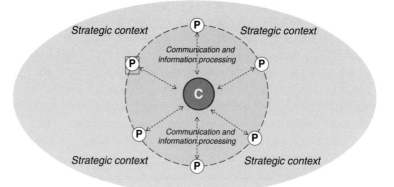

P - employees execute initiatives in the periphery of the organization close to the strategic context
C - executives plan and monitor outcomes from the administrative center of the organization

Interaction between periphery (P) and center (C) is embedded in the organization's communication and information processes

Figure 4.3 Interaction between central and peripheral actors

emerging initiatives. The strategic actions derive from managerial decisions that interact with numerous individuals inside and outside the organization and thus constitute nonlinear processes. Central planning, although it may invite the views of many individuals, is characterized by rational deduction and linear computations to comprehend and create a more certain way forward. Hence, a basic characteristic of the combined central and peripheral processes of integrative strategy making is that it establishes a contrasting difference between linear and nonlinear processing modes. When the two processes are brought together in the same dynamic system, the interaction between them becomes complementary, where they mutually depend on each other. The central process provides direction and scope for decentralized responsive actions that in turn provide new experiential insights to the central interpretive analysis of the strategic context. This dynamic process will furnish a gradual adaptation of organizational activities to match the emerging changes in the competitive environment.

The adaptive strategic renewal of the firm has been conceptualized as *dynamic capabilities* expressed as the organization's ability to "integrate, build and reconfigure internal and external competences to address rapidly changing environments."[25] Dynamic capabilities can be ascribed to the knowledge and competencies of executives, managers, and specialized actors in the organization and therefore constitute a multifaceted and complex construct.[26] However, the dynamic system formed by interactions between central, forward-looking planning activities and decentralized, backward-looking learning from responses to emerging events provides a useful, and possibly more straightforward, basis for the analysis of adaptive processes.

Responding to environmental change

The dynamic capabilities of the organization arguably depend on an ability to sense emerging changes in the environment, seize new opportunities, and reconfigure the organization to exploit new opportunities offered by the changing competitive environment.[27]

From this perspective, corporate adaptation will require capabilities to:

1. *sense* opportunities (and risks) and shape responses
2. *seize* the identified opportunities (and fend off the risks)
3. *reconfigure* resources around responses to retain competitiveness.

To achieve this, management has to organize processes to sense the new customer needs, competitive activities, and technological–scientific developments that shape opportunities for new products, services, and process improvements. This cannot be left solely to the creativity and learning of a few people scattered throughout the organization, although the involvement of individuals and their experiences are important to the dynamic adaptation process. The employees located at the organizational periphery engage in daily business activities and interact directly with customers, suppliers, distributors, and other colleagues. Consequently, they are often the first to observe the subtle changes that take place in the environment and these insights can reveal important information. The prevailing communication and information flows among individuals, managers, and executives are instrumental to the ensuing process of filtering, analyzing, and

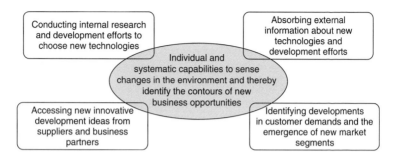

Figure 4.4 A strategic opportunities sensing framework. Source: adapted from Teece (2009)

interpreting these observations from the surrounding competitive environment.[28] Hence, we can think of a broader sensing system that extracts observations from internal and external informants and analyzes ongoing environmental changes to identify strategic opportunities for the firm (Figure 4.4).

This is a dynamic system of current observations at the organizational periphery that regularly and relatively frequently performs analytical interventions attempting to make sense of updated information flows about the competitive environment. This approach is somewhat different from that proposed by industrial economics (exemplified by Porter's five forces model), where the strategy deliberations try to deal with the pressures of existing rivalry and competitive forces. In contrast, the sensing of environmental changes identifies new opportunities and considers the prevailing industry structure as temporary and in continuous flux, where dynamic capabilities must develop appropriate responses. Hence, the organization can pursue unique value-creating opportunities by collaborating with relevant industry peers and complementing firms where activities co-evolve among interacting stakeholders. This reflects a cooperative view supported by ideas about open innovation as a superior approach to create viable solutions through collaborative efforts and gain sustainable buy-in among a broad set of market participants. Hence, the underlying organizational setting builds on a culture of (open) innovation that depends on the involvement of engaged individuals whose unique insights and

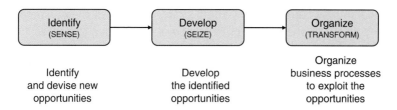

Figure 4.5 A stepwise path to strategic adaptation. Source: inspired by Teece (2009)

specialized knowledge are instrumental for the sensing and opportunity development processes.

However, it is not enough to sense emerging environmental changes, analyze, and interpret them to identify new opportunities the firm can pursue. It is equally important to be able to recombine and configure available resources into viable solutions that seize the identified opportunities. That is, you must be able to build the "machine" before you can use it. Finally, the organization must be able to reorganize and coordinate existing processes and transform the current structure to exploit the new opportunities, i.e., you must be able to install the "machine" to utilize it. This corresponds to the three steps in the firm's strategic adaptation process suggested by David Teece (Figure 4.5).

The strategic adaptation process becomes increasingly important as the competitive landscape changes. These environmental changes are characterized by increasing use of information, communication, and computational technologies that can accommodate flexible structures and fast organizational responses based on individualized knowledge. However, the new competitive context also creates corporate exposures with higher levels of uncertainty, where it is impossible to forecast future developments. This calls for strategic response capabilities that allow the organization to "respond fast when change or surprise occurs," based on flexible strategies, adaptive organizational structures, and a managerial mindset geared to (open) innovation and collaborative learning efforts.[29] The ability to adapt to changing competitive conditions and match the firm's strategic position to the current environmental requirements is a fundamental concern in strategic management as good strategic fit is the basis for persistent and sustainable profitability. The fit-creating adaptations can be expressed as *strategic responsiveness*, where the firm is in possession of "a bundle of capabilities to assess the environment, identify firm resources, and mobilize them in effective responsive actions."[30] Furthermore, the ability to respond and adapt to maintain strategic fit over time is associated with both higher and more stable economic returns (see Box 4.2 *Effects of strategic responsiveness*).

The strategic responsiveness perspective analyzes effects of general response capabilities for strategic fit at an aggregate organizational level and does not consider the details of an integrative strategy-making process that can accomplish ongoing adaptation. However, the preceding discussion points to the importance of forward-looking considerations informed by experiences gained from autonomous initiatives taken by individuals throughout the organization. Hence, the execution of proposed solutions and responsive actions rely on more than a single strategy-making mode since there is a need for *central* analytical capabilities as well as a structure to support *decentralized* responses. In many ways it reflects the need for an overarching sense-making process to create strategic *intent* and coordinate execution of corporate actions, combined with an ability to respond to *emerging* events along the way and learn from them.

One argument for integrative coordinated analysis is that connected operational activities are vulnerable to abrupt changes from unexpected events. Hence, we are often unable to analyze strategic issues in isolation because they are part of a complex system where elements are tightly coupled so things can evolve in unpredictable ways. For example, the Deepwater Horizon oil spill in the Gulf of Mexico in 2010 was part of a complex structure (the rig was owned by Triton Asset Leasing GmbH, operated by Transocean Ltd., and leased by British Petroleum) with unprecedented technological challenges that deflected responsibilities and thwarted precautionary behaviors. While some contingencies can be planned in advance, it is difficult in a competitive landscape exposed to uncertainty and unpredictability. Here there is a need to take local action and respond more immediately to events as they evolve because the necessary situational and technical expertise is available locally for quick and effective handling. However, given the complexity of the business environment, we also need to interpret and assess the emerging responses from an integrative organizational perspective.[31] In short, we are faced with a competitive context that requires an analytical overview of tightly coupled corporate activities combined with a degree of structural decoupling that can facilitate autonomous responses to unexpected events.

It is argued that the business environment generally is becoming more complex, dynamic, and unpredictable, as observed from the unprecedented economic effects from the global financial crisis and credit crunch after the Lehman Brothers collapse. These kinds of turbulent conditions can lead to unprecedented socio-political events, technology shifts, competitive moves, etc. Under these circumstances the corporation is exposed to a high degree of complexity and coupling between events as well as a high degree of uncertainty and change. This is particularly challenging and probably reflects what most firms are confronting in a globally connected business environment. In this case, there is a need for *central handling* of events to consider the effects of complex interdependencies, and at the same time being able to engage with *decentralized responses* as unexpected events occur, to remain vigilant and responsive (Figure 4.6).

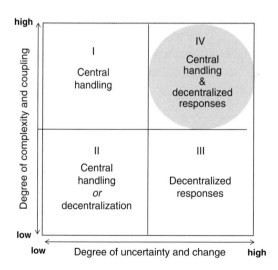

Figure 4.6 Responding to turbulent environmental conditions. Source: Andersen (2010)

The central handling of events can be accomplished through *central planning* activities with integrated analyses that coordinate organizational activities across functional entities (see Chapter 2). The central planning process creates a common strategy focus and integrates current activities with the intent of optimizing outcomes and coordinating strategic actions for effective execution. The decentralized responses are achieved from *decentralization*, where dispersion of decision power encourages alertness to environmental changes and gives authority to respond locally. The decentralized responsive initiatives can be conceived as experimentation in the form of small-stakes probes that test identified opportunities that could become future strategic options for the firm. The empirical evidence supports the proposed advantages of an integrative structure that combines central planning and decentralization (Figure 4.7).[32] Hence, those firms that use a central planning process to conduct integrated analyses and at the same time decentralize to enhance local responsiveness are associated with higher performance outcomes and lower variation in performance. That is, they display a favorable risk–return profile.

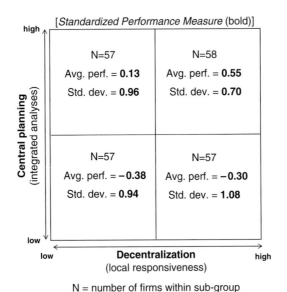

Figure 4.7 Effects of combined strategy-making modes. Source: Andersen (2010)

Complementary strategy-making modes

Integrative strategy making can be depicted as complementary strategy-making modes comprised of central and decentralized processes. The rational analytical strategy approach outlined in the conventional strategic management model constitutes a *central strategy-making* process used to form direction and *strategic intent* for the firm. The ability of dispersed managers to engage and take action in view of emerging events constitutes a *decentralized strategy-making* process that displays the key characteristics of *emergent strategy*.

The rational analytical approach reflects central planning that includes mission statement, long-term goals, short-term action plans, and regular strategic controls (see Chapter 2). This approach has merit across all types of businesses operating in all environments because the fact-based analyses and related strategy discussions help develop new insights and form a common understanding of the competitive situation among key decision makers across the firm. The active involvement of middle managers in these discussions provides diversity of views as well as creating commitment, even if there is less than full agreement on all issues. The planning discussions can both develop innovative ideas and serve as a vehicle to shape new business opportunities for the firm as well as a forum that is able to coordinate actions across different business functions.

However, planning cannot stand on its own, particularly in firms that operate in turbulent environments where corporate actions are highly dependent on individual knowledge and expertise. In this environmental context there is a need for observations and responses among managers and frontline employees in the operating entities so emerging events can be sensed and interpreted through trial-and-error learning. Hence, autonomy allows local managers to deal more effectively with new events because they are close to where the relevant and detailed information is available for decision making. The immediate responses to new developments provide experiential insights about what seems to work and what does not, i.e., it is a decentralized way of learning. Involving these managers in the strategic decision-making process provides a mechanism to communicate and engage these updated insights into the forefront of the firm's strategic considerations.

Hence, there are two distinct ways in which dispersed managers can exert an influence on activities in the firm. One is to participate in important strategic decisions so different views and insights can help inform discussions about alternative solutions and thereby develop better decision outcomes based on information from different functional areas. Another way is to distribute decision authority to lower-level managers so they can take action locally without asking for permission at headquarters, i.e., they have sufficient autonomy to respond at their own discretion. This makes it possible to react faster when things happen and gain new insights about what is going on. The implied learning can feed into the planning discussions and deliberations around strategic decisions that provide information otherwise unavailable. Hence, central planning and decentralized strategy making complement each other and therefore lead to better strategic outcomes associated with higher corporate performance (Figure 4.8). Hence, the prior success of Hewlett-Packard Company (HP), at times referred to as "the HP way," can be explained by a corporate culture and central structure that nurtured decentralized ideas and initiatives and let them

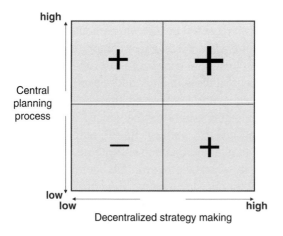

Figure 4.8 The performance effect of integrative strategy

persevere. The principle was that development of new business opportunities was made as low as possible in the organization whereas crucial infrastructure and corporate processes were centralized.[33] Empirical studies support this proposition and corroborate the underlying argumentation. Central planning is important and firms that engage in planning are associated with higher performance and even more so in turbulent industries.[34] The decentralized decision-making approaches, both autonomy and participation, are similarly associated with higher corporate performance, particularly under turbulent conditions where there is a need for local responses and diverse insights. However, organizations that pursue central planning and decentralized strategy making at the same time and are able to combine the two modes clearly outcompete their peers in the industry.

The basic elements of the *integrative strategy* approach are made up by slow learning from central planning activities that consider the performance of the entire organization and fast local learning from autonomous initiatives and responsive actions taken in the decentralized strategy-making process (Figure 4.9). Central planning is a top-management-driven process where strategy is reassessed in longer-cycled *strategic learning* loops. Decentralized strategy making is instigated by lower-level

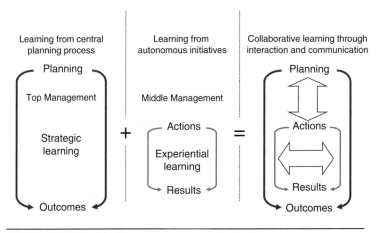

Learning from central planning process   Learning from autonomous initiatives   Collaborative learning through interaction and communication

Planning

Top Management   Middle Management

Strategic learning   **+**   Actions   **=**   Actions

Experiential learning

Results

Outcomes   Results   Outcomes

⬦⎰ • meetings and communication links

Figure 4.9 The integrative strategy approach

employees and middle managers who gain updated experiences from short-cycled *experiential learning* loops. The ability to learn collectively from these complementary processes depends upon effective communication and information systems that link managers throughout the organization. The horizontal communication between managers across different functional entities facilitates exchange of specialized knowledge and insights and coordinates responses through mutual adjustment of responsive activities. The vertical communication between managers at different hierarchical levels facilitates exchange of experiences from the short-cycled learning loops into the long-cycled strategic learning process and vice versa to create common understanding of the competitive situation based on updated environmental information. Hence, the availability of effective communication links is a necessary prerequisite to benefit from collaborative learning. These links are formed as personal discussions for example in meetings and as technology-facilitated communication. This is important because the ability to deal with complex situations is extended by intense collaborative efforts between people with diverse insights that escape the limitations of individual cognition. That is, the information required to solve ambiguous problems exceeds the capacity of a single person and therefore makes collaborative learning essential.[35]

Slow, *long-cycled planning* interacting with fast, *short-cycled actions* tied together by formal and informal communication channels are the core elements of the integrative strategy process. The interaction between slow and fast action-processing systems among diverse people in a group is by nature collaborative and has the ability to deal with turbulent and unpredictable conditions.[36] There is a need for central analysis of the surroundings to form an overarching direction based on ongoing interpretations of decentralized experiences gathered from autonomous responsive initiatives taken in day-to-day transactions with important stakeholders. The collection of diverse people in the organization comprised of central and decentralized decision makers represents a dynamic system of slow (central) and fast (peripheral) processes. Hence, the perceptions about the business environment are obtained from experiences gathered by managers throughout the organization and the collective understanding of the competitive reality evolves from the central analytical considerations in the planning process.

It should be noted that communication derived from personal interactions at meetings and technology-enhanced information exchanges has different cost–benefit characteristics. Face-to-face discussions constitute the richest means of communication, but they are also time consuming and resource demanding, particularly if they involve many and large groups of people. In contrast, information-technology-enhanced communication can have significant benefits by integrating communication links across organizational, geographical, and time-bound divides at low cost. Hence, the participatory decision-making processes offer rich exchanges but are relatively costly because meetings require management time and divert attention from ongoing operations. Conversely, decentralized decision making is less costly, particularly when communication and information technologies (CIT) give access to relevant data and facilitate mutual coordination.[37] This speaks for the need to think through the best decision structures that provide appropriate participatory forums as well as delegated decision structures supported by distributed information access. Hence, a combination of participatory decision making involving key informants and dispersed decision power to capable operating managers in functional entities supported by inclusive communication and information systems seems appropriate.

Cisco Systems, for example, has worked on its strategic decision processes with the ambition of optimizing the value-creating potential of current business operations while at the same time driving new business initiatives forward to build future corporate growth.[38] This was accomplished partially by establishing different cross-functional forums to hone promising business propositions identified in the organization (see Box 4.3 *Cisco's collaborative model*). Cisco CEO John Chambers found that "the biggest market transition is the shift to a more collaborative world, which is only made possible by what we call an 'intelligent, network centric' world."[39] To accommodate these ideas the company implemented a process where strategic priorities were managed by cross-functional, collaborative councils and boards rather than exclusively by top management. However, this approach was abandoned in 2011 as the company faced unsatisfactory revenue growth and profitability following the financial market crisis. The extraordinary market turmoil illustrated the potential shortcomings of an extensive participative decision-making structure as the inclusion of many committee members challenges the authority and clarity of direction while imposing additional costs in terms of time and resources consumed in the process. Hence, it is clearly not easy to find the right balance between central strategic direction, participation in decisions, and support for autonomous responsive actions.

In many ways the challenge of combining central planning and decentralized strategy making resembles the ideas about building ambidexterity. This way the organization can operate to execute planned business activities effectively and simultaneously experiment with and develop new business opportunities for tomorrow. Being *ambidextrous* refers to a person who can use both hands equally well and thereby obtains unusual skills. Hence, the ambidextrous organization is able to optimize the way things are operated at the moment and at the same time experiment to find new and better ways to operate. There are basically two ways to think about this in an organizational context. The proponents of *structural ambidexterity* argue that the experimental development activities should be separated from day-to-day business activities to reduce the influence of current pressures and provide freedom to think and act in new ways.[40] In contrast, proponents of *contextual ambidexterity* argue that the individual employees should take adaptive initiatives in the course of their daily work activities.[41] This organizational context is arguably enabled by a particular managerial focus and social support system in the firm. In view of the prior discussion about interacting central (slow) and peripheral (fast) processes, we can add that creativity and ideas about responsive changes must be related to the external reality and the way the organization is set up to deal with it. This supports the idea that ambidexterity has to be engrained in the organizational context and the way people think, behave, and work. The individuals in such an ambidextrous organization will engage in initiatives beyond their daily routines and collaborate broadly to develop new opportunities.[42]

Hence, organizations that are able to combine intended and emergent strategy modes, such as an integrative strategy process comprised of centrally planned activities and autonomous responsive initiatives, are likely to have ambidextrous qualities. Central planning engages in forward-looking thinking that coordinates contributions from functional entities in the organization. This will tend to improve strategic effectiveness and economic efficiencies in ongoing operations. Autonomous responsive initiatives taken by lower-level managers with delegated authority within their areas of responsibility provide the means to understand emerging environmental changes through experiential learning that sow the seeds for future business opportunities. For example, it is argued that Google's past success is linked to the freedom of employees to pursue their own ideas as long as their decisions are backed by supportive data based on the principle that new products that provide value to the customers will always succeed.[43]

This implies that organizational activities are adapted to accommodate the changing environmental requirements and thereby provide viable avenues for strategic renewal in the face of unexpected competitive challenges. This duality of streamlining and renewing operations is important and can be interpreted as an adaptive dynamic system of interacting central and peripheral processes. Empirical studies suggest that strategic emergence arising from participatory strategic decisions (participation) and autonomous responsive initiatives (autonomy) enhances adaptive behavior and leads to higher performance (Figure 4.10).[44] The strategic planning activities increase the effectiveness of adaptive moves, and the implied alignment of organizational activities from the intended strategy leads to further improvements in economic efficiencies. In other words, the ability to use experiences and autonomous initiatives from within the organization to develop adaptive solutions seems to drive performance, although the planning activities make them more effective. This begs the question of how the firm can draw on this important information about emerging changes residing inside the organization and respond to them while using the implied learning to update the centrally planned activities.

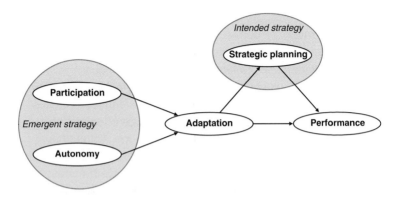

Figure 4.10 The dynamic relationships of integrative strategy. Source: Andersen and Nielsen (2009)

Strategic monitoring and control

This brings us back to the issue of strategic control. The idea is that a strategic control system can measure results and compare them with the predetermined strategic performance goals. Hence, the *balanced scorecard* is typically adopted to report on essential performance measures and monitor internal processes and external outcomes against set priorities. One potential advantage of this approach may be to develop a deeper understanding of the business model and identify key elements in the underlying value creation and thereby form a common understanding of the strategic value drivers. Furthermore, imposing a more balanced range of performance indicators broken down to business entities and individual actors within the organization has the potential to create inclusion and shared commitment.

Hence, the balanced scorecard can be seen as an attempt to document the links between strategic performance measures and the underlying value-creating business model.[45] In principle, the scorecard identifies a small number of financial and non-financial measures and targets them to see whether performance meets expectations in a conventional control perspective. However, four elements arguably set it apart: (1) it has a few high-level financial return measures, (2) it includes measures that depict how the customers derive value, (3) it shows efficiency indicators on internal business processes, and (4) it tries to identify where the firm can learn and improve. These essential scorecard parameters, or key performance indicators, identify the essential value-creation process and may, therefore, also serve as performance targets. So, the balanced scorecard is often used to benchmark against perceived competitors, or admired "best-in-class" companies to use the common jargon. In many firms it is also used as the basis for setting incentive pay according to performance against KPI targets even allocated to the level of individual employees. The potential pitfalls if used inappropriately include the risk of enforcing a predominant understanding of the strategy context at the expense of more diverse views, which can limit the ability to observe and interpret emerging changes. Similarly, a stringent adherence to allocated KPIs, particularly at the individual level, can become a straitjacket that restrains responsive behaviors.

To the extent actual realized outcomes show a discrepancy against planned intended performance goals, then something is not going as expected, and there is a need to take corrective action. Yet, there may be significant uncertainties associated with the interpretation of the business model where assumptions could be wrong or conditions might change dramatically in the interim. According to Goold and Quinn: "Strategic objectives (competitively set milestones for non-financial targets) are often hard to define with specificity, clarity and precision."[46] So, it is good to describe the underlying business model because it can form a common understanding about how customers gain value and how operations can deliver products and services at a profit. However, the model can be incomplete and might become obsolete when conditions change. Hence, including broad measures in the scorecard is better than including narrow measures because it adds more nuances to the evaluation of performance. Goold and Quinn suggest that "an amalgam of several qualitative indicators may be more suitable than an attempt to focus exclusively on any single (or small number of) quantifiable factors." Benchmarking against different targets, such as financial ratios, customer satisfaction, efficiency, productivity and quality indicators, etc., at all levels can be useful. But one should beware that an excessive focus on KPIs runs the risk of narrowing the analytical scope and vision by forcing organizational actors to consider only their KPIs and nothing else. The ability to remain open and alert is important to enable responsive initiatives that can help adapt the organization from within.

The realized outcomes may differ from the planned performance for two basic reasons. First, the effects of planned interventions might turn out differently than expected, possibly because working conditions were different than anticipated, new technologies emerged, or the criteria for the activities were modified along the way. That is, the advance knowledge about means–ends relationships used when the activities were planned might be wanting and could affect the predictability of outcomes. Second, the external environment in which the firm operates could be turbulent and unpredictable. This means that knowledge about competitive effects of proposed strategic actions is lacking, which influences the ability to assess the strategic outcomes. If we know a lot about both the external competitive effects in the market and the relationships between efforts and outcomes, then we can meaningfully engage in both results and action controls. Then we can monitor whether actors perform the intended actions as planned (internal process controls) as well as whether the realized results correspond to the planned outcomes (external reporting controls). The real problem arises when uncertainties are high on both accounts, in which case neither of the control approaches gives sufficient insight to determine the causes for performance shortfalls (Figure 4.11). In these extreme situations, that resemble the hypercompetitive conditions, it is suggested that firms must rely on so-called *clan control*.[47] That is, when conventional control measures are insufficient, a strong corporate culture with core values shared by everyone can align internal activities and responses in the face of uncertainty and change. Hence, the mission statement might be a particularly helpful construct for firms operating under these environmental conditions.

These challenges highlight the importance of ongoing observations by managers throughout the organization to detect signs of impending changes while communicating those impressions freely to collectively interpret developments and devise appropriate responses. The responsive initiatives taken by managers in operating entities when confronted by new

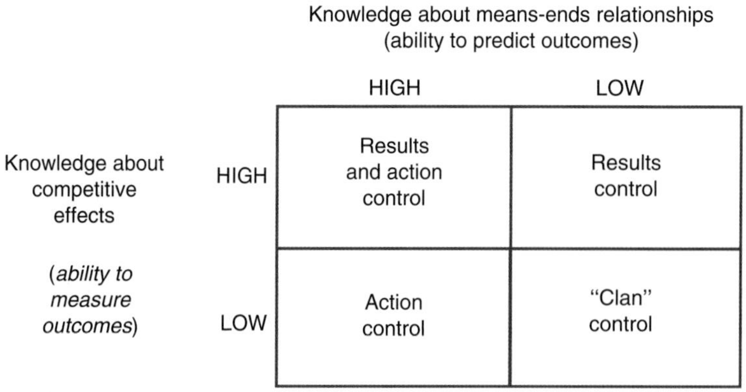

Knowledge about means-ends relationships
(ability to predict outcomes)

		HIGH	LOW
Knowledge about competitive effects	HIGH	Results and action control	Results control
(*ability to measure outcomes*)	LOW	Action control	"Clan" control

Figure 4.11 Demands of the strategic control systems. Source: adapted from Goold and Quinn (1990)

environmental requirements are important to the firm's capacity to adapt. Hence, Burgelman describes strategy evolution as the managerial redirection of resources toward viable business opportunities (in)formed by initiatives taken by autonomous individuals within the organization.[48] Andy Grove notes: "The process of adapting to change starts with the employees, who through their daily work, adjust to the new outside forces."[49] In other words, frontline employees respond to evolving business challenges and gain updated knowledge about developments as they observe the effects of their actions. So, the incremental changes in the environment are initially observed by organizational actors that are embedded in the real actions. As frontline employees engage in business execution they gain detailed insights about changing conditions, stakeholder sentiments, and the quality of internal competencies in dealing with those changes.[50]

The ability to make sense of observations and learn from ongoing events depends on communication between individuals with different insights in various parts of the organization. The *horizontal communication* links allow individuals to exchange information and gain feedback on ongoing observations and orchestrate coordinated (autonomous) responsive actions in the business entities. The *vertical communication* channels can send information and field observations from the business entities to top management and thereby update prevailing assumptions and

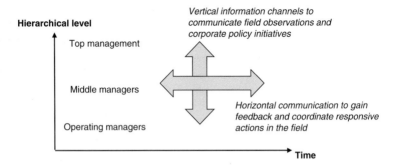

Figure 4.12 Horizontal and vertical communication channels

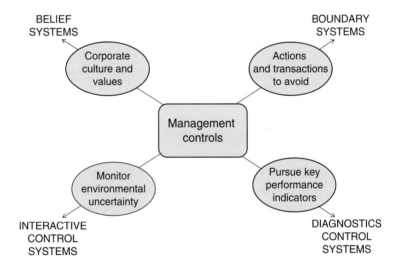

Figure 4.13 Strategic control systems. Source: adapted from Simons (1995)

enhance forward thinking. This can also communicate policy initiatives down the management levels and explicate intended strategy implications (Figure 4.12). In short, the presence of versatile communication channels facilitates the organization's information-processing capabilities that constitute the means to integrate central planning activities and peripheral strategic responses.

Organizations can be managed through different types of controls, including belief systems, boundary systems, diagnostic control systems, and interactive control systems (Figure 4.13).[51]

The *belief systems* are made up of core values in the corporate culture that drive the behavior of organizational actors and largely correspond to the concept of "clan" control. The *boundary systems* tell us what the firm is about and what core businesses it operates in, and explicates what business activities it will not entertain. Both forms of control are comprised by the strategic management model figuring as part of the formal mission statement and engrained in the strategic positioning approach. Hence, Porter argues: "Strategy is making trade-offs in competing. The essence of strategy is choosing what *not* to do."[52] These control systems provide guidance to organizational decision makers under uncertainty and ensure a certain alignment across responsive initiatives. The *diagnostic control systems* are closest to the conventional control approach where critical performance variables are monitored with regular intervals and adjusting actions are evaluated in linear feedback loops. This is the thinking behind the strategic control concept and applies to balanced scorecards, even though they are based on more nuanced performance indicators. The *interactive control systems* are control processes used by top managers as the basis for discussing emerging developments with subordinates. This approach goes beyond the concern for critical success factors that relate to what we think we already know. Instead it becomes a vehicle to interactively address imminent uncertainties, i.e., things we don't know directly among executives and lower-level managers.

Interactive control systems are particularly interesting because they can tie forward-looking reasoning among executives at the corporate center with current experiences acquired by operating managers in the organizational periphery and thereby interactively uncover new risks and opportunities. The interactive control principle can be applied to a number of existing control systems, such as planning and budgeting systems, project management systems, intelligence systems, human resource management systems, etc. So, there is no need to invent new systems, but one can apply an interactive management principle on control processes already in place. A control system is interactive when it (1) is used regularly by the highest management level, (2) receives frequent attention from operating managers across the organization, (3) has face-to-face discussions between superiors

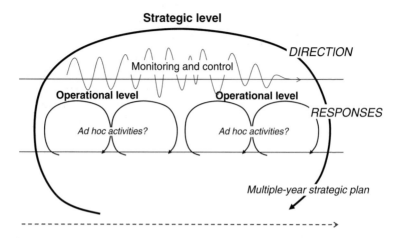

Figure 4.14 Monitoring and control in integrative strategy making

and subordinates, and (4) creates ongoing debate.[53] This way, top management can be updated on experiences from lower-level employees as they deal with daily business challenges and the responsive experiments in the business units are aligned with overarching strategic concerns. Hence, the interactive *monitoring and control* process constitutes a mechanism with the potential to tie experiences from ongoing *responses* at the *operational level* to the process of forming *direction* at the *strategic level* (Figure 4.14).

The more frequently the intervening meetings are held in the interactive control process, the closer the tie we create in the integrative strategy making between central planning considerations and decentralized (autonomous) responses in the operating entities. Other types of management information systems and practices may also support these types of interactive multi-level management discussions, including various enterprise risk management (ERM) systems (see Box 4.4 *Strategic risk management at LEGO Systems A/S*).

However, strategic issues may arise between the planning cycles when unexpected things happen in the competitive environment that uncover new risks and opportunities. Ansoff identified a strategic issue as "a forthcoming development, either inside or outside of the organization, which is likely to have an important impact on the ability of the enterprise to meet its

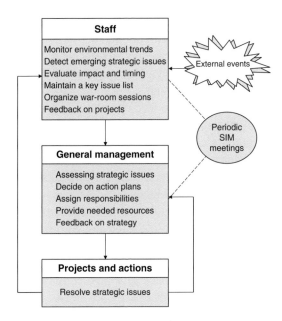

Figure 4.15 The strategic issue management process. Source: adapted from Ansoff (1980)

objectives."[54] He proposed a systematic *strategic issue management* (SIM) process to deal with these emerging issues. In this set-up, designated staff monitor environmental events to detect emerging strategic issues and engage general management in periodic meetings to generate fast responses that can circumvent potential adverse effects and enhance positive outcomes. These meetings would be conducted frequently and cut across hierarchical levels so top and line managers interact with managers from relevant business units to devise appropriate adaptive responses (Figure 4.15).

The frequent interaction between top management and operational managers can enhance adaptive improvements in small steps that respond to ongoing changes in the environment, which arguably is a superior way to adapt.[55] Hence, interactive controls and strategic issues management constitute processes that can tie together the strategic and operational levels in frequent updates of corporate responses through the intervention of designated staff and the active involvement of middle managers.

The middle managers can act as messengers and information-exchange gates between top management and the active frontline employees in the operating entities. They serve as decision influencers that bring experiential insights from ongoing business activities into the strategic decision discussions and bring adjusted strategic directives back to the field operators. The ability to take decentralized initiatives provides immediate responses that help uncover the contours of the changing environment and the insight obtained from initial responses may suggest possible solutions that can be brought forward for further consideration at the periodic meetings. This entire process provides a basis for gradual modifications of firm activities to match the requirements of the surrounding environment and therefore reduce the need for major structural changes. Yet, firms may still be exposed to the *innovator's dilemma*, where small, innovative business propositions seem uneconomical if applied to a large corporate scale.[56] However, providing sufficient leeway to take small, responsive initiatives at the local level in the form of low-risk probes that are developed gradually and tested against emerging strategic issues can ensure a continuous flow of alternative business propositions. Hence, the ability to gradually hone and promote these kinds of grass-roots responses while holding them against developments in the competitive situation can also reduce the pressures on top management to engage in a high-odds investment game of revolutionary change.

Part of the trick seems to be to develop responsive initiatives along the way as risks and opportunities emerge and intervene regularly to adjust strategic actions. The periodic SIM meetings might be suitable for these interventions that intertwine insights gained from initiatives taken in the operating business entities with adjustments to the central strategic direction. The SIM process can be set up physically as a so-called war-room format where the competitive situation is assessed systematically, involving the views of all key managers (Figure 4.16).[57] This set-up adheres to the logic of the rational analytical strategy process and starts with updates on external developments, for example, conducted within a PEST framework followed by competitor analysis, assessment of customer needs, opportunity identification, and response evaluations. The final outcomes from the meeting would

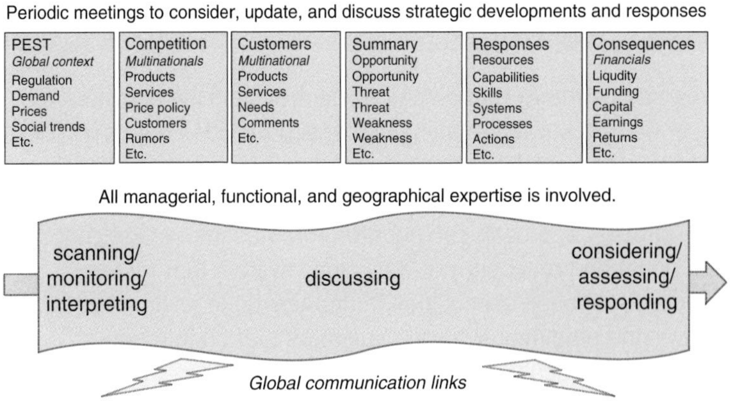

Periodic meetings to consider, update, and discuss strategic developments and responses

PEST	Competition	Customers	Summary	Responses	Consequences
Global context	*Multinationals*	*Multinational*	Opportunity	Resources	*Financials*
Regulation	Products	Products	Opportunity	Capabilities	Liqudity
Demand	Services	Services	Threat	Skills	Funding
Prices	Price policy	Needs	Threat	Systems	Capital
Social trends	Customers	Comments	Weakness	Processes	Earnings
Etc.	Rumors	Etc.	Weakness	Actions	Returns
	Etc.		Etc.	Etc.	Etc.

All managerial, functional, and geographical expertise is involved.

scanning/
monitoring/
interpreting

discussing

considering/
assessing/
responding

Global communication links

Figure 4.16 The strategic meeting room set-up

be to decide on concrete updated action plans to deal with the
identified issues. These periodic meetings connect expertise from
different functional areas and business entities that can enrich
strategy discussions and help reach timely and effective solutions.
The meetings can be facilitated by video-conferencing technologies
and the like in geographically dispersed organizations. Hence, a
strategic meeting room setting can provide a mechanism to
confront central plans with insights gained at the organizational
periphery in interpretative discussions to update and revise
strategic actions.

Thus we argue that effective strategic response capabilities
that enable firms to adapt to changing environmental conditions
and retain high profitability depend on an integrative strategy
approach that incorporates central direction and coordination with
decentralized initiatives and experiential insights gained from
these responses. Since these kinds of central and peripheral
processes follow different cycle times and operate on different
organizational levels, it is important to link them across
management ranks and over time. The interactive control systems,
strategic issue management processes, strategic risk
management practices, and periodic strategic meetings discussed
above represent specific vehicles and managerial interventions
to accomplish just this.

Conclusion

Integrative strategy that combines central planning activities with decentralized strategy-making processes provides the basis for streamlining ongoing business operations and at the same time responding locally to observed changes in competitive conditions. This strategy approach can be interpreted as interacting central and peripheral processes in a dynamic system that fosters effective response capabilities in unpredictable environments. Hence, the empirical evidence suggests that an integrative strategy approach is associated with higher firm performance and lower risk outcomes, i.e., they seem to have superior risk–return effects. The need to manage the link between central planning activities and current insights gained from decentralized responsive initiatives can be accomplished through a number of defined management control systems.

The need to respond to changing environmental conditions is higher the more complex, dynamic, and unpredictable the business context is. Firms that operate across different business activities, customer segments, and geographical regions will obviously face more confounded and uncertain business conditions. However, it turns out that the integrative strategy approach can deal with these conditions as well. We will discuss this and related topics in the following chapter.

Box 4.1 The "new" brain metaphor

Humans have two ways of thinking, embedded in a fast and a slow system. The world is observed in the fast system and the observations are interpreted in the slow system. Modern cognitive science has brought together the slow and fast mental processes between conscious understanding and unconscious observations from physical interaction with the real world. The body is always on duty and continues to experiment on-line through encounters with the environment. In contrast, the mental processes operate off-line and speculate about longer-term consequences. Emotions are important to the way the fast and slow brain systems operate and how information is exchanged between the fast and slow systems. Two parts of the brain are particularly important in this context: (1) the *frontal lobes* that generate conscious reasoning and (2) the *limbic system* where two areas, the *amygdala* and the *hippocampus*, are heavily involved in the dynamic systems processes (see figure). They interfere in the interactions between the consciousness of the slow brain system and the urges of the fast system. Emotions influence how we think, learn, and store things in memory where positive feelings increase the ability to observe and think creatively.

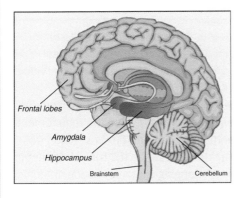

Human creativity and innovation can be interpreted as evolving properties of the interacting slow and fast processes. Cognition derives from the dual process of reasoning (judgment) and deciding (taking actions) carried out in two sub-systems. *System 1* is old in evolutionary terms and humans share it with other animals. *System 2* is only human and came about more recently in the evolution. The cognitive processes of systems 1 and 2 are complementary and formed by the relationship between fast and slow processes. Ideas can develop in both sub-systems, but the judgment of which ideas are better is based on the slow system 2. Alternative initiatives are considered, and the slow system 2 assesses their consequences. When initiatives are carried out, the decentralized processes of the fast system are active. They create new experiential insights from ongoing actions and pass them to the slow system for forward consideration. This forms the interacting effects between actions induced by the slow system, immediate exploratory actions taken in response to external events, and continuous observance of outcomes in the fast system.

Box 4.2 Effects of strategic responsiveness

The strategic responsiveness model assumes that some individual firms have an ability to assess environmental changes, identify and assemble available resources in viable solutions, and mobilize them in effective responses to address current market requirements. Hence, firms compete to achieve the best possible match between the requirements imposed by the environment (c) and the firm's position (d) against those requirements at all times (t). This competition can relate to fulfillment of changing customer needs, matching output to current demand, adopting the most effective technologies, etc. Each of these factors affects firm profitability (P) as a better match between firm position, and the requirements imposed by the environment will lead to higher revenues and/or increased efficiencies expressed in lower costs. So, a better match or strategic fit reduces the discrepancy between environmental requirements and firm position at any time ($c_t - d_t$) and leads to a lower loss of profit potential compared with the optimal possible return in the industry (K) from a potential mismatch (see equation below). The coefficients a and b in the formula are linear and exponential functions that make it possible to modify the model to reflect a given industry context over a given time period.

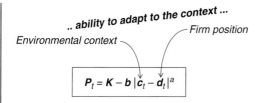

Hence, it is intuitively seen from this that a firm able to adapt its position on all important strategic dimensions to the requirements of the changing environmental context will achieve the highest returns possible in the industry at all times and thereby also display the lowest variations in realized returns. That is, we will observe that for each firm, higher average returns are associated with lower variability in returns. Assuming that firms in an industry have different abilities to respond and adapt, their return-variability relationships will vary where poor adaptors display extreme negative returns with major swings from one period to the next. In turbulent industries, adaptability is more challenging and the response capabilities vary more across firms, which is displayed in more extreme inverse return-variability relationships. The validity of this initial intuition can be demonstrated both mathematically and by simulations based on the simple model, and it also corresponds to the empirics observed in different industries (see figure below).

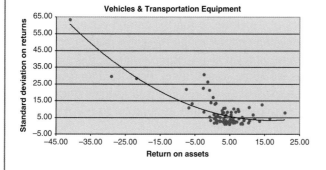

Box 4.3 Cisco's collaborative model

The initial modelling of the collaborative structure in Cisco started in 2001 as an effort to ensure the company engaged across all key business areas to achieve its overarching strategic goals. It was believed that a system of cross-functional councils and working groups would help enhance productivity, create innovation, incorporate diverse expertise, and develop responses to change. The inclusion of larger groups of senior people should lead to more informed decisions and more effective alignment of resources in the execution of projects as well as support the development of new sustainable business opportunities.

To this end the company created a structure of *councils* to deal with US$10 billion opportunities, *boards* to deal with US$1 billion opportunities, and various *working groups* to deal with smaller innovation initiatives. This was practiced for more than eight years inspired by a top management vision of the future business 5–10 years ahead to discipline the creative thinking. New business ideas were broadly encouraged as long as they were supported by sustainable competencies that would differentiate the company. The ongoing assessments of opportunities were summarized into efforts to be implemented over a 2–4-year time horizon with concrete steps executed within a 12–18-month time horizon. So, instead of having ten people in top management running the whole company, this set-up engaged 500 people from different functional areas with diverse sets of expertise to run things and prioritize new business developments through the collaborative work of council, board, and working group members. The expected advantages would be to get direct input from smart people with diverse expertise and insights and to think through the often complex strategic issues as a group to reach better and more implementable solutions.

The establishment of boards and councils was a way to form social-network groups among diverse individuals and have the group members collaborate to find better solutions and ensure that key decisions were executed effectively throughout the company. Hence, the councils and boards would propose new strategic initiatives to the operating committee (comprised of the full top management team) based on their development work supported by detailed business plans. These business proposals should answer to the overarching vision of the company and be supported by sustainable differentiation factors that can be successfully executed within a few years.

Hence, the council and board structure would consist of an operating committee at the top comprised of the CEO and ten group executives plus nine councils with a collection of people from different functional areas in the company overlooking particular customer-product segments and cross-functional opportunities for improvement. The nine councils covered five business segments and four cross-sectional areas:

Segment councils:
- Enterprise
- Commercial
- Service provider
- Small
- Consumer

Cross-segment councils:
- Emerging solutions
- Connected architecture
- Emerging countries
- Connected business operations

Sources: Collaborative Management Model, Management Approach, Cisco Systems Website; HBR Interview with John Chambers, *Harvard Business Review*, November 2008; McKinsey Conversations with global leaders: John Chambers, *McKinsey Quarterly*, Issue 4, 2009.

Box 4.4 Strategic risk management at LEGO Systems A/S

The emphasis on strategic risk management was initiated at the LEGO Group in late 2006 as senior management wanted more focus on strategic risk issues as an overlooked element of the corporate risk portfolio. The strategic risk management (SRM) process has since then evolved to comprise four elements: preparing for uncertainty, active risk and opportunity planning (AROP), enterprise risk management (ERM), and operational risk management (see figure below). The SRM process is adopted to challenge managerial assumptions, test the robustness of strategic decisions, ensure that promising business opportunities are identified and executed prudently, and define an appropriate corporate risk profile for future growth and prosperity.

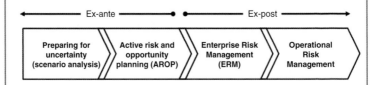

Prepare for uncertainty

This is a forward-looking exercise where scenario discussions among executive decision makers challenge existing perceptions of the global competitive situation and test the robustness of the corporate strategy and key projects. A look at major trends in the world helps identify important environmental uncertainties and define extreme, but not unlikely, future *business scenarios*. The major issues associated with each scenario are identified and fed into discussions about the corporate responses required to deal with these challenges. The process alerts decision makers to environmental uncertainties and urges preparedness to deal with the unexpected.

Project risk management

The core risk management principles are applied to all major projects in the company as a way to anchor risk awareness across important corporate actions. The projects reflect resource-committing decisions that change or update corporate activities and thereby execute intended strategies as well as emerging initiatives. The active risk and opportunity planning (AROP) process follows the conventional risk considerations of identification, assessment, intervention, and monitoring applied both to *downside* risks and *upside* opportunities.

Enterprise risk management

This framework identifies potential risk factors collected from all business units and incorporates them in a central register. The risks are prioritized based on an impact-likelihood metric and aggregated into a *corporate risk profile* for simulation-based analysis. The aggregate exposures are expressed in a "risk barometer" to assess whether current risk levels exploit the available corporate resources and capabilities satisfactorily. The risk portfolio is presented and discussed regularly with the top management team and the board of directors.

Operational risk management

Detailed mitigation plans are developed for all prioritized risks and ongoing *risk handling* is assigned to designated *risk owners* in the relevant operational entities. The associated exposures are reported on a regular basis to monitor the completion of assigned risk responses. The corporate risk register is updated accordingly and serves as a source for historical trend analysis and forward-looking exposure simulations.

Source: M. L. Frigo, H. Læssøe (2012) Strategic risk management at the LEGO Group, *Strategic Finance* 93(8): 27–35.

Notes

1 See, for example, J. G. March, The business firm as a political coalition, *The Journal of Politics* 24(4): 662–678, 1962; G. R. Salancik, J. Pfeffer, Who gets power – and how they hold on to it: A strategic contingency model of power, *Organizational Dynamics* 5(3): 3–21, 1977.

2 C. C. Markides, *Game Changing Strategies: How to Create New Market Space in Established Industries by Breaking the Rules*, Jossey-Bass: San Francisco, CA, 2008.

3 J. Manas, *Napoleon on Project Management: Timeless Lessons in Planning, Execution, and Leadership*, Nelson Business: Nashville, TN, 2006.

4 For major studies see, for example, D. C. Hambrick, High profit strategies in mature capital goods industries: A contingency approach, *Academy of Management Journal* 26(4): 687–707, 1983; G. G. Dess, P. S. Davis, Porter's (1980) generic strategies as determinants of strategic group membership and organizational performance, *Academy of Management Journal* 27(3): 467–488, 1984; D. Miller, Configurations of strategy and structure: Towards a synthesis, *Strategic Management Journal* 7(3): 233–249, 1986; D. Miller, P. H. Friesen, Porter's (1980) generic strategies and performance: An empirical examination with American data, Part II: Testing Porter, *Organization Studies* 7(3): 255–261, 1986; A. I. Murray, A contingency view of Porter's "generic strategies," *Academy of Management Review* 13(3): 390–400, 1988.

5 C. Campbell-Hunt, What have we learned about generic competitive strategy? A meta-analysis, *Strategic Management Journal* 21(2): 127–154, 2000.

6 See, for example, Y. Korem, *Computer Control of Manufacturing Systems*, McGraw-Hill: New York, 1983; T. Tolio, *Design of Flexible Production Systems – Methodologies and Tools*, Springer: Berlin, 2009; J. Pine, *Mass Customization: The New Frontier in Business Competition*, Harvard Business School Press: Boston, MA, 1992; J. Pine *et al.*, Making mass customization work, *Harvard Business Review* 72(6): 108–119, 1993.

7 See I. Nonaka, H. Takeuchi, *The Knowledge-Creating Company: How Japanese Companies Create the Dynamics of Innovation*, Oxford University Press: New York, 1995; J. K. Liker, *The Toyota Way: 14 Management Principles from the World's Greatest Manufacturer*, McGraw-Hill: New York, 2004; J. P. Womack, D. T. Jones, *Lean Solutions: How Companies and Customers Can Create Value and Wealth Together,* Simon & Schuster: London, 2005.

8 S. Gregory, Walmart's latest move to crush the competition, *Time Business*, Wednesday, Sept. 9, 2009.

9 W. C. Kim, R. Mauborgne, *Blue Ocean Strategy*, Harvard Business School Press: Boston, MA, 2005; M. M. Andersen, F. Poulfelt, *Discount Business Strategy: How the New Market Leaders are Redefining Business Strategy,* Wiley: Chichester, 2006.

10 See, for example, M. E. Porter, What is strategy? *Harvard Business Review* 75(6): 61–78, 1996; A. Osterwalder, Y. Pigneur, *Business Model Generation*, Wiley: Hoboken, NJ, 2010.

11 J. March, Exploration and exploitation in organizational learning, *Organization Science* 2(1): 71–87, 1991.

12 T. J. Andersen, P. W. Schrøder, *Strategic Risk Management Practice*, Cambridge University Press, 2010.

13 D. Kahneman, *Thinking Fast and Slow,* Farrar, Straus and Giroux: New York, 2011.

14 The fast observant system is reflected in backward-looking, experience-based, *on-line* decision making where new insights are gained from current actions in trial-and-error learning. The slow interpretive system corresponds to forward-looking, cognitive-based planning driven by *off-line* reasoning. See G. Gavetti, D. Levinthal, Looking forward and looking backward: Cognitive and experiential search, *Administrative Science Quarterly* 45(1): 113–137, 2000.

15 H. Mintzberg, Planning on the left side and managing on the right, *Harvard Business Review* 54(4): 49–58, 1976. While making a point, the left/right brain dichotomy is probably an oversimplification. See, for example, T. Himes, Left brain/right brain mythology and implications for management and training, *Academy of Management Review* 12(4): 600–606, 1987.

16 See, for example, J. Child, R. G. McGrath, Organizations unfettered: Organizational form in an information-intensive economy, *Academy of Management Journal* 44(6): 1135–1148, 2001; H. W. Volberda, Toward the flexible form: How to remain vital in hypercompetitive environments, *Organization Science* 7(4): 359–374, 1996.

17 T. J. Andersen, K. Fredens, Strategy as complementary interaction between central and peripheral processes, *Strategic Management Society Annual International Conference*, Miami, FL, 2011.

18 J. Hendry, Strategic decision making, discourse and strategy as social practice, *Journal of Management Studies* 37(7): 955–977, 2000; S. Hill *et al.*, Decentralization, integration and the post-bureaucratic organization: The case of R&D, *Journal of Management Studies* 37(4): 563–585, 2000; S. E. Page, *The Difference: How the Power of Diversity Creates Better Groups, Firms, Schools, and Societies,* Princeton University Press, 2007.

19 M. Allingstrup, PROFILEN: Søren Tvilsted – chef for TDC Musik, Kollegaerne grinte af PLAY, *Berlingske Business*, April 8, 2008.

20 R. Pfeifer, J. Bongard, *How the Body Shapes the Way We Think: A New View of Intelligence,* MIT Press: Cambridge, MA, 2009; J. A. S. Kelso, D. A. Engstrøm, *The Complementary Nature,* MIT Press: Cambridge, MA, 2006.

21 A particular research stream emphasizes the executive role in adaptive processes conceptualized as *dynamic managerial capabilities* and *strategic renewal.* See, for example, R. Adner, C. E. Helfat, Corporate effects and dynamic managerial capabilities, *Strategic Management Journal* 24(10): 1011–1025, 2003; R. Agarwal, C. E. Helfat, Strategic renewal of organizations, *Organization Science* 20(2): 281–293, 2009.

22 See, for example, D. C. Hambrick, P. A. Mason, Upper echelons: The organization as a reflection of its top managers, *Academy of Management Review* 9(2): 193–206, 1984; D. C. Hambrick, Putting top managers back in the

strategy picture, *Strategic Management Journal* 10: 5–15, 1989; S. Finkelstein, D. C. Hambrick, A. A. Canella, *Strategic Leadership: Theory and Research on Executives, Top Management Teams, and Boards,* Oxford University Press: New York, 2009.

23 J. L. Bower, C. G. Gilbert (eds.), *From Resource Allocation to Strategy,* Oxford University Press, 2005.

24 See, for example, T. J. Andersen, Integrating decentralized strategy making and strategic planning processes in dynamic environments, *Long Range Planning* 33(2): 184–200, 2000; S. Hart, C. Banbury, How strategy-making processes can make a difference, *Strategic Management Journal* 15: 251–269, 1994; A. Miller, G. G. Dess, Assessing Porter's model in terms of its generalizability, accuracy, and simplicity, *Journal of Management Studies* 30(4): 553–585, 1993.

25 D. J. Teece *et al.*, Dynamic capabilities and strategic management, *Strategic Management Journal* 18(7): 509–533, 1997.

26 C. E. Helfat *et al.*, *Dynamic Capabilities: Understanding Strategic Change in Organizations,* Blackwell Publishing: Malden, MA, 2007.

27 D. J. Teece, Explicating dynamic capabilities: The nature and microfoundations of (sustainable) enterprise performance, *Strategic Management Journal*, 28(13): 1319–1350, 2007.

28 Inspired by D. J. Teece, *Dynamic Capabilities and Strategic Management: Organizing for Innovation and Growth,* Oxford University Press: New York, 2009.

29 See, for example, R. A. Bettis, M. A. Hitt, The new competitive landscape, *Strategic Management Journal* 16 (Summer – special issue): 7–19, 1995.

30 T. J. Andersen, R. A. Bettis, The risk–return effects of strategic responsiveness: A simulation analysis, Chapter 3 in T. J. Andersen (ed.), *Perspectives on Strategic Risk Management,* CBS Press: Copenhagen, 2006; T. J. Andersen, J. Denrell, R. A. Bettis, Strategic responsiveness and Bowman's risk–return paradox, *Strategic Management Journal* 28: 407–429, 2007.

31 Inspired by C. Perrow, *Normal Accidents: Living with High-Risk Technologies,* Princeton University Press, 1999.

32 T. J. Andersen, Combining central planning and decentralization to enhance effective risk management outcomes, *Risk Management* 12(2): 101–115, 2010.

33 See, for example, C. H. House, R. L. Price, *The HP Phenomenon: Innovation and Business Transformation,* Stanford University Press, 2009; D. Packard, *The HP Way: How Bill Hewlett and I Built Our Company,* HarperCollins: New York, 1995.

34 T. J. Andersen, Integrating decentralized strategy making and strategic planning processes in dynamic environments, *Journal of Management Studies* 41(8): 1271–1299, 2004; C. C. Miller, L. B. Cardinal, Strategic planning and firm performance: A synthesis of more than two decades of research, *Academy of Management Journal* 37(6): 1649–1665, 1994.

35 P. Antonenko *et al.*, Using electroencephalography to measure cognitive load, *Educational Psychology Review* 22: 425–438, 2010.

36 J. Sweller, Cognitive load during problem solving: Effect on learning, *Cognitive Science* 12(2): 257–285, 1988; F. Paas *et al.*, Cognitive load theory: New conceptualizations, specifications, and integrated research perspectives, *Educational Psychology Review* 22: 115–121, 2010.

37 See, for example, T. J. Andersen, Information technology, strategic decision making approaches and organizational performance in different industrial settings, *Journal of Strategic Information Systems* 10(2): 101–119, 2001; T. J. Andersen, The performance effect of computer-mediated communication and decentralized strategic decision making, *Journal of Business Research* 58(8): 1059–1067, 2005.

38 I. Sidhu, *Doing Both: How Cisco Captures Today's Profit and Drives Tomorrow's Growth,* FT Press: Upper Saddle River, NJ, 2010.

39 J. Chambers, B. Fryer, T. A. Stewart, The HBR Interview: Cisco sees the future, *Harvard Business Review* 86(11): 72–79, 2008.

40 M. L. Tushman, C. A. O'Reilly, Ambidextrous organizations: Managing evolutionary and revolutionary change, *California Management Review* 38(4): 8–30, 1996.

41 C. B. Gibson, J. Birkinshaw, The antecedents, consequences, and mediating role of organizational ambidexterity, *Academy of Management Journal* 47(2): 209–226, 2004.

42 J. Birkinshaw, C. B. Gibson, Building ambidexterity into an organization, *MIT Sloan Management Review* Summer: 47–55, 2004.

43 See S. Levy, *In the Plex: How Google Thinks, Works, and Shapes Our Lives,* Simon & Schuster: New York, 2011.

44 T. J. Andersen, B. B. Nielsen, Adaptive strategy making: The effects of emergent and intended strategy modes, *European Management Review* 6(2): 94–106, 2009.

45 See, for example, R. S. Kaplan, D. P. Norton, *The Strategy-Focused Organization: How Balanced Scorecard Companies Thrive in the New Business Environment*, Harvard Business School Press: Boston, MA, 2001; R. S. Kaplan, D. P. Norton, *Strategy Maps: Converting Intangible Assets into Tangible Outcomes*, Harvard Business School Press: Boston, MA, 2004.

46 M. Goold, J. J. Quinn, The paradoxes of strategic controls, *Strategic Management Journal* 11(1): 43–57, 1990.

47 W. G. Ouchi, A conceptual framework for the design of organizational control mechanisms, *Management Science* 25(9): 833–848, 1979; W. G. Ouchi, Market, bureaucracies, and clans, *Administrative Science Quarterly* 25(1): 129–141, 1980.

48 R. A. Burgelman, A process model of strategic business exit: Implications for an evolutionary perspective on strategy, *Strategic Management Journal* 17(S1): 193–214, 1996.

49 A. S. Grove, *Only the Paranoid Survive: How to Exploit the Crisis Points that Challenge Every Company and Career*, HarperCollins Business: London, 1997.

50 C. Halin *et al.*, Executive expectations and forecasts versus employee sensing: An unequal prediction contest? Working Paper, Copenhagen Business School, 2012.

51 R. Simons, *Levers of Control: How Managers Use Innovative Control Systems to Drive Strategic Renewal*, Harvard Business School Press: Boston, MA, 1995.

52 M. E. Porter, What is strategy? *Harvard Business Review* 74(6): 61–77, 1996.

53 R. Simons, The role of management control systems in creating competitive advantage: New perspectives, *Accounting, Organization and Society* 15(1/2): 127–143, 1990; R. Simons, Strategic orientation and top management attention to control systems, *Strategic Management Journal* 12(1): 49–62, 1991; R. Simons, How top managers use control systems as levers of strategic renewal, *Strategic Management Journal* 15(3): 169–189, 1994.

54 H. I. Ansoff, Strategic issue management, *Strategic Management Journal* 1: 131–148, 1980.

55 See, for example, C. Zook, J. Allen, *Repeatability: Build Enduring Businesses for a World of Constant Change*, Harvard Business Review Press: Boston, MA, 2012.

56 C. M. Christensen, *The Innovator's Dilemma: When New Technologies Cause Great Firms to Fail*, Harvard Business School Press: Boston, MA, 1997.

57 S. M. Shaker, M. P. Gembicki, *The WarRoom Guide to Competitive Intelligence,* McGraw-Hill: New York, 1999.

5 Multinational corporate strategy

Learning points

- Outline the contours of the multinational corporation
- Discuss the trade-offs of business and geographical diversity
- Describe the tensions between integration and responsiveness
- Consider applications of integrative strategy making

When firms conduct business the strategic outcomes are affected by decisions made in various parts of the organization and the associated actions pursued over time. An engineer might see an opportunity in the firm's technological competencies to accomplish new ends and then develop these in response to identified customer needs. Sales managers might observe new customer requirements or concrete requests for adaptations to existing products and services and therefore engage production and engineering to accommodate those demands in new market offerings. They might also note that some customers express an interest in establishing overseas sales relationships as their activities move outside the home country. Operating managers might see applications of new technologies and practices that can provide more flexibility in product deliveries and be open for more efficient sourcing channels overseas. At the same time, executives might come across potential acquisition candidates among close competitors or firms operating in adjacent industries, possibly with activities in different countries, and persuade the board to back decisions to acquire or merge with these companies. These examples illustrate how decisions and activities pursued in different parts of the organization can lead to the development of a broader product-market focus in the firm that also may entail a certain internationalization of business activities.

As a consequence, it is a fact that most firms today operate in more than one product market and their activities reach across

	Single business	Multiple businesses
Single country	**Business strategy**	**Corporate strategy**
Multiple countries	**International business strategy**	**Multinational corporate strategy**

Figure 5.1 Multinational corporations. Source: adapted from Ghemawat (2002)

more than a single national market place. Of course, this is a matter of degree. Some firms produce a variety of more or less related products and services whereas others focus on a fairly narrow range of business activities. Conversely, some firms are selective in their geographic presence and focus on specific national markets whereas other firms operate in countries across the globe as true multinational outfits catering to every nation on earth. In conclusion, the majority of firms manage more than one product market across more than a single country or nation.[1] Hence, we will use the term *multinational corporation* in reference to firms that manage multiple business activities across multiple national contexts (Figure 5.1).

So far we have not explicitly considered the potentially complicating dimensions imposed by a broader scope of different business and geographical activities. In principle, we have dealt "only" with the *business strategy* related to a single product market within a single country setting. If this context is extended to more than one country we might refer to an *international business strategy* perspective. This situation can easily arise. In a small open economy like the Danish one, a business becomes international when commercial transactions cross the bridge from Copenhagen to Malmö in Sweden on the other side of the sound. So, you become international because you cross a national border even though it might be difficult for a stranger to see any difference between the two sides. Most countries, irrespective of their size, have regions with slightly different characteristics that can be exploited. For example, Oticon A/S (part of William Demant Holding), the Danish producer of hearing aids, had production located in Northern Jutland due to its skilled and reliable workforce whereas development and central administration were placed north of Copenhagen. So, even companies that operate in a relatively small national context may take advantage of regional differences as they organize their business activities. This is clearly a possibility in the US across fifty states where business conditions and resource endowments can vary considerably between, say, Arizona, California, Florida, Massachusetts, North Carolina, and Texas. The economic base might differ and you can find different industry and research clusters, and the population and its consumer needs may show significant differences across individual states. However, the interstate transactions formally take place within the same national context and are considered domestic.

Within the European Union there have been many efforts to set commercial standards and shape a common internal market, even with a single currency, for all business transactions. Yet, they are still conceived as international when they cross the border between member countries. Hence, the definition of an international business and multinational organization is not all that clear cut, but the presence of national differences will impose new risks on the firm and create business opportunities as well. However, many of the implied risks and opportunities already exist in the national context, and therefore the issues related to internationalization and multinational activities are not necessarily that different from domestic business concerns. We do observe, though, that the characteristics of national markets, including languages, customs, business conduct, and financial systems, typically become increasingly disparate the more distant the overseas markets are, and can impose new challenges on the multinational corporation. These challenges derive from the increasing diversity of markets and resemble the issues related to managing a portfolio of disparate business activities where the level of complexity increases. The management of multiple businesses is a key concern of *corporate strategy*. Therefore, due to the commonalities between business and geographical diversification, and since most firms must deal with both at the same time anyway, we will consider these twin aspects in what we may refer to as *multinational corporate strategy*.

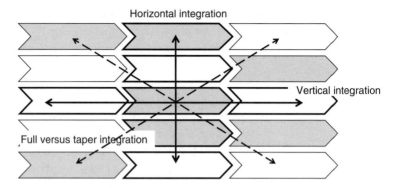

Figure 5.2 Corporate business structures

The different businesses in a corporate portfolio can be analyzed on the basis of their product-market characteristics. Within a given industry the predominant business activities can be classified as *primary* activities that provide general production inputs, such as raw materials, semi-produce and support services, *secondary* manufacturing or production activities, and *tertiary* retail services that distribute goods to the end-consumers. Hence, Rio Tinto, the British–Australian global mining company, operates in primary industries. Andersen Inc., as a producer of windows and doors with fifteen manufacturing locations in places such as Minnesota, Wisconsin, Iowa, Illinois, Texas, Ohio, Georgia, and New Jersey as well as Ontario, Canada, operates in secondary industries. Wal-Mart Stores Inc., the US-based international retailer, operates in a tertiary industry.

A corporate business portfolio might also contain activities along all three parts of the industry value chain, in which case we usually talk about *vertical integration* (Figure 5.2). For example, Royal Dutch Shell is a global group of energy companies engaged in exploration, generation, refining, and distribution across the entire energy value chain. The vertically integrated corporation controls all business activities along the value chain and may thereby shield off some of the uncertainties imposed by a dynamic environment but also requires more coordination of corporate processes.[2]

The corporate business portfolio may also be comprised of comparable business activities at the same stage in the industry value chain but reaching across different industries, in which case we refer to *horizontal integration*. A horizontally integrated corporation can benefit from scope economies where similar processes are applied to accommodate comparable business activities and related managerial skills are used across different industry contexts. As an example, Flextronics, the Singapore-based global manufacturing services company, caters to companies operating in many different industries where it levers its production design solutions. When the corporate business portfolio reaches across the entire spectrum of industries and incorporates different stages in the economy, we refer to *full integration*. Fully integrated corporations are practically nonexistent, but some business conglomerates have aspired to this model. A more common approach in recent years has been to selectively incorporate business activities in distinct industries at different industry stages, often referred to as *taper integration*, as a way to integrate relevant resources and competencies into the corporate operating structure. For example, General Electric Company (GE) operates in manufacturing and services across a broad spectrum of industries, such as appliances, electronics, jet engines, power distribution, health care, rail, software, and financial services. It should be noted, of course, that many of the individual business activities are located in multiple countries around the world.

The hundred-million-dollar question now is which one of these constellations of corporate business activities is the most effective. Alfred Chandler observed and described how a new breed of multi-business conglomerates emerged in the US market as industrialization evolved where the increasing diversity of activities called for divisional corporate structures.[3] He also observed an increase in the number of large conglomerates engaged in many unrelated business activities. However, Richard Rumelt's pioneering work was one of the first attempts to grapple with the performance implications of the relatedness of activities across a corporate business portfolio.[4] To this end he defined a "related ratio" as the proportion of corporate revenues ascribed to the largest group of related business activities ranging from zero to one, where a ratio above 0.7 would indicate a related business portfolio (Figure 5.3).[5] He further defined a "specialization ratio" as the proportion of revenues derived from the largest single

Related ratio : proportion of revenues from largest group of related businesses

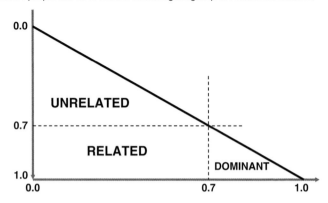

Specialization ratio: proportion of revenues from largest single business

Figure 5.3 Business diversification. Source: adapted from Rumelt (1974)

product-market activity in the corporate business portfolio and set a threshold at 0.7 above which the business portfolio would be dominant. Hence, a *related diversified* business portfolio was identified by a related ratio above 0.7 and a specialization ratio below 0.7, an *unrelated diversified* business portfolio by related and specialization ratios below 0.7, and a *dominant* business portfolio by related and specialization ratios above 0.7. This classification scheme made it possible to compare performance outcomes across corporations with different types of business portfolios.

The initial analysis found that corporations with related diversified business portfolios outperformed conglomerates of unrelated diversified businesses, which could be explained by the relative ease of using skills and competences across comparable business contexts. These general results have been confirmed in subsequent studies that also uncovered potential advantages from joint business development and promotional activities among corporate businesses operating in related industry contexts.[6] DuPont (E. I. du Pont de Nemours and Company) is an example of a related diversified corporation. This US-based chemical company is involved in the production of polymer products, such as neoprene, nylon, Teflon, Mylar, Kevlar, NOMEX, and Lycra. The company has also developed Freon for refrigeration and synthetic pigments for paints. Litton Industries is an example of an unrelated diversified corporation, founded in 1953 as an electronics company in navigation, communications, and electronics. The company diversified to grow and engaged in shipbuilding and the manufacture of microwave ovens, among other things. During the 1990s the company focused on military equipment, with other commercial activities split into separate entities, and was eventually acquired by Northrop Grumman in 2001.

So, excessive diversification of business activities seems to have negative performance effects, so much that large conglomerates with activities across many unrelated businesses actually lost value for their shareholders.[7] Hence, various studies have systematically shown that bidding firms typically get caught up in the hype of acquiring a target company and thereby, subconsciously or possibly with intent, overestimate potential acquisition gains to justify transactions. The evidence shows that shareholders of target companies normally benefit from takeover attempts at the expense of shareholders in the bidding company. Studies of corporate acquisitions are also consistent with the relatedness findings as shareholders in bidding companies experience significantly lower market returns when the acquisition target leads to further diversification of the business portfolio. This adversity is enforced when the target is a high-growth company and also coincides with poor managerial performance in the acquiring company.[8] To illustrate the lack of consensus about corporate strategy, Porter displayed the poor acquisition track record among large US companies during the 1960s and 1970s.[9] He demonstrated that they divested more acquisitions than they kept over a thirty-five-year period and eliminated rather than created shareholder value in the process. No surprise, then, that corporate raiders flush with cash from issuance of junk bonds began to take over large conglomerates to break them up. Hence, we saw a string of spectacular corporate buy-outs during the 1980s, with subsequent sales of individual business activities that generated significant profits to the involved intermediaries. The US$25 billion leveraged buy-out of R. J. R. Nabisco in 1988 arranged by Kohlberg, Kravis, Roberts (KKR) was a trendsetter at the time.[10] However, these types of levered transactions have remained an important element of the market for corporate control.[11]

So far, we have discussed competitive strategy from the vantage point of a single business entity (Chapter 2). *Corporate strategy* deals with the kind of business activities the corporation should engage in and how it should manage those businesses it owns or controls. However, the underlying earnings potential of the corporation still depends on the success, or competitive advantage, of the individual business activities and the way they are dealt with by corporate headquarters. Therefore effective corporate strategy combines business strategies applied to the relevant industry contexts and appropriate corporate structures set up to manage the individual business units. The structure determines, for example, how resources are shared across business activities and how business activities are coordinated, e.g., through management control and information systems, the degree of autonomy, incentive systems, etc.[12] Hence, according to Goold *et al.*, the "primary wealth creation takes place only at the business level" and "the parent must work through its businesses to create value."[13] The concept of *parenting advantage* speaks to this as the particular contribution the corporate headquarters can provide to support each of the business entities. It is argued that a strong contribution requires a good fit between the corporate structure and the characteristics of the individual businesses. Hence, a portfolio of related technology-intense business activities may gain value if the corporate headquarters provides coordination mechanisms to share processes and exchange knowledge between business units. In contrast, a portfolio of basic unrelated businesses needs little coordination of activities but may rather benefit from decentralized responsibility supported by appropriate priorities, financial targets, incentives, and control systems.

Many empirical studies have looked into relatedness performance effects and the general conclusions to be drawn from these research efforts were summarized in a meta-study that aggregated all these results.[14] The accumulated insights from those studies are largely consistent with the initial findings that related diversification outperforms both dominant businesses and portfolios of unrelated business activities (Figure 5.4).

Hence, some diversity in product-market perspectives seems to spur value-creating business opportunities whereas a very narrow focus imposes limitations on creative business development.

Performance

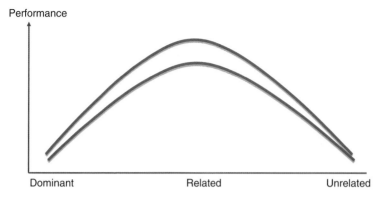

Dominant   Related   Unrelated

Figure 5.4 Business relatedness effects. Source: adapted from Palich *et al.* (2000)

Conversely, a too broad focus on different business activities makes it difficult to integrate the diverse business perspectives in new value-creating activities.

Economic trade-offs

A number of arguments support the urge to extend the corporate business portfolio. For example, an increase in the size of the enterprise can increase *bargaining power* in the markets where it operates. It might be possible to share central administrative functions and thereby *save costs*. Resources may be pooled for common purposes across business activities to realize *economic efficiencies*. Diversity in business and market practices may enhance *innovation* and the ability to create valuable product and service offerings. An increase in business volume within a single business as well as across related business activities may provide the basis to achieve *scale economies* through standardization and mass production and *scope economies* by sharing large-scale processes across comparable business activities. These effects constitute the potential positive contributions from a large agglomeration of businesses under a single corporate umbrella where particularly the scale and scope economies carry weight. However, the proposed effects, to the extent they materialize, are likely to have *diminishing return* characteristics, so the more they are pursued, the lower will be the incremental benefits from a marginal extension of business activities.

There are also a number of potential negative effects associated with the handling of a large business portfolio that often seem to be overlooked. First of all, a set of disparate corporate businesses requires more efforts to coordinate activities, particularly for firms operating in dynamic and complex industries, which can impose additional *coordination costs*. Given the cognitive limitations of human beings, the executive capacity to manage a broad business portfolio may fall short, particularly in dealing with complex, unrelated, diversified business activities. The *executive capabilities* derive from the specific experiences they have gained in their past careers that form their "dominant logics."[15] However, this experience base can be incompatible with the skills and insights required to deal with the challenges across a highly diverse set of business activities. Even though there seem to be the necessary complementary capabilities available across the combined business portfolio, essential resources may be *overstretched* in the attempts to reach aspired outcomes.

The various cost elements generally increase with higher complexity and incompatibility between unrelated business activities. Diminishing returns from positive effects and increasing negative effects suggest that there is an inverse curvilinear relationship between corporate diversification and performance. As corporate activities expand from a dominant business focus toward more related business areas, the benefits are expected to increase faster than the incremental costs. But further expansion into diverse activities will provide smaller and smaller positive effects, whereas as the associated costs increase exponentially, the more the firm engages in unrelated activities. In this situation scale and scope economies are weak or nonexistent whereas coordination costs are high and the executive challenges substantial.

There are many commonalities between the extension of corporate business activities and geographical expansion of the corporate presence. Both aspects emerge as natural elements of the central aim to grow revenues and expand business volume. Hence, a common perspective on the internationalization process describes it as a gradual expansion of business activities initially pursued in the near markets and then eventually extended to more distant and "exotic" markets as the corporation grows.[16] The expansive geographical reach of large corporations was observed in the increasing significance of foreign direct investments that seem to reflect a certain *multinationality advantage* ascribed to large global firms with a presence in many countries.[17] These developments triggered fundamental questions about underlying economic rationales that might explain the observed trend toward larger and more influential multinational enterprises. A predominant framework identified *ownership* of assets, specific conditions of the market *location*, and *internal* governance capabilities as three essential advantages associated with international expansion (see Box 5.1 *The eclectic (OLI) paradigm*).[18] However, a number of other elements have been advanced to explain the value-creating potential of multinational business activities, many of which resemble the arguments discussed in the context of business diversification. These include the potential cost efficiencies of a multinational business portfolio, business development opportunities spurred by access to diverse capabilities, enhanced innovation through collaboration within a global network, and creating strategic fit among the structural elements of the multinational enterprise.[19]

Many of the arguments adopted to explain business diversification effects also apply to the discussion of geographical diversification effects associated with *multinational expansion* or the business *internationalization* process, either directly or in modified form. Hence, the arguments for positive scale and scope economies can also apply to a geographical expansion of business activities. As the degree of *multinationality* increases, the firm will have business activities in more and more countries. This provides opportunities for central mass production of goods that can be distributed to a larger number of markets, or it makes it possible to share process capabilities across comparable regional activities.[20] The ability to act in different national business environments that are different from the firm's domestic context may provide insights that inspire the development of new business opportunities and can also give access to diverse resources that foster *innovation* and new product and service developments.[21] The fact that business conditions and factor endowments differ across national economies can provide opportunities to form a

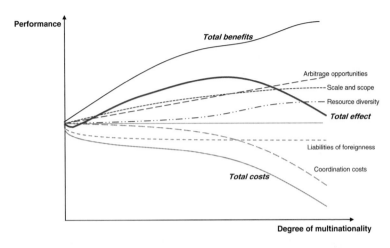

Figure 5.5 Multinational performance. Source: inspired by Lu and Beamish (2004)

global structure and orchestrate corporate activities that gain cheaper access to essential factor inputs and advantageous sales channels. In addition, it can provide *arbitrage* opportunities from transactions between national markets.[22] Maintaining a multinational structure of business activities can provide additional *flexibilities* that allow the firm to adjust activity levels across foreign entities and thereby adapt better to changing economic conditions.[23]

The potential positive effects associated with these factors can be evaluated and assessed for different degrees of international expansion. Hence, the proposed advantages might show linear or curvilinear relationships as the degree of multinational expansion increases.[24] Adding together these effects can provide insights about the total advantages to be derived from an extended international presence (Figure 5.5).

We should also take account of the potential negative effects associated with multinational expansion. A major adverse effect can arise from the increasing *coordination* costs associated with the handling of an extended multinational business presence. These costs might show an exponential increase as the degree of multinationality becomes higher.[25] Part of the reason for this relates to the increasingly diverse national environments the firm needs to accommodate in handling multinational business transactions. Furthermore, establishing foreign operations in more distant geographical markets may lead to significant increases in communication costs, travel expenses, legal fees, etc. It may also require significantly more executive attention, time, and meeting hours that divert scarce management resources. However, these implied costs from necessary coordination efforts to establish the overseas operational structure are often overlooked in the official management accounting systems. The specific demands imposed by the distinctiveness of national market characteristics are sometimes referred to as *liabilities of foreignness*.[26] That is, the national environments have their own unique cultural, linguistic, and historical heritage that forms a special economic infrastructure, and unique administrative practices in the country that influence the way people and business agents act and behave. Countries in the vicinity typically operate in quite similar ways to how things are done at home, but the more distant the international expansion becomes, the more economic systems and behaviors are likely to differ in substantive ways from those known in the home market. The implied diversity in business operations and human interactions will impose costs on business transactions made across national borders and they might increase exponentially if the cultural challenges become excessive. Conversely, if the organization can learn how to deal effectively with the implied cultural differences, it might be possible to contain the associated costs within a certain range.

By aggregating the costs and holding them against the total benefits we can get an overview of the expected net effects from a multinational expansion of business activities. Ideally, it will amount to a positive net gain, although the performance relationship may show an inverse u-shaped relationship to the degree of multinationality. That is, multinational expansion, or geographical diversification as it is, may display a performance pattern comparable to that observed in the case of corporate business diversification. To the extent this is the case we can think of an optimal point for the multinational corporation that combines considerations for both business and geographical diversification (Figure 5.6). This is obtained for a degree of business

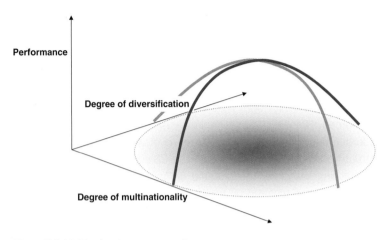

Figure 5.6 Multinational corporate performance

diversification somewhere between dominant and unrelated business activities and a multinational structure adapted to the firm-specific conditions with some overseas presence but not excessively so.

The performance effect of a multinational presence is highly dependent on the particular industry context in which the firm operates.[27] The increased flexibility and responsiveness provided by multinationality are particularly enhanced in industry contexts characterized by information-driven and knowledge-based business activities. In these types of businesses we generally observe the curvilinear performance relationship displayed in Figure 5.6. One reason for this is that much of the information and knowledge used in these businesses can be stored in operating procedures and practices, in computerized memories as electronic bits, and within the heads of key people. All of these essential information and knowledge resources are relatively easy and costless to move around from one geographical location to another and thereby facilitate the reorganizing of corporate activities as market demands change. It also makes it easier to combine and link essential information and knowledge in search of new solutions and the development of responsive business opportunities. Hence, this context appeals to flexible and nimble maneuvering against frequent and abrupt changes in global market conditions. This means that a diverse multinational presence can be exploited better in this particular business context. These types of business activities include areas such as information services, accounting, auditing, consulting, engineering, and other professional advisory services. The Rambøll Group, a global multi-disciplinary engineering, design, and consultancy company, exemplifies this kind of organization. AECOM Technology Corp., a global provider of professional technical and management support services in transportation, facilities, environment, energy, and water, is another example.

However, the same performance benefits have not been identified among multinational firms that operate in different manufacturing and network industries. The network industries comprise business activities in areas such as transportation, energy, and telecommunication that typically require a substantial network infrastructure to offer their services with sufficient operational coverage. The relatively high capital intensity and immobility of economic assets render these types of business activities less flexible and thus more exposed to changing environmental conditions. Hence, the manufacturing firms in general show little, if any, benefit from a multinational presence in terms of gaining upside business potential or deflecting adverse outcomes. So, even though we may argue for the flexibility embedded in a multinational operational structure, the costs associated with their maintenance can simply equal the benefits derived from them. In the case of corporations in network industries, the effects of multinational activities show overall negative performance effects, partially due to the double exposures derived from heavy investment in productive assets dispersed across multiple overseas locations and operating under restrictive local regulations and licensing arrangements. Hence, multinational expansion has often been associated with heavy investment commitments and exposure to significant country and political risks. AES Corporation is a global power company with generation and distribution businesses around the world and thus belongs to this challenging industry segment. Another example was Enron Corporation, the energy, commodities, and services company. Before its bankruptcy in 2001, it was one of the world's leading electricity, natural gas, and communications companies.

In short, multinational expansion is affected by different economic trade-offs of potential benefits and costs, and firms should understand the economic dynamics in their respective industry contexts as they assess their multinational expansion strategies.

Portfolio considerations

The multinational corporate strategy perspective deals with the management of a portfolio of business activities that may be extended across different geographical locations. The *GE business matrix* is a simple plotting technique used to analyze the viability of different product markets. It can be used to get an overview of which areas to expand, contract, and continue to invest in across an existing portfolio of business activities. This framework was developed by McKinsey for General Electric in the 1970s and is conceptually similar to the better known BCG matrix (see Box 5.2 *The BCG business matrix*). It is a simple plotting tool where business activities are arranged in a two-dimensional grid according to one axis indicating *industry attractiveness*, e.g., measured by profitability, or fit with existing competencies, and another axis indicating *competitive strength,* measured by, for example, price premium, level of service, etc. (Figure 5.7).

The potential advantage of this simple plotting framework is that it can display at the same time both the external *market potential* and the fit with *internal capabilities*, while also providing

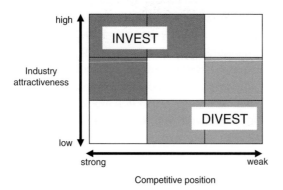

Figure 5.7 Extended business matrix

some nuances to the measures used to inform the two axes or scales. Based on this framework, a simple decision rule is to *invest* in and commit more resources to the business activities that show high industry attractiveness combined with a strong competitive position where current capabilities provide a good fit to support the efforts. Conversely, we should *divest* business activities that have low industry attractiveness combined with a weak competitive position. The plotting framework can be refined further to map the individual business activities or products with pie charts indicating the proportional size of the sales volume or total revenues in the market, with a slice of the pie presenting the market share enjoyed by the company. The business activities and products that appear in the top left corner of the matrix are generally attractive for investment and the company has a resource-based competitive advantage to support the investment. Business activities and products in the bottom right-hand side of the matrix are unattractive and poorly supported by internal competencies. The areas in the middle between these extremes are less clear cut and therefore need further scrutiny. Whereas the GE matrix overcomes some of the oversimplification problems of the BCG matrix, it has its limitations. For example, it does not indicate possible relationships and dependencies across business areas, such as potentials for scale and scope economies, commonalities between the competencies, and skills that can support multiple businesses, or potential dynamic spill-over effects from learning and exploration in related product-market activities.

The tension between an exclusive focus on external market conditions and considerations about internal supportive competencies is also reflected in the contrasting perspectives of the market positioning school and the resource-based view in strategy. This theme appeared in the previous strategy discussion where the simple solution was to reconcile these views and combine the external and internal considerations in SWOT analysis (see Chapters 1 and 2). However, this obviously becomes more complicated when the firm is engaged in multiple business activities. As the multi-business firms emerged, they established business divisions as senior executives realized that they were unable to handle the diversity of functional issues in a timely manner and lacked the detailed information required to deal effectively with daily business operations.[28] For the most part, the new divisions or business units were organized around specific product-market areas and this approach was broadly advocated by management consultants. Therefore, Prahalad and Hamel referred to the "tyranny of the SBU" to point out that the corporations were partially blinded by their primary focus on strategic business units defined by the market position of the end-products.[29] As they argued: "Obviously, diversified corporations have a portfolio of businesses. But we believe in a view of the company as a portfolio of competencies as well." Their reasoning was that the particular focus on business units discarded the importance of essential resources and competencies that could be used with advantage across all business activities even though this was not apparent from the industry classification of the final products. Hence, they introduced the concept of *core competencies* as bundles of resources, capabilities, and skills that can provide important core product or service offerings. For example, Honda Motor Co. developed core competencies in the construction and building of engines and power trains that gave it a strong position in diverse markets for cars, motorcycles, lawn mowers, and generators. Canon Inc. developed core competencies in optics, imaging, and microprocessor controls applied to enter diverse markets for copiers, laser printers, cameras, and image scanners (Figure 5.8). Similarly, FedEx Corporation developed core competencies in logistics and computerized tracking systems that supported its worldwide express delivery business but also opened for inventory tracking, replenishment, and other supply chain services.

The introduction of core competencies re-emphasized the importance of common resources and capabilities that reach across multiple business activities. Hence, the development of strong core competencies relies on collaborative work efforts across organizational boundaries between levels and functions. It also requires a central executive focus on the core competencies and core products that may support various end-products in different markets. However, it is not easy to identify the true core competencies and determine whether they should be developed going forward. That is, the underlying idea is compelling but hard to

Core competencies

Products	Precision mechanics	Fine optics	Micro-electronics
Cameras	•	•	•
Printers	•		•
Fax machines	•		•
Calculators		•	•
Copiers	•	•	•
Videos	•	•	•
Imaging	•		•
Aligners	•		•

Figure 5.8 Core competencies (example). Source: adapted from Prahalad and Hamel (1990)

practice. The ability to match internal capabilities against diverse market opportunities is constrained by the cognitive capabilities of corporate executives formed by their managerial experiences. In other words, the fit between the experiential base of executives and the business context of the corporation might matter as much as the relatedness between business activities. If the business activities in the corporate portfolio are too diverse, the executive experience might simply not be able to contain this, to the detriment of corporate performance. If the corporate business activities fall within the same vertical stage of the industry value chain, this should make it easier to match executive competencies to the underlying strategic challenges. So, corporations with high business relatedness as well as managerial relatedness should outperform. The empirics indicate that executives in the forest products industry and highly diversified companies display these relationships, although this is not the case among vertically integrated oil companies.[30] In other words, compatible managerial experience matters, but there are notable exceptions to the general rule. Hence, executive experiences applied across industries at the same stage on the value chain in horizontally integrated businesses generally enhance performance, but not in the oil industry where vertical integration outperforms.

Consequently, there is no simple answer, but the results seem to reflect the presence of industry-specific intangible assets and competencies where appropriate corporate structures across business activities are required to exploit them.

In view of the specific business conditions that surround different industry contexts, some of which may be quite unique, it is apparent that the corporate structure should be able to accommodate those industry-specific contingencies. In other words, the corporate structure should match the requirements imposed by the industry contexts of the businesses to effectively support management in the individual business units. That is, to realize a potential parenting advantage there must be a certain fit between the characteristics of the parent and the characteristics of the individual business, where the corporate structures, systems, and processes support each of those businesses.[31] Hence, value is created at the business level, but decisions made at the parent company, head office, or headquarters, as may be, will affect how the business units are allowed to perform. So, part of the challenge is to set up an appropriate corporate structure to deal effectively with the business portfolio in a manner that creates internal fit between the structural elements and a strategic fit with the requirements imposed by the industry contexts of the businesses' activities.

According to Collis and Montgomery, "alignment is driven by the nature of the firm's resources – its special assets, skills, and capabilities. The firm's resources are the unifying thread, the element that ultimately determines the others."[32] They suggest that appropriate fit is achieved by matching high-quality corporate resources against strong product-market positions and configuring an organization that can lever those resources in each of its businesses. The corporate structure should be configured so it is compatible with the nature of the corporate resources. Hence, the degree to which the underlying resources are specialized or general determines how they can be applied across the businesses in the corporate portfolio (Figure 5.9). That is, corporations with predominantly specialized resources will engage within a relatively narrow range of related business activities whereas corporations with more general resources typically engage in more diverse, unrelated businesses.

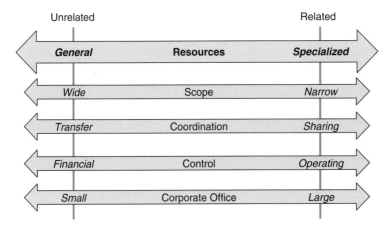

Figure 5.9 Structural fit with the business portfolio. Source: adapted from Collis and Montgomery (1998)

Corporations with specialized resources are typically engaged in related business activities. The corporate office has a relatively large staff involved in coordination processes where (core) competences and skills are shared between entities while imposing control on operating processes at the business level. For example, Sharp Corporation, the Japanese consumer information products and electronic components company, is engaged in related businesses such as audio-visual, communication, health, environmental, and information equipment.[33] The company has developed core competencies in specialized optoelectronics technologies, including liquid crystal displays (LCDs), that provide support for many of its product offerings. The company has a functional structure where central corporate staff are involved in ongoing technology investments and sharing of technological competencies across business activities. Multiple cross-unit and corporate committees are engaged in the coordination efforts between specialized functional and product managers. These intricate relationships call for a corporate control system focused on operating process standards and behavioral norms.

When corporate resources are more general, the company is typically engaged in a wider spectrum of unrelated businesses. In this case the corporate office should have a small staff because there is little need to engage in internal coordination and operating-control processes. Standard practices, best-in-class operating procedures, and management systems can be readily transferred to all business entities, with little intervention from central staff. Hanson Trust plc was a British-based international building materials company known for its successful acquisitions of underperforming companies.[34] It is known for several notable takeovers, including United Drapery Stores (1983), Imperial Tobacco Group (1986), and Consolidated Gold Fields (1988). Hence, the corporate portfolio included many unrelated businesses. The philosophy applied to these companies was that good basic quality of essential goods and services can be offered at high profitability. They set high aims and standards for performance measured by stringent financial targets and related incentive systems. Management responsibilities were decentralized and financial controls were centralized. Hence, this particular corporate structure required only a small central staff.[35]

It is also suggested that corporate structures can be set up in a way that creates flexibility and adaptive capacity under turbulent market conditions by allowing various business activities to be recombined in new ways as the environment changes.[36] Hence, the ability to apply (core) competencies and skills across different business units is essential for corporate adaptation where commonality in the structural elements facilitates their flexible utilization and reorganization. The principle of *patching* can be applied to reorganize corporate business activities in response to changing market opportunities. This means that parts of an existing core business can be separated to form a new promising business activity. Hence, parts of Hewlett-Packard's laser-jet printer unit were used to form a new business for network printers. The company also used competencies in other units to launch new businesses in ink-jet printers and scanners while recombining activities across business entities to improve economic efficiencies and enhance focused innovation. This approach promotes relatively small and frequent adjustments formed around effective adaptive routines. It is facilitated by a structure of well-defined and focused activities pursued in comparable ways across different business units as well as a compensation system that operates consistently across all parts of the corporation. Some of the key principles for an effective patching technique are to act quickly without undue delays, consider alternative options, experimentation before launch, and planning of the initial phase in the reorganization. The patching technique may also include entry into new business areas through acquisition of small, related companies, as practiced, for example, by Cisco Systems.

However, it is generally difficult to acquire business development capabilities through acquisitions. Hence, a study of innovation in Johnson & Johnson, the US multinational pharmaceutical and consumer goods company, found that internal development generally was more effective than innovating through acquisitions.[37] Whereas more frequent reconfigurations of business units created more value, especially around acquired companies, most of the innovations took place in internally created business units. That is, the ability to share essential knowledge around commonly understood core competencies seems essential for effective business development efforts and this is hard to achieve by acquiring other firms.

Many of the concerns expressed in corporate strategy about the need for resources and development of competencies applied to a spectrum of product markets are also recognized in the considerations around multinational strategy. The need for central integration and coordination as well as decentralized resource commitments in local markets have been highly influential elements in these discussions framed around an integration–responsiveness trade-off perspective.[38] Hence, the multinational corporation must operate around the tensions created between two overarching pressures in the global business environment. One is the pressure to reduce operating and administrative costs and optimize efficiencies in coordinated corporate activities. Another is the pressure to satisfy the requirements imposed by specific national business conditions and customer demands that can be quite diverse across geographical regions. So, the basic challenge can be described as tensions between the ability to produce price-competitive goods and services and responding to unique local demands in national markets.[39] The concern for differentiation and integration was initially applied in analyses of organizational structure that identified an increasing need for specialized business entities and their coordinated efforts to

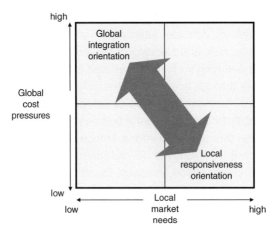

Figure 5.10 Generic strategy orientations. Source: inspired by Bartlett and Ghoshal (1998)

achieve a common corporate purpose.[40] In a similar way, multinational management must be able to respond to specific market needs through differentiated local activities while at the same time integrating these diverse business activities to gain economic efficiencies. Hence, predominant pressures to satisfy local market needs would push the firm toward a *local responsiveness* orientation whereas global cost pressures would urge a move toward a *global integration* orientation, although joint pressures require a certain balance between the two orientations (Figure 5.10).

A *global integration orientation* entails a centralized operational management structure where resource-committing decisions across national boundaries are coordinated through centralized planning efforts in pursuit of an overall corporate strategy. The global organization is a centralized structural configuration with complex interdependencies, with intense coordination requirements. Major decisions are planned centrally and scaled globally where local entities primarily pursue headquarters strategies.[41] A *local responsiveness orientation* entails a multinational organization that can respond to unique national market conditions through adaptive actions pursued within a decentralized decision structure. Locally responsive companies delegate authority and decision power to managers with regional market responsibilities and develop resources across national business entities. The organizational structure is characterized by loosely coupled and dispersed decision processes.

However, different business activities and product-market offerings can be exposed differently to these underlying forces, depending on, for example, the importance of multinational customers, multinational competition, universal needs, differentiated distribution channels, host government demands, etc. If customer demands converge between countries and there are substantial scale economies, there should be a drive in those industries toward global integration, whereas national rules and comparative advantages could drive other industries toward local responsiveness. Hence, it is argued that industries such as food products, consumer goods, and metal fabrication typically assume a local responsiveness orientation whereas semiconductors, computers, and automobiles assume a global integration orientation (Figure 5.11).[42]

Computer products and consumer electronics industries face global standards and high cost pressures and therefore should adopt a global integration orientation. Food products, clothes, and

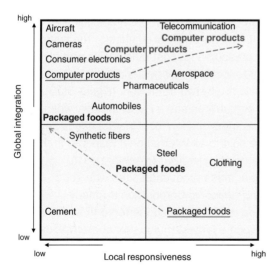

Figure 5.11 The strategic orientations of industries. Source: inspired by Beamish *et al.* (2000)

other household goods are more exposed to specific national market demands and restrictions that would require a local responsiveness orientation. However, availability of local market technologies might call for more diverse sourcing of intangible assets where flexible manufacturing and mass-customization techniques can enable the offer of locally adapted products in cost-efficient ways. Hence, firms in technology-intensive business activities such as *computer products* may move toward a combined position of global integration and local responsiveness.[43] At the same time, many common goods products, for example in the food-processing and clothing industries, are increasingly offered in the form of branded products with standardized quality where the global brand recognition provides a good basis for scale economies. Hence, we may see that *packaged goods* firms, from being geared to respond to local traditions and customs, increasingly pursue global integration as a viable strategic solution. In short, industry conditions are dynamic and constantly change and firms operating in different product markets should be cognizant of these changes and reconsider the strategic orientations accordingly.

The relative importance of global integration and local responsiveness as driven by global cost pressures and local market needs has been used to identify four archetypical approaches to the multinational strategy challenge. The distinction between high and low pressures for cost efficiencies and high and low pressures to adapt to local market needs defines four strategy typologies identified in a two-by-two framework (Figure 5.12).[44]

A company should arguably pursue a *global strategy* when there are high global cost pressures and low local market needs because the same products are sold in all international markets. In this situation products can be standardized to achieve scale economies from regional mass production sites with good distribution capacities. Panasonic Corporation (formerly Matsushita Electric Industrial Co.), headquartered in Kadoma, Osaka, is one of the world's largest multinational electronics companies and competes alongside Canon, Sony, and Toshiba in a range of products sold on a global scale. The intense competition in these goods pushes a need to consider a global strategy focus. Procter & Gamble (P&G), the US multinational corporation

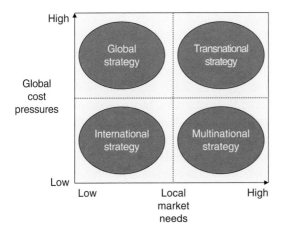

Figure 5.12 Strategy typologies for the multinational firm. Source: inspired by Bartlett and Ghoshal (1989)

headquartered in Cincinnati, Ohio, is a worldwide manufacturer and marketer of a range of consumer goods. They include household care products with known brands, such as Always, Ariel, Cher, Crest, Dash, Duracell, Gillette, Tide, Vicks, etc. The brand recognition makes a global strategy of standardized products in all overseas markets a sensible approach.

A company can pursue an *international strategy* when there are low global cost pressures and low local market needs because the products can be sold internationally and produced locally. McDonald's Corporation, headquartered in Oak Brook, Illinois, may be an example of this strategy. It is a leading global foodservice retailer with more than 33,000 local restaurants in 119 countries where over 80 percent of the restaurants are operated by local owners. The company strives to be the favorite local place for the Big Mac, the Quarter Pounder, and Chicken McNuggets. The general brand recognition allows for global sales of standardized food offerings. However, the perishable nature of the raw materials speaks for a distributed supply chain anchored in nearby regional markets and the franchise financing model calls for access to local ownership engagement.

A company adheres to a *multinational strategy* – at times also referred to as *multidomestic strategy* – when there are low global cost pressures and high local market needs, in which case production and distribution should be close to the market to abide by local regulatory requirements and customs. Royal Philips Electronics (Koninklijke Philips Electronics N.V.) is often used as an example of this strategy. This Dutch multinational electronics company, headquartered in Amsterdam, has a broad market presence as a diversified company. It is organized in three main divisions: Philips Consumer Lifestyle (formerly Philips Consumer Electronics and Philips Domestic Appliances and Personal Care), Philips Healthcare (formerly Philips Medical Systems), and Philips Lighting. The company has a history of innovation, including the audio tape, compact cassette, and video cassette recorder, and it teamed up with Sony to launch the compact disk that evolved into DVD and Blu-Ray. However, a complex corporate structure, including many overseas acquisitions of technology companies, such as Amperex, Magnavox, Marconi, Mullard, and Signetics, has increased the challenges of gaining economic efficiencies.

A company should ideally follow a *transnational strategy* when it is exposed both to high global cost pressures and high local market needs. In this case, the firm must fulfill the dual requirements for cost efficiencies and local market responses, which may be the reality faced by most companies in today's market environment. Incidentally, these requirements resemble those captured in the discussion about the need to choose between low-cost and differentiation strategies (Chapters 2 and 4). Yet, in the international business literature it is presented as an ideal typology that many corporations should try to accommodate. Hence, we see a general trend toward multinational corporations striving to heed both the cost efficiency and responsiveness requirements at the same time. For example, McDonald's now complements many of its standardized branded food items with national specialties or traits that appeal to local customers and also offers lighter complements such as salads catering to the more health-conscious customer segments, with a strong footing in some national markets. Similarly, Dell Inc. has attempted to offer customized computers on competitive terms in all overseas markets even though it has been challenging to transpose a largely US-based business model to other national environments, particularly in emerging markets.

There has been much effort devoted to examining the validity of the four strategy typologies, but the evidence has been quite mixed.[45] It is often an underlying premise that if multinational firms adopt the generic typology that has the best fit with the underlying global cost pressures and local market needs, it would also lead to superior performance outcomes. However, this has only been sporadically assessed. Specific industry studies may find clusters of firms that are commensurate with the four strategy typologies, but these clusters show no significant differences in performance. The examples amply illustrate that it may be overly ambitious to impose the often highly complex multinational corporate structures into the confines of a simple two-by-two framework. Furthermore, in corporations with more diverse business portfolios, the various activities and product-market offerings may cater to different global contexts that require a multifocal approach where each set of business activities adopts its own strategic approach.

In conclusion, we can consider the integration–responsiveness framework that identifies the four strategy typologies as an analytical framework rather than a schematic frame for easy solutions. It can help the multinational corporate strategist assessing the environmental pressures that circumscribe the international aspects of the corporate business activities and thereby provide qualified background analysis for discussions about viable solutions for the multinational corporation.

Structure and processes

Most of the multinational companies also preside over a portfolio of different business activities that in extreme cases take extraordinary proportions and increase the complexity of managing the multinational corporation. There have been different approaches to structuring the often diverse activities of the multinational corporation. One approach is to assume a worldwide *functional structure* where all the overseas functional activities report to a functional department or division at corporate head office. This structure may be preferred when the corporation has a strong emphasis on supportive technological know-how and core competencies anchored in operational activities. Alternatively, the corporation can set up an *international structure* where foreign subsidiaries report to an international division at headquarters. This approach may be preferred when the products sold internationally are fairly standardized, with little diversity, and where there is low involvement from the foreign entities. This largely corresponds to the conditions around the global strategy approach where cost pressures speak for centralized product development efforts that cater to all overseas markets combined with large-scale, efficient manufacturing facilities. This can be extended to a *worldwide product structure*, where focused product divisions at headquarters assume the responsibility for a particular product or product groups in the overseas entities. This may be required in situations where the product portfolio is very diverse and therefore requires special attention. Another alternative is a *geographical structure* where the international markets are divided into regions that report into designated area divisions at headquarters. This structural set-up may be preferred when the products are relatively standardized and undiversified but there is a need for foreign market involvement due to country-specific requirements as foreign sales have become worldwide in reach.

When there are multiple requirements at play at the same time there is a need for more flexible corporate structures. There may be a need to focus on functional specialization to protect operational competencies as well as a regional focus due to diverse geographical requirements. If the business portfolio is comprised of diverse activities and products there may be a need to focus on particular product groups and business lines. The implied requirements for dual focus on core functional, geographic, and business concerns can be accomplished through different *matrix structures* (Figure 5.13).

Hence, a multinational management matrix may combine a dual focus on functional competencies and geographical concerns so employees are responsible both to the country management that reports to a central global division and to the relevant functional departments at headquarters. Similarly, a corporate management matrix can combine the dual focus on functional competencies and product concerns so employees report both to designated product divisions and to functional departments at

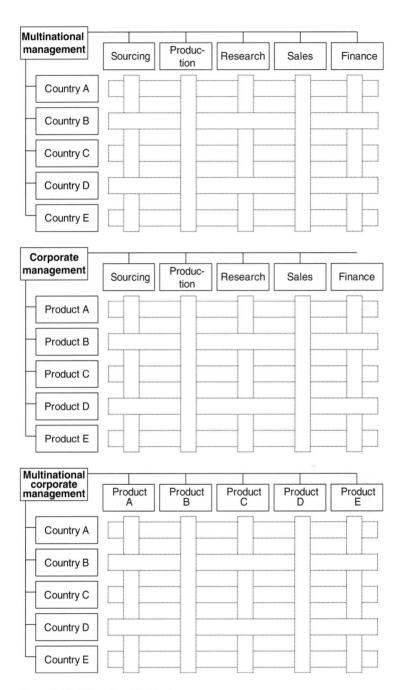

Figure 5.13 Different matrix structures

headquarters. Furthermore, a multinational corporate matrix may combine geographical and business portfolio concerns where employees report both to country managers under the global division and to product divisions at headquarters. If functional specialization remains important, it may even be possible to add a third reporting line to the functional divisions at headquarters, thereby creating a *three-dimensional matrix* structure.

The underlying idea is that the mixed structures will ensure focused prioritizations of core competence development, business portfolio demands, global cost, and adaptation pressures with appropriate coordinative efforts. A better fit between multinational corporate structure and the strategy applied to deal with the global competitive conditions should make it easier for key employees to act and thereby support better strategic outcomes. However, the added corporate and multinational dimensions make the competitive environment considerably more complex and thereby increase the information-processing requirements imposed on the multinational corporation. Setting up an appropriate structure can help ensure that decision making, reporting lines, and management control systems are construed to accommodate the underlying information-processing requirements.[46] This implies that employees and managers across the multinational corporation have relevant information to take the necessary actions, and that top management is sufficiently informed and updated about activities in foreign operations and corporate businesses.

A matrix structure can also deal with organizational settings where people with particular skills are assigned to work with different projects and business initiatives. Hence, the engineering department, for example, is responsible for engineering services in general and assigns qualified engineers to different projects who report to other project managers where the employees might report to several managers on different aspects of the project. This structure could be relevant for project-centered organizations that work with different types of customers in multiple overseas locations and where the services are provided through project teams. This is in contrast to a "pure" matrix organization as discussed before where responsibilities are distributed across central divisions with functional, business line, or regional specializations. Yet, in these organizations there may also be special project teams where project responsibilities are shared across the matrix. There are supposedly two advantages associated with a matrix structure: (1) information across essential focal areas is more readily shared for mutual adjustment of activities, and (2) focus on specialized knowledge areas is retained for professional development. The disadvantages relate to potential confusion about reporting lines and responsibilities that can be neutralized by employing proper management control, incentive, and shared corporate value systems.

The matrix structure can ideally harvest the advantages from cross-functional collaborative work practices and avoid the shortcomings of centralization in the increasing complexity of the firm as it grows and extends its business and geographical activities. Hence, the international coffee house chain Starbucks Corporation used a matrix structure to combine a functional focus on strong operating practices with a product focus to enhance high-quality customer experiences. The challenge of dual reporting lines was addressed by developing a team spirit where employees are empowered and trained in hard skills as well as soft interpersonal behaviors.

Multinational matrix designs with reporting to regional divisions are also common in large corporations with an extended global reach, such as Procter & Gamble and Unilever. These structures are complex organizational forms attempting to accommodate the forces of global competition and specific customer requirements in specific national markets. The matrix designs try to impose a flatter and less hierarchical organization that gives individuals more leeway to respond to the multiple demands of the multinational environment. At the same time, it can also provide structure and focus on essential corporate concerns to balance the decentralized responses with centrally coordinated development efforts.

The many possibilities in matrix designs reflect the emergence of the globally networked corporation. The implied network structures build on the cooperative strategy model where firms not only compete for market value against each other in a zero-sum game, they might also collaborate in open networks where the various elements of the network evolves through co-evolutionary

Geographic, product, and functional matrix organization

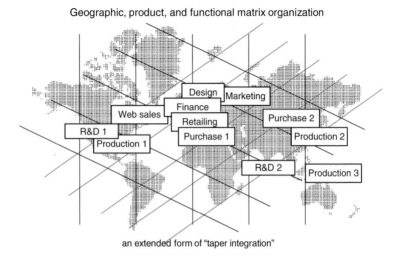

an extended form of "taper integration"

Figure 5.14 Networked global business structure

contributions among partners, collaborators, and complementing businesses (see Box 5.3 *Porter's dynamic model of global competitiveness*).[47] Hence, a networked organization can contract some of its business functions to other companies if this is considered more efficient. This may call for new, flexible types of matrix structures that combine functional, product, and geographical concerns where corporate business activities are scattered across an extended form of "taper integration" (Figure 5.14).

The multinational corporate managers who operate within such a network structure coordinate and monitor the external relations with the help of enabling information-technology solutions. For example, the Swedish retail-clothing company Hennes & Mauritz AB (H&M) became more flexible and nimble as its in-house designers developed the clothes and worked with buyers who outsourced production to a network of external manufacturers and thereby gained a cost advantage. The Danish-based international developer, manufacturer, and marketer of quality footwear, ECCO Shoes A/S, is a typical example of a vertically integrated, networked, multinational company. Hence, the company sourced the best-quality leather in central Europe and superior rubber soles from Germany, and produced the shoes in Portugal, Indonesia, Thailand, and Japan. Global marketing was performed by experts in Amsterdam and e-sales out of New York. Design and development were handled in collaboration with overseas research centers, while central administration was maintained in Bredebro. This entire entourage has been bound together by advanced communication and information technologies that were unavailable just a few decades ago. Hence, computer-mediated communication creates cost-efficient information-handling capabilities that allow multinational corporations to coordinate activities and enhance business development more effectively in view of the inherent turbulence associated with international business.[48]

Integrative–responsive strategy making

The discussion of matrix organizations and network structures illustrates that it matters how the multinational corporation sets up its business activities and devises its internal management processes. There are no simple solutions to the identified tensions between demands imposed by national market conditions and global competitive pressures. However, as in the case of the dual demands for quality products and services and continuously improving economic efficiencies, the answer relates to the ability to establish collaborative settings where creativity and innovation can devise viable solutions to emerging challenges. This was neatly uncovered by Doz et al. as they suggested a number of "administrative solutions" to deal with the underlying tensions (Figure 5.15).[49]

Hence, the underlying challenge is enforced by the sheer complexity of business activities that increases as the firm expands into more diverse product markets located in an increasing number of national environments. At the same time, the dynamic changes that take place in the global competitive environment will increase the frequency of decisions that need to balance local needs against global cost pressures.

As the complexity and dynamic changes enforce the underlying tensions, the traditional *unidimensional approach* of centrally

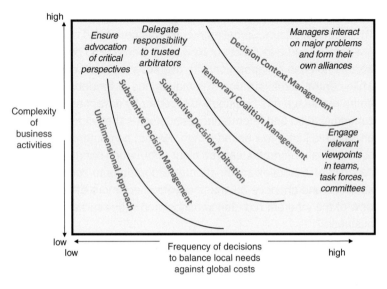

Figure 5.15 Managing MNC tensions. Source: adapted from Doz *et al.* (1981)

planned decisions falls short and there is a call for decision-making processes that involve people with diverse field insights. One such approach is referred to as *substantive decision management*, which simply means that top management ensures that the critical views of different management groups in the firm are heard before major decisions are made. A second approach is *substantive decision arbitration*, where the responsibility to balance important forces or pressures is delegated to one or more trusted agents as arbitrators in the process. Even though there is some delegation of responsibility, it still leaves the door open for possible executive intervention in the final decision. The third approach is *temporary coalition management*, where top management assembles a group of qualified managers with relevant diverse backgrounds to make the specific decisions. So, here top management retains the flexibility to appoint the members who influence the decision while also determining the decisions that should be considered. In the fourth approach, *decision context management*, top management sets up an organizational context where managers are motivated to interact in ways that will reconcile the different tensions. It is a "context in which managers form the necessary alliances themselves to deal with the issues." This implies that decision power has been delegated to lower-level functional managers who interact and communicate openly to find the best solutions to emerging problems. In the interim approaches, we see elements with a strong resemblance to the concept of *logical incrementalism*, the process of *fast decisions* in high-velocity industries, and *participatory* decision making (see Chapter 3). In the last approach we see something with a strong resemblance to *decentralization* of decisions backed by supportive incentive and value systems.

The challenges that affect the multinational corporation have the same roots as the strategic management challenges discussed previously, although garnered with additional concerns for business and geographical diversification issues that make things somewhat more complex. However, the global environment has also changed toward more knowledge-based and information-rich business conditions where, according to Doz *et al.*, "the challenge is to innovate by *learning from the world*."[50] Hence, the so-called *metanational advantage* to be gained in this competitive context arguably depends on three distinct types of capabilities the multinational firm must possess. They should have *sensing* capabilities that allow the firm to extend its existing capabilities by identifying new valuable customer needs and finding relevant technologies to address them. They should have *mobilizing* capabilities that make it possible to convert the new insights into concrete product offerings and market opportunities. They should have *operationalizing* capabilities so once the product offerings and the supporting business model are tested they can be scaled for a global reach with potential local adaptations. From this argumentation we see a clear resemblance to the dynamic capabilities framework of sensing, seizing, and reconfiguring firm resources in responses to new competitive conditions. Hence, the same strategic considerations apply to the meta-national conditions as discussed in the context of increasingly turbulent and knowledge-intensive competitive environments in general.

The tensions created between the dual forces of global cost efficiencies and local market adaptations in effect constitute an international business version of the generic strategy schism we referred to as *stuck in the middle* (see Chapter 4). The solution to these situations is that global standardization and local adaptation as well as cost efficiency and product differentiation are not dichotomies that represent either/or choices. Rather, they represent significant underlying tensions in the competitive environment that we need to handle at the same time. Hence, it may come as no surprise that the integrative strategy approach that combines decentralized strategy making with central planning is particularly effective in the face of the extraordinary turbulence faced by firms that expand their business activities internationally.[51] Whereas we already discussed in Chapter 4 how firms that are able to handle both decentralized strategy making and central planning outperform their peers, this is particularly so among firms that are very international, i.e., where foreign sales make up a high percentage of total sales.

A detailed study of strategic planning in a multinational firm illustrates how the strategy-making process is influenced by the people engaged in the overseas operating entities. Even though the strategy process is initiated by top management, a common strategy emerges over time through the involvement of different organizational actors. The influence derives from participation in the planning deliberations and partially reflects the outcomes and experiences from prior decisions made in the local markets. The associated strategic discourse among organizational members entails both formal communication and informal contacts through interpersonal relationships, partially influenced by self-interests, resistance, and internal power positions (see Box 5.4 *Strategy making at Chr. Hansen A/S*).[52] Another study of overseas subsidiaries finds that headquarters policies affect how new subsidiary initiatives are utilized effectively.[53] The multinational leadership and its corporate staff are often ambivalent between central control and responsive initiatives taken locally. But if handled appropriately, the overseas subsidiaries and corporate business units in general can contribute, with new market and product development initiatives that respond to observed changes in both the global and the local competitive environments. If these initiatives are uncovered, tested, and advanced, when successful they can be exploited by corporate business units and subsidiaries located in other markets. This approach, in effect, is comparable to the approaches discussed for a purely domestic firm with regional business entities except that the diversity of the multinational environment is more extensive.

By choosing to engage in related business activities and locate in overseas markets with different product adaptations, technology applications, logistical structures, institutional settings, etc., the multinational corporation can form an enterprise with access to a unique set of competencies and knowledge-based resources. The diverse skills, competencies, and insights gained from different market contexts can be a source for developing responsive initiatives that deal effectively with changes in the global competitive environment. This provides a unique platform to create new corporate ventures that can exploit changing business conditions and where an extended portfolio of opportunities increases corporate maneuverability in the face of a turbulent environment.[54] Hence, the empirical evidence suggests that some business diversity and multinationality will have favorable performance implications associated with lower downside risk effects and reduced earnings volatility as well as a higher upside potential for opportunity gains. Interestingly, these effects arise relatively quickly. That is, a firm needs only a few related business areas and a presence in 2–3 distinct and well-chosen overseas countries or regions to obtain these advantages. So, just as in the case of the purely domestic firm that exploits comparative advantages across regions, this is also the case in a multinational context, although probably on a grander scale.

Conclusion

Adding different business activities to the corporate portfolio as well as expanding business activities to different overseas markets creates more complexity in the strategic management challenge. We find that some diversity across related business activities in the corporate portfolio can enhance performance, while access to different overseas markets can provide a basis for developing new business opportunities. However, there are obvious trade-offs between these incremental advantages and various costs associated with the extended business and geographical diversification that should be considered carefully. Yet, it is possible to find a superior combination of business activities and national market presence that allows better utilization of existing competencies and where the exchange of related knowledge in innovative activities can develop new products and processes. The corporate multinational challenge of dealing with the dual pressures of global competition and local responsiveness is not unlike accommodating the call for cost efficiency and differentiation advantages identified in strategic management. The integrative strategy approach that combines central planning with decentralized strategy making is a possible solution to both aspects as an effective way to give direction, generate viable responses to emerging competitive changes, and coordinate adaptive corporate actions.

In sum, the integrative strategy approach that combines a central analytical strategy-making process with decentralized autonomous response capabilities provides a dynamic interaction that can deal effectively with the turbulence of a global competitive context. However, this raises the issue as to how this can be accomplished by strategic leadership. This is the topic of the next chapter.

Box 5.1 The eclectic (OLI) paradigm

The profitability of multinational expansion in overseas business activities through foreign direct investments arguably depends on the superiority of the firm's own intangible assets that can be transferred to overseas markets and exploited with advantage. There may also be benefits or efficiencies to be gained in the local national markets to which the economic assets are transferred because they are more favorable than the home market. Both these effects depend on the firm's ability to apply its internal governance structure properly.

$$FDI = O + L + I$$

FDI = foreign direct investment
O = ownership advantage (firm-specific advantages)

L = location advantage (country-specific advantages)
I = internalization advantage

The ownership (O) advantage is displayed when foreign direct investment in productive assets leads to higher returns than is generally obtained by local production. The ownership superiority could relate to things such as more efficient production technologies, more effective management systems, better leadership, governance structures, etc. It could also derive from the presence of unique, knowledge-based intellectual capital and know-how embedded in technology innovation and development of management competencies.

The location (L) advantages would be expressed by the fact that a firm's overseas entities display higher economic gains, thus reflecting that business conditions are superior in those national locations. The relative benefits could accrue from better factor cost conditions, higher demand conditions, access to superior competencies, or unique research and development practices, etc. It could also relate to a more efficient economic infrastructure in the host country, including cultural artifacts that facilitate more efficient behaviors.

The internalization (I) advantages bound in internal managerial competencies may explain why some firms are better at exploiting their assets in overseas locations. The internationalizing firms might buy comparable assets in the overseas markets but choose to use their own presumably because they are unique and thus require a unique internal governance structure and related management capabilities to exploit them properly. Hence, the ability to exploit location advantages may hinge upon similar learned competencies that exist in a superior form only within the corporation.

The unique knowledge-based advantages embedded in the intellectual capital owned by the corporation can be extended if an internal governance structure provides the means to exchange these resources to develop new business opportunities that respond better to local market requirements. Hence, the knowledge-based advantages construed around a unique network of multinational competencies and market insights can be transferred more efficiently and hence exploited better within an internal management system. Given the industry- and firm-specific differences in the underlying intangible assets, we would expect the multinational advantages to differ across industry contexts as well as across firms.

Box 5.2 The BCG business matrix

The BCG matrix (Boston Consulting Group portfolio diagram) was introduced by the Boston Consulting Group and widely applied during the 1970s. The matrix provides a two-by-two framework to chart the corporation's existing product lines, product markets, and business activities or different business units. Hence, it can provide an overview of the distinct products and markets where the corporation is present and the divisions assigned to govern these activities. They are ordered by relative market share and growth, which can help allocation of resources across a portfolio of business activities from low to high prospects.

The plot identifies four quadrants:

Cash cows are activities with high market share in slow-growth markets – they generate cash and should be milked without investing too much.

Dogs are activities with low market share in slow-growth markets – they generate sufficient cash to retain the market position but there is no cash generated for dividends and therefore they should be sold.

Question marks are high-growth activities that use lots of cash to support expansion but still have low market share – a question mark has potential to become a star and then a cash cow, once the market grows and matures.

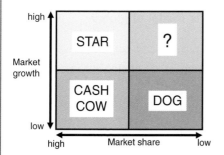

Stars are activities with high market share in fast-growing markets – they have the potential to become *cash cows* where market leadership requires further investment but it is rewarding.

The framework can help decide which business activities to fund and which ones to dismiss or divest, where the idea is to use funds from the cash cows to develop the stars and support the question marks while getting rid of the dogs. It maps the generic strengths and weaknesses of product-market positions and may help balance the business portfolio across cash flows and future growth potential. Hence, it can be a neat tool to gain a quick overview of business activities and assess cash flows for future business development.

The framework has limitations and provides misleading results if it is over-interpreted or inappropriately specified. It may disregard the fact that mature industries can be profitable with the right kind of proactive initiatives, and some argue that it caused some firms to dangerously diversify toward unrelated, high-growth business activities. The framework applies only to corporations with a diversified business portfolio so they may manage cash flows and resource allocation better. It ranks according to market share and growth rate but overlooks industry characteristics and thus is exposed to subjective assessments of future market conditions that can lead to misplaced investment in over-optimistic business activities. It ignores differentiation and product renewal opportunities and takes market conditions as a given, with little room left for entrepreneurship and innovation.

Box 5.3 Porter's dynamic model of global competitiveness

In a global context the competitive challenge is to understand why firms that originate from specific national contexts are more successful internationally than others. The success derives from dynamic capabilities in the national environments where firms compete by innovating on an ongoing basis to improve their competitive position. The ability of a national context to maintain a competitive environment depends on four general attributes: (1) the factor conditions, (2) the demand conditions, (3) the related and supporting industries, and (4) firm strategy, structure, and rivalry (see the figure below, often referred to as "the diamond").

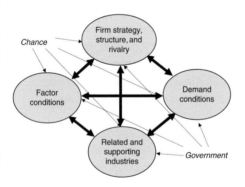

Source: adapted from Porter (1990)

The *factor conditions* refer to the fact that national economies have access to different factors of production or input factors, including labor, land, capital, infrastructure, intangible assets, etc., the relative munificence of which can provide conditions of economic advantages expressed in differentiated factor costs and availability of essential resources. The *demand conditions* in the home market affect the ability to develop competitive products and services, particularly when the market has durable growth potential and customers impose relatively demanding and sophisticated requirements that force innovation and improvement. The *related and supporting industries* are important to ensure high-quality supplies of primary inputs as well as more sophisticated semi-produce and key services that support collaborative development initiatives and improve the industrial infrastructure.

Firm strategy, structure, and *rivalry* matter because the strategic approach taken by firms in the industry must fit with the national character and customs to exploit the peculiarities of the country setting, and intense rivalry among these firms will keep them on their toes in the effort to improve and remain competitive. In addition to this, the *government* can intervene in different ways that may affect the competitiveness of firms in the country, e.g., by imposing demanding requirements on high-quality management practices, subsidizing economic activities, investing in essential economic infrastructure, research, education, etc. Furthermore, *chance* plays a role since unpredictable events create risks and opportunities that provide the background to excel in the face of competitive challenges.

The diamond framework of international competitiveness takes a different view on competition than the five forces framework. The five forces model considers the competitive forces that can enhance the firm's bargaining power and suggests ways to position the firm to gain as much as possible from this zero-sum game. The diamond model sees competition and rivalry in the national industry as a positive thing that creates value by continuously improving competitiveness to stay ahead of the game and improve firms' international competitiveness. In this model, collaboration with suppliers and customers will help create value as joint innovation advances the competitiveness of all industry participants.

Box 5.4 Strategy making at Chr. Hansen A/S

"Knowledge is our core competence and essential for us to fulfill our vision, create organizational excellence and remain competitive. Through our employees, their knowledge and contributions we reach our business goals."
[www.chr-hansen.com]

Chr. Hansen is a Danish-based multinational producer of ingredients to the food, health, and animal feed industries, drawing on expertise in bioscience and insights from the international markets where the firm operates. More than 500 million people around the world consume Chr. Hansen products every day, although the corporate name is unknown to most of them. The company is a global market leader in enzymes for cheese and cultures for dairy, wine, and meat products, and has a global market share of around 30 percent in natural colors. It has built its market position around innovative product applications, production processes, and long-term customer relationships. The corporate activities are organized in three business divisions – cultures and enzymes, health and nutrition, and natural colors – with three functional divisions focused on stakeholder relations, global sales, and finance and IT.

The multinational activities are set around overseas entities in thirty-two countries on all continents, with the largest contingents of people located in Denmark, the US, France, Germany, and Brazil. This extended global presence spans a range of unique market conditions that must be understood to gain access and fulfill the aspiration of continued growth. All the while this type of knowledge-intensive, technology-based company relies on state-of-the-art technological capabilities and ongoing development efforts. The product areas vary considerably in terms of prices, customers, practices, and industry dynamics. For example, the market for cultures has protected technologies, high entry barriers, and relatively stable factor prices, whereas the global market for colors is more competitive, commoditized, and price elastic.

The divisional structure around products signifies these differences that call for specific attention. The sales division reflects the strategic focus on international growth by expanding business relations in existing markets where local market knowledge is essential. The stakeholder relations division recognizes the importance of investors, collaborative partnerships, and not least the involvement of knowledgeable and engaged employees.

The management of the multinational corporation is built around principles of delegated responsibility in a defined structure, with clear guidelines to ensure that everyone everywhere in the organization works in the same direction toward common goals. There is a stated attempt to establish open and honest communication, free of bureaucracy and politics, with an emphasis on personal development and contribution. The strategy is rolled out through a centralized process where the HR function (part of the stakeholder relations division) ensures that all managers throughout the multinational organization are informed about the mission and planned strategic intent to give *aspiration* for the ongoing efforts to execute corporate strategy.

The HR function is used as a vehicle to link business, people, and organization in the strategy-making process. The central communication of strategic intent is a precursor for intense local workshops used to discuss strategic opportunities in the individual units as an integral part of management development. The CEO is involved in most of these workshops to help instill strategic direction and provide executive backing while giving top management a better feel for the local market challenges. The experiences from prior and new market initiatives are collected from these encounters to give *inspiration* to the strategic considerations at headquarters.

The organizational conduct is reviewed in all business units from August to December, involving all local unit managers and divisional executives to identify areas for improvement and new initiatives. The process serves to uncover new opportunities, potential problems, and "red flags" for further consideration and thereby facilitates necessary strategic adjustments. The top management team and divisional executives discuss the audit reports in January as part of the central planning process.

Source: T. J. Andersen, D. Minbaeva (2012). The role of human resource management in strategy making, SMG Working Paper, Copenhagen Business School.

Notes

1 Partially inspired by P. Ghemawat, Semiglobalization and international business strategy, *Journal of International Business Studies* 34(2): 138–152, 2002.

2 See, for example, J. D. Thompson, *Organizations in Action: Social Science Bases of Administrative Theory*, Transaction Publishers: New Brunswick, NJ (first published in 1967), 2008.

3 A. D. Chandler, *Strategy and Structure: Chapters in the History of the Industrial Enterprise*, MIT Press: Cambridge, MA, 1962.

4 R. P. Rumelt, *Strategy, Structure, and Economic Performance*, Harvard University Press: Boston, MA, 1974.

5 We may refer to *constrained related* businesses when they share product content, technologies, and various process activities within the same industry context. The *related linked* businesses have less direct sharing of content, may comprise up- and down-stream activities along the value chain, and include complementary services from within the industry value network.

6 See, for example, R. A. Bettis, Performance differences in related and unrelated diversified firms, *Strategic Management Journal* 2(4): 379–393, 1981. The examples of related and unrelated diversified firms, DuPont and Litton Industries, are included in this study and are thus representative of the findings.

7 M. H. Lubatkin, R. C. Rogers, Diversification, systematic risk, and shareholder return: A capital market extension of Rumelt's 1974 study, *Academy of Management Journal* 32(2): 454–465, 1989; C. C. Markides, Consequences of corporate refocusing: Ex ante evidence, *Academy of Management Journal* 35(2): 398–412, 1992.

8 See, for example, G. A. Jarrell, J. A. Brickley, J. M. Netter, The market for corporate control: The empirical evidence since 1980, *Journal of Economic Perspective* 2(1): 49–68, 1988; R. Morck, A. Shleifer, R. W. Vishny, Do managerial objectives drive bad acquisitions? *Journal of Finance* 45(1): 31–48, 1990; R. Roll The hubris hypothesis of corporate takeovers, *Journal of Business* 59(2): 197–216, 1986; M. H. Lubatkin, P. J. Lane, The merger mavens still have it wrong, *Academy of Management Executive* 10(1): 21–39, 1996.

9 M. E. Porter, From competitive advantage to corporate strategy, *Harvard Business Review* 65(3): 43–59, 1987.

10 B. Burrough, J. Helyar, *Barbarians at the Gate: The Fall of RJR Nabisco*, Harper & Row: New York, 1990.

11 See, for example, D. Scharfstein, The disciplinary role of takeovers, *Review of Economic Studies* 55: 185–199, 1988.

12 R. E. White, R. G. Hamermesh, Toward a model of business unit performance: An integrative approach, *Academy of Management Review* 6(2): 213–223, 1981.

13 M. Goold, A. Campbell, M. Alexander, *Corporate Level Strategy: Creating Value in the Multibusiness Company*, Wiley: New York, 1994.

14 L. E. Palich, L. B. Cardinal, C. C. Miller, Curvilinearity in the diversification-performance linkage: An examination of over three decades of research, *Strategic Management Journal* 21: 155–174, 2000.

15 C. K. Prahalad, R. A. Bettis, The dominant logic: A new linkage between diversity and performance, *Strategic Management Journal* 7(6): 485–501, 1986; R. A. Bettis, C. K. Prahalad, The dominant logic: Retrospective and extension, *Strategic Management Journal* 16(1): 5–14, 1995.

16 J. Johanson, J. E. Vahlne, The internationalization process of the firm: A model of knowledge development and increasing foreign commitments, *Journal of International Business Studies* 8(1): 23–32, 1977.

17 See S. H. Hymer, *A Study of Foreign Direct Investment*, MIT Press: Cambridge, MA, 1976.

18 See, for example, P. Buckley, The limits of explanation: Testing the internalization theory, *Journal of International Business Studies* 19: 181–194, 1988; J. H. Dunning, The determinants of international production, *Oxford Economic Papers* 25: 289–336, 1973; J. H. Dunning, The eclectic (OLI) paradigm of international production: Past, present and future, *International Journal of the Economics of Business* 2: 173–190, 2001.

19 For an authoritative presentation of key theories adopted to explain the multinational firm, see, for example, M. Forsgren, *Theories of the Multinational Firm: A Multidimensional Creature in the Global Economy*, Edward Elgar: Cheltenham, 2008.

20 See, for example, P. J. Buckley, M. C. Casson, *The Future of the Multinational Enterprise*, Macmillan: London, 1976; R. E. Caves, Industrial corporations: The industrial economics of foreign investment, *Economica* 38: 1–27, 1971; S. J. Kobrin, An empirical analysis of the determinants of global integration, *Strategic Management Journal* 12: 17–37, 1991.

21 See, for example, C. A. Bartlett, S. Ghoshal, *Managing Across Borders: The Transnational Solution* (second edn.), Random House: London, 1998; V. Govindarajan, A. K. Gupta, *The Quest for Global Dominance: Transforming Global Presence into Global Competitive Advantage*, Jossey-Bass: San Francisco, 2001; B. Kogut, U. Zander, Knowledge of the firm and the evolutionary theory of the multinational corporation, *Journal of International Business Studies* 15: 151–168, 1993; M. D. Lord, A. L. Ranft, Organizational learning about new international markets: Exploring the internal transfer of local market knowledge, *Journal of International Business Studies* 31: 573–589, 2000.

22 See, for example, A. M. Rugman, *Inside the Multinational: The Economics of International Markets*, Croom Helm: London, 1981; D. J. Teece, The multinational enterprise: Market failure and market power considerations, *Sloan Management Review* Spring: 3–17, 1981.

23 B. Kogut, Designing global strategies: Profiting from operational flexibility, *Sloan Management Review* Fall: 27–38, 1985; B. Kogut, N. Kulatilaka, Operating flexibility, global manufacturing and the open value of a multinational network, *Management Science* 40: 123–138, 1994.

24 Partly inspired by J. W. Lu, P. W. Beamish, International diversification and firm performance: The S-curve hypothesis, *Academy of Management Journal* 47(4): 598–609, 2004.

25 See, for example, G. R. Jones, C. W. L. Hill, Transaction cost analysis of strategy-structure choice, *Strategic Management Journal* 9: 159–172, 1988; K. Roth, S. O'Donnell, Foreign subsidiary compensation strategy: An agency theory perspective, *Academy of Management Journal* 39: 678–703, 1996.

26 See, for example, S. Zaheer, Overcoming the liabilities of foreignness, *Academy of Management Journal* 38: 341–363, 1996; S. Zaheer, E. Musakowski, The dynamics of the liability of foreignness: A global study of survival in financial services, *Strategic Management Journal* 18: 439–464, 1997.

27 T. J. Andersen, Multinational risk and performance outcomes: Effects of knowledge intensity and industry context, *International Business Review* 21: 239–252, 2012; T. J. Andersen, Multinational performance relationships and industry context, SMG Working Paper 15/2008, Copenhagen Business School, 2008.

28 See, for example, A. D. Chandler, The functions of the HQ unit in the multibusiness firm, *Strategic Management Journal* 12: 31–50, 1991.

29 C. K. Prahalad, G. Hamel, The core competence of the corporation, *Harvard Business Review* 68(3): 79–91, 1990.

30 A. Y. Ilinitch, C. P. Zeithaml, Operationalizing and testing Galbraith's center of gravity theory, *Strategic Management Journal* 16: 401–410, 1995.

31 M. Goold, A. Campbell, M. Alexander, *Corporate-Level Strategy: Creating Value in the Multibusiness Company*, Wiley: New York, 1994.

32 D. J. Collis, C. A. Montgomery, Creating corporate advantage, *Harvard Business Review* 76(3): 71–83, 1998. See also D. J. Collis, C. A. Montgomery, *Corporate Strategy: Resources and the Scope of the Firm*, Irwin McGraw-Hill: Boston, MA, 1997.

33 This example is drawn from Collis and Montgomery (1998) and has many commonalities with the core competencies introduced by Prahalad and Hamel (1990).

34 This example is inspired by Goold, Campbell and Alexander (1994).

35 The company ended as a diversified conglomerate by breaking into four companies: Hanson plc, Imperial Tobacco, The Energy Group and Millennium Chemicals. After Lord Hanson stepped down as chairman in 1997, the company focused on building materials and was eventually acquired to become a division of Heidelberg Cement in 2007.

36 K. M. Eisenhardt, S. L. Brown, Patching: Restitching business portfolios in dynamic markets, *Harvard Business Review* 77(3):72–82, 1999.

37 S. Karim, W. Mitchell, Innovating through acquisition and internal development: A quarter-century of boundary evolution at Johnson & Johnson, *Long Range Planning* 37: 525–547, 2004.

38 C. K. Prahalad, Y. L. Doz, *The Multinational Mission: Balancing Local Demands and Global Vision*, Free Press: New York, 1987.

39 Interestingly, we recognize the same kind of tension from the strategy discussion around the choice suggested by Michael Porter (1980) between a low-cost/high-efficiency strategy and a high-cost/differentiation strategy. This might be no coincidence since both discussions derive from scholars at the Harvard Business School.

40 P. R. Lawrence, J. W. Lorsch, Differentiation and integration in complex organizations, *Administrative Science Quarterly* 12: 1–47, 1967.

41 C. A. Bartlett, S. Ghoshal, *Managing Across Borders: The Transnational Solution* (second edn.), Random House: London, 1998; S. Leong, C. Tan, Managing across borders: An empirical test of the Bartlett and Ghoshal (1989) organizational typology, *Journal of International Business Studies* 24: 449–464, 1993; A. Harzing, An empirical analysis and extension of the Bartlett and Ghoshal typology of multinational companies, *Journal of International Business Studies* 31: 101–120, 2000.

42 P. Beamish, A. Morrison, P. Rosenzweig, A. Inkpen, *International Management: Text and Cases* (fourth edn.), Irwin McGraw-Hill: Homewood, IL, 2000; M. E. Porter, *The Competitive Advantage of Nations*, Free Press: New York, 1990; G. S. Yip, *Total Global Strategy*, Prentice Hall: Upper Saddle River, NJ, 1995.

43 T. J. Andersen, M. P. Joshi, Strategic orientations of internationalizing firms: A comparative analysis of firms operating in technology intensive and common goods industries, SMG Working Paper (WP 11/2008), Copenhagen Business School, 2008.

44 C. A. Bartlett, S. Ghoshal, J. Birkinshaw, *Transnational Management: Text, Cases, and Readings in Cross-Border Management* (fourth edn.), McGraw-Hill/ Irwin: Boston, MA, 2004.

45 J. Birkinshaw, A. Morrison, J. Hulland, Structural and competitive determinants of global integration strategy, *Strategic Management Journal* 16: 17–31, 1995; J. Johnson, An empirical analysis of the integration-responsiveness framework: US construction equipment industry firms in global competition, *Journal of International Business Studies* 26: 621–635, 1995; J. H. Taggart, Strategy shifts in MNC subsidiaries, *Strategic Management Journal* 19: 663–681, 1997; S. Veniak, D. F. Midgley, T. M. Devinney, A new perspective on the integration-responsiveness pressures confronting multinational firms, *Management International Review* 44: 15–48, 2004.

46 W. Egelhoff, Strategy and structure in multinational corporations: A revision of the Stopford and Wells model, *Strategic Management Journal* 9: 1–14, 1988; J. R. Galbraith, R. K. Kazanjian, *Strategy Implementation: Structure, Systems and Processes*, West Publishing: St. Paul, MN, 1986; M. M. Habib, B. Victor,

Strategy, structure, and performance of US manufacturing and service MNCs: A comparative analysis, *Strategic Management Journal* 12: 589–606, 1991; J. M. Stopford, L. T. Wells, *Managing the Multinational Enterprise*, Basic Books: New York, 1972.

47 M. E. Porter, *The Competitive Advantage of Nations*, Free Press: New York, 1990.

48 T. J. Andersen, N. J. Foss, Strategic opportunity and economic performance in multinational enterprises: The role and effects of information and communication technology, *Journal of International Management* 11: 293–310, 2005.

49 Y. L. Doz, C. A. Bartlett, C. K. Prahalad, Global competitive pressures and host country demands: Managing the tensions in MNCs, *California Management Review* 23(3): 63–74, 1981.

50 Y. L. Doz, J. Santos, P. Williamson, *From Global to Metanational: How Companies Win in the Knowledge Economy*, Harvard Business School Press: Boston, MA, 2001.

51 T. J. Andersen, Integrating the strategy formation process: An international perspective, *European Management Journal* 22(3): 263–272, 2004.

52 P. Jarzabkowski, J. Balogun, The practice and process of delivering integration through strategic planning, *Journal of Management Studies* 46(8): 1255–1288, 2009.

53 T. C. Ambos, U. Andersson, J. Birkinshaw, What are the consequences of initiative-taking in multinational subsidiaries? *Journal of International Business Studies* 41(7): 1099–1118, 2010.

54 T. J. Andersen, Risk implications of multinational enterprise, *International Journal of Organizational Analysis* 19: 49–70, 2011.

Learning points

- Outline the role of the strategic leader
- Discuss leadership in the integrative strategy-making process
- Consider the implications for strategic management

The previous chapters have provided a general background to strategic management and introduced a variety of models, theories, and approaches to analyze and understand the competitive dynamics that affect the strategic position of the firm. A rational analytical planning framework was used to identify superior strategic positions and uncover alternative ways to reach them as the backdrop to formulate a strategic path, or plan, to guide future actions. However, the rational planning approach is an idealized normative depiction of the strategy-making process. What actually happens when strategy is executed, or implemented, cannot be described as a linear process but is a complicated amalgam of intended actions and ongoing learning from dispersed activities pursued in different parts of the organization in response to emerging events. Hence, we outline an integrative strategy-making approach that combines central planning activities as a way to create direction and common understanding with decentralized responses in the operating entities as they react to dynamic changes around the daily transactions.

These dispersed actions taken by operating managers throughout the organization constitute small-stake/low-risk probes that experiment with new ways to perform business activities as the competitive situation changes. If the experiences from these autonomous initiatives are fed into the planning process they can give valuable information to the analysis of the evolving environmental conditions and thereby support the forward-looking strategy considerations. This interaction between central strategic planning and decentralized strategy making can form a dynamic system where experiences from ongoing activities update the common understanding of the surrounding business environment. New operating solutions are developed in various parts of the organization and become part of a strategic options reservoir that can be incorporated in the central strategy considerations. Hence, the intentionally planned and emerging responsive actions are complementary elements of corporate strategy formation and as a consequence strategic planning and ongoing learning do not represent either/or choices. There is a need for both processes and they must interact to create an effective adaptive organization. Some diversity in the firm's business activities and geographical scope is advantageous for the ability to generate innovative solutions that deal effectively with new risks and opportunities. However, it must take place across related business areas where resources, capabilities, and core competencies can be shared and communicated across specialist functions, business entities, and geographical areas. It is within this general reality of the complex strategy-making process that we must consider strategic leadership.

AES Corporation, the global power generation and distribution company headquartered in Arlington, Virginia, was a prime example of the empowered organization where frontline employees were given authority to make important decisions without top management interference.[1] However, faced with volatile energy markets and demanding economic conditions, the company fell upon hard times in the early 2000s and had to impose more structure on its business activities, with more corporate direction and discipline.[2] The company pursued an aggressive global expansion during the 1990s, heeding a loose entrepreneurial management structure, but lost economic focus in the process and was on the brink of declaring Chapter 11 in 2002. As a consequence the engagement of the corporate office was extended to trim the portfolio of overseas investments in power plants while imposing a corporate culture based on responsibility, collaboration, and individual excellence. This illustrates why there is a need to combine decentralization and local empowerment with central direction and corporate structure.

Chr. Hansen Holding (CHH) is another illustrative example. CHH was a rather successful Danish conglomerate with operations in the global food-processing and pharmaceutical industries. The company agreed to divest its food ingredients and color business to a leading private equity fund in 2005 that continued activities under the Chr. Hansen name (the company was eventually listed on the NASDAQ OMX Nordic markets exchange in 2010). The Chr. Hansen organization was considered a pleasant place to work, operating in a flat corporate structure with high trust relations. But it was also somewhat undermanaged, with little accountability and no performance culture. To unleash the human potential in this knowledge-intensive business, the acquired company engaged in a transformation process to establish a clear strategic direction and engage individual managers throughout the organization directly in the local business initiatives. That is, they retained the decentralized engagement but imposed a more focused and structured process where the local initiatives became part of a general management development process.[3] Hence, autonomy, decentralization, and empowerment in and of itself will not suffice as local and decentralized actions need direction and central coordination to work properly.

Conversely, strong central direction is also insufficient by itself. Hence, Sony Corporation, the Japanese electronics company known for its introduction of the Walkman and successful forays into flat screens, momentarily lost its competitive edge and the ability to generate innovative initiatives from within the organization. Similarly, a process-oriented focus on efficient development and production of competitive mobile phones to the world market seems to have demolished the innovative drive of Nokia Corporation, the Finnish communications company, despite its undisputed engineering skills. In dominant markets, the mobile phone was gradually becoming a flexible network-based interface with content and functionality rather than a mere communication tool. This provided inroads for new competitors such as Apple and Google that could lever their core competencies in this environment. However, these trends observed by many individuals within the company were ignored by decision makers, including top management that continued to run the business as a global manufacturer of communication devices – connecting people.

Nokia's old-time competitor, Motorola Inc., the US telecommunications company, is a good example of what can happen when strategy is formed by high-stakes investment commitments pursued centrally by top management. Motorola invested billions of dollars to create a global network of communication satellites that turned out to be a fiasco due to failed assessments of technology developments and market demand. As commented in the press, eighty-eight half-ton satellites could soon drop to Earth: "Not killer asteroids, but $4 billion worth of Iridium global communication satellites ... for which no one in the world can seem to find a use."[4] As a consequence of these digressions, Motorola lost the lead in 1998 and Nokia took over as the world's largest producer of mobile phones. But a decade later Nokia was itself outpaced by Samsung Electronics, the flagship subsidiary of the Korean Samsung Group. This shows the need to balance a central direction and forward-looking aspirations with the ability to engage managers in thoughtful execution of actions throughout the organization authorizing responsive initiatives that can probe environmental developments.

It is in this context of effective integrative strategy making that we must see the challenge of *strategic leadership*, by which we understand the key priorities of all influential decision makers in the organization, notably the top management team and members of the board of directors. That is, strategic leadership must be able to instill purpose, values, and direction into the organization and promote rational analytical capabilities to facilitate facts-based insights that can form a common understanding of the competitive reality faced by the firm. It must also set up an organizational structure that enables and facilitates autonomous initiatives by individual managers operating throughout the firm to explore new developments and experiment with responsive solutions that can work. The central planning and decentralized response processes should be combined through open (possibly technology-enhanced) communication and information systems whereby forward-looking strategic reasoning can be updated with ongoing experiential insights from the operating entities monitored by supportive management control systems. Hence, the strategic role of top management is very much about the establishment of an appropriate setting for the enterprise, with the right values and attitudes among organizational members and corporate structures, processes, and systems to support the ongoing activities they pursue.

So, strategic leadership should enable engagement of all actors throughout the organization as potentially important contributors to achieve effective strategic outcomes. This means that the strategy process driven by a strong and charismatic CEO as often portrayed in the popular press must be considered somewhat of a misnomer. The empirical evidence suggests that while charismatic executives generally are paid better, they make no difference to corporate performance. Charisma is here understood as the leader's ability to display persuasiveness, excitement, high expectations, and pursuit of a strong vision. Whereas superior organizational results often are ascribed to good leadership that strengthens the perception of the CEO's charisma, there is no evidence that strong CEO charisma by itself is associated with higher subsequent performance outcomes.[5] Similarly, extraversion, where the leader acts in a dominating, assertive, outgoing, and talkative manner, is found to work in the context of passive employees but leads to low performance when applied to proactive and engaged employees.[6] The collapse of Lehman Brothers in September 2008 vividly illustrates what can happen when a dominant executive is able to create a powerful position.[7]

According to Collins and Hansen: "The best leaders we studied did not have a visionary ability to predict the future ... they were more disciplined, more empirical, and more paranoid."[8] Therefore, the painstaking truth is probably less glamorous and more engrained in a persistent focus and relentless effort to steadily improve things in a highly competitive environment. As Mintzberg argues: "Great enterprises are built slowly and thoughtfully by people who are fully engaged."[9] This means that it takes time to form an appropriate corporate setting with a structure that engages everyone in the process of uncovering appropriate strategic moves. So, the owners, and the managers they engage throughout the organization on their behalf, should have the patience to find the right solutions without aiming for unwarranted shortcuts in pursuit of short-term gains. It also means that top management should extend the scope from being the main source of a "strategic plan" to be more concerned with a corporate setting that can engage everyone in the organization to act and search for the right strategic path in an uncertain environment. In other words, there should be a stronger tie between the strategy-making process and the actual doings in various parts of the organization where managers engage in the transactions employees conduct as they interact with important stakeholders. As suggested by Mintzberg, it is important to "get managers out of their offices, away from their meetings, and into the places where their organization serves its basic purpose."[10] Setting the stage for the integrative strategy-making process should enable this fruitful interaction between thoughtful central reasoning and decentralized activities where the daily business is transacted.

Cynthia Montgomery claims: "Strategy has lost breadth and stature. It has become more about formulation than implementation, and more about getting the idea right at the outset than living with a strategy over time."[11] To get away from this and emphasize the longer-term evolution of strategy, strategic leadership has to impose a corporate structure and decision processes that enable the organization to form a common sense of direction as its members work to accommodate current customer needs. All the while, organizational members should be cognizant of subtle changes in market requirements and continuously work to find better responses to new competitive challenges. Hence, a common trait of successful companies seems to be their consistency of actions throughout the organization where less successful companies seem much more inclined to pursue aggressive and centrally imposed growth initiatives.[12] The entrepreneurial view of strategy making (discussed in Chapter 3) suggests that operating and functional managers act as corporate entrepreneurs who respond to the emerging opportunities they encounter and find new solutions to the changing competitive conditions.

So, it is argued that entrepreneurial organizations should act by taking small, exploratory steps, learn from them incrementally, and then gradually extend the product/service offerings and internal practices from the insights gained along the way.[13] This reflects a firm-level perspective that applies to a relatively small entrepreneurial organization whereas the challenge becomes different as the company grows in size and complexity. Then the question is more how to facilitate effective business expansion in an organization comprised of an increasingly complex set of operating functions with many functional experts. In this situation it makes sense to engage individual managers throughout the organization in a kind of "effectuation" approach that takes form as small-stakes experimental probes when they encounter new risks and opportunities. As individual managers gain experiential insights from these decentralized responsive ventures they should be agglomerated and incorporated into the forward-looking strategy analysis for the firm, or corporation, as a whole. That is, an important challenge for strategic leadership is to form the dynamic link between the ongoing actions taken by lower-level managers in the organization and the forward-looking considerations performed at the executive level.

The CEO and the top management team are located at the corporate center and assume the formal responsibility for all business activities that take place in the many parts of the organization. We know that the executives at the center and the operating managers in charge of specific business and functional responsibilities spend an inordinate amount of their time trying to collect information from within and around the organization.[14] These reconnaissance efforts are often highly unstructured and informal, conducted on the fly as a way to gather what is going on in the firm and its surrounding business environment. Much of this information is obtained through oral communication and stored in a nonverbal tacit form that constitutes privileged information assembled by the individual managers themselves. So, the managers scan their immediate environments and monitor ongoing activities within their areas of responsibility for their own purposes. But they also share these insights in internal conversations and thereby disseminate observations through the internal communication networks. However, the CEO and the top management team and the operating managers reporting to them have only a limited sight of all the things that go on inside the firm, including actions taken by employees at the periphery of the organization as they deal with various external stakeholders (Figure 6.1).

The many and varied activities that go on every day throughout the organization can be managed directly, indirectly through people, or by managing information as the basis for requests for adaptive actions. That is, the available information can be managed in a way that influences the actions taken by employees.

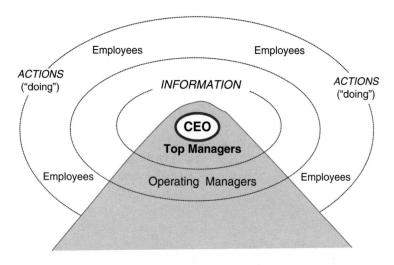

Figure 6.1 The CEO and the organization. Inspired by Mintzberg *et al.* (2003)

However, managing by information is passive, indirect, and two steps removed from where the action takes place and where the actual "doing" of things is performed. In other words, there is little current information and substantial distance between managerial decisions and the updated insights derived from the ongoing activities. An alternative is to manage through people, or operating managers, who are closer to the real actions but still one step removed from the actual doings. This is achieved by imposing a corporate structure with general policies, assigned responsibilities, and decision authority distributed to lower-level managers and employees. This brings management closer to the real actions where environmental insights can be updated through intense communication and interactive controls. Finally, management can be directly involved in all the ongoing doings of individual employees.[15] However, direct interference is not realistic or warranted in a complex organization where knowledgeable individuals handle things. The remoteness of information management also has limitations. So, the appropriate solution is a decentralized decision structure with open communication channels and interactive controls that integrate updated insights from actions taken within the organization with the forward-looking considerations performed at the corporate center. This set-up complies with a claim that "the real planning of organizations takes place significantly in the heads of its managers and implicitly in the context of their daily actions."[16]

Hence, the insights obtained from responsive lower-level initiatives dispersed throughout the organization can contribute with updated knowledge that can enhance the analytical efforts to understand the changing competitive environment. So, where effectuation in (corporate) entrepreneurship may suggest that strategy formation is based on *acting* and *creating* rather than on engaging in *thinking* and *analysis*, it actually introduces a false dichotomy.[17] The two strategy perspectives do not represent an either/or choice; instead they must co-exist and complement each other. Hence, we see the strategic leadership challenge as commensurate with the ability to orchestrate central planning and decentralized response processes at the same time and have them interact. That is, the doing, learning, and development loops at the individual management level provide new insights and experiences around activities conducted in the organization close to the real actions and daily transactions with influential stakeholders. The rational analysis to consider and coordinate forward-looking strategic actions is performed centrally around the strategic apex of the organization and should ideally be informed by the ongoing experiential insights from the dispersed responsive initiatives. Hence, an important aspect of the strategic leadership challenge is to organize the strategy-making processes and supportive management information systems in ways that effectively integrate the central and decentralized process elements.

Strategic leadership should be focused on strategy formulation as well as the ensuing decision-making processes driven by strategic intent as well as adaptive responses to emerging events. This is effectively how strategic outcomes are formed by actions taken in different parts of the organization. It speaks for a central process that engages organizational members in the development of a common understanding of the competitive situation and the strategic intent in dealing with it as a necessary motivation for ongoing execution of planned actions and responsive initiatives. Therefore, strategic leadership should support a central planning process that drives strategic intent as well as enabling and engaging organizational members in the pursuit of flexible and meaningful execution of strategic actions. As John Pisapia argues: "Strategic leadership is not just within the purview of executives as traditionalists suggest. It must reach to the lowest levels of the organization."[18] So, what is the key strategic role of corporate executives? Is it the role of the focused strategist and inspirer? Is it the role of the instigator and engaged analyst? Is it the role of the organizer and process facilitator? Is it the role of orchestrator, motivator, and comforter? Well, the preceding discussion suggests that it comprises elements of all these categories, which obviously makes the challenge so much more complicated.

The strategic leadership role is not accomplished by formulating the corporate strategy and then retreating to "official" duties while leaving it to organizational members to implement the planned actions. As we discussed in Chapter 3, strategy implementation often fails because executives disengage from the ensuing execution of activities that need close attention and follow-up. Yet, executives are heavily influenced by previous experiences that color their views and limit their sense-making abilities where they use analogies to make strategic decisions.[19] That is, managerial decision makers are often distorted by different biases that can lead to bad decisions and "important decisions made by intelligent, responsible people with the best information and intentions are sometimes hopelessly flawed."[20] So, executives should not dominate important decisions but must be challenged by the deep insights of relevant operating managers and updated environmental insights from the actions taken by individual employees operating in the periphery of the organization. Hence, a leadership style that actively seeks the opinions of managers and promotes new ideas and experimentation throughout the organization is found to have a positive moderating effect on corporate performance.[21] However, there are many barriers to gaining management knowledge through dispersed experimentation because "companies tend to adopt practices in an all or nothing way – either the CEO is behind it so everyone does it, or at least claim to do it, or it isn't tried at all."[22] In other words, there is a true strategic leadership challenge associated with the ability to restrain undue influence while attracting the right expertise to partake in the decision-making process as well as encourage experimentation that can create important insights into the competitive environment.

The potential executive mistakes are nowhere better displayed than in the corporate acquisitions history, where even experienced senior executives can get caught up in the hype and glamour around major investment transactions and lose track of the underlying strategic rationale. Major acquisitions are, due to their size, typically confined to secretive and secluded discussions among senior officials and important people but with little involvement from the holders of the core competencies and key insights in the organization. A typical argument in favor of the acquisitions is that there are significant synergies to be gained, either associated with major savings from joint and streamlined administrative and operational functions, or through combined efforts of seemingly compatible core competencies that can lead to new, promising market opportunities. However, the savings rarely materialize as predicted and the prospective market gains often fall short.

The synergy argument applies to many other cost-saving and business-enhancing initiatives imposed by corporate headquarters. However, if corporate executives took a more balanced and skeptical view on these important strategic initiatives, many mistakes could be avoided.[23] Goold and Campbell claim that corporate executives are exposed to four essential biases: a synergy bias, a parenting bias, a skills bias, and an upside bias. These biases can make executives believe that significant economic synergies exist, that head office must coordinate activities to exploit superior competencies in the corporation, and that the prospective gains are significant, even if this might not be the case. But rather than adopting a disciplined approach to evaluate whether the economic synergies actually exist and can be realized, the proposals are often seen as a justification for the executive function itself. "It reflects executives' real fear that they would be left without a role if they were not able to promote coordination, standardization, and other links among the various businesses they control." As a consequence, the desperate urge to seek corporate synergies can drive executives to make unwise investment decisions without consulting the expertise available inside the organization. The need to engage in organizational restructuring seems overrated, where the criteria instead should be to provide the context for sound decision-making processes that can ensure superior performance outcomes. Hence, the managerial decisions made in different parts of the organization are part and parcel of good strategy execution and corporate performance.[24]

There is a need to balance the decision processes so the strategic directions formed through the central analytical planning considerations incorporate relevant knowledge and expertise from organizational members. It is also important that this information is updated by current insights gained from responsive initiatives taken throughout the organization where managers explore new ways to deal with emerging challenges. These organizations let their employees operate under broad goals and high aspirations, with active participation in essential decisions while giving some freedom to develop new opportunities. This calls for a more dynamic role of the financial management function where resources can be allocated in flexible processes with room to maneuver rather than being restrained by rigid procedures.[25] But executives can still be in the way for a more open and engaged leadership style if they feel a need to be in direct control of all activities. If top management imposes its own ideas without proper consultation, it disregards valuable expertise inside the organization and exposes itself to executive biases. Hence, a lack of enthusiasm among employees is not necessarily a sign of unwillingness to cooperate but may rather express a genuine concern for the viability of proposed actions. The operating managers may simply find that the arguments behind the executive decisions are wrong. According to Goold and Campbell: "If business-unit managers choose not to cooperate, they usually have good reasons."[26] Therefore, the strategic leadership challenge of top managers may also entail the ability to overcome professional pride and possibly adopt a more subdued role.[27]

There are good examples of successful organizations being led by these types of executives. The former CEO of Colgate Palmolive, Reuben Mark, who retired from the company in 2007 after spending twenty-three years at the helm, was heralded as one of the most successful CEOs while remaining unknown to the public.[28] He did not do interviews or go on TV because he felt that celebrity was incompatible with business leadership and that magazine profiling would take away credit from those who worked in the company. "Colgate, under Mark, has been a case study in an old-school brand of management – one that emphasizes execution over grand strategy, continual improvement over bet-the-company adventures, and teamwork over celebrity."[29] Hence, the key to success came through incremental and consistent gains through continuous improvement and financial discipline while paying tribute to innovative initiatives taken by employees around the world to achieve these gains.

Another example is the leadership of Nucor Corporation, the large steel producer headquartered in Charlotte, North Carolina. The former CEO of Nucor, Ken Iverson, did not condone executive perks, was accessible, and answered his own phone. The corporate structure gave almost complete autonomy to the business entities but at the same time had an active and free exchange of ideas and solutions across geographical and functional boundaries. According to Iverson: "Our goal is to just let people go ahead and *do* things."[30] The company to this day retains a strong culture focused on customer service and technological innovation that gives common direction and a decentralized management structure with performance pay and equal benefits that ensure collaborative engagement and experimentation to improve. In the company's own words: "Nucor Corporation is made up of 11900 teammates whose goal is to 'Take Care of Our Customers.'" The management control system is simple, with a weekly summary sheet per entity combined with the ability to engage in informal communication as and when it is considered necessary. Hence, the decentralized structure pushes the power to make decisions of strategic importance down to the business entities as they take responsive actions and invest in new activities geared toward the market.

However, getting the right balance between a central structure without a stifling bureaucracy of rigid rule-based procedures and a flexible decentralized structure where engaged employees have leeway to respond to emerging events is not easy. As discussed in Chapter 4, John Chambers, the CEO of Cisco Systems, observed a need to deal with an identified shift toward a more collaborative networked environment and decided to impose an elaborate structure of councils, boards, and working groups of key managers to deal with new business propositions. The idea was that the new set-up would reduce the direct pressures on top management to make the many and diverse resource-committing decisions by involving relevant managers with a diversity of insights and expertise in the ongoing assessment of important strategic initiatives.[31] Chambers argued: "I'm a command-and-control guy ... but that's not the future. The future's going to be all around collaboration and teamwork, with a structured process behind it."[32] While this sounds highly plausible, the result of the exercise was a rather time-consuming decision process with somewhat diffuse responsibilities that obscured clear communication lines and fast responsive decisions to amend action plans. As a consequence this decision structure was eventually abandoned and replaced by a central control structure supported by management information systems, leaving room for local initiatives and inputs.

The durable and successful business enterprises, such as Colgate Palmolive and Nucor Corporation, seem to excel around core business activities defined by product, customer, and technology commonalities as the basis for building and extending their competitive advantage. Hence it is argued that sustainable value creation can draw on common capabilities in technical know-how, business processes, and information management.[33] This is consistent with the findings from three decades of research around the multinational corporation where the evidence attests that some business diversity within related business activities is superior to unrelated diversification and a dominant business focus. We also deduced that some geographical diversification has similar effects, particularly in areas that are less capital intensive, as it gives new market insights and access to different competencies. These effects can arguably derive from creativity and innovation where a degree of diversity provides new combinations of skills and competencies that have not hitherto been available to the firm and thereby enhance development of better product offerings and business processes. These diversification effects can be achieved fairly quickly through a relatively low number of diverse business activities and locations, e.g., 3–4 businesses or geographical regions.[34] However, it requires that these diverse areas have commonalities that make it possible to communicate and exchange knowledge in ways that are generally understood among organizational members at all levels and in all functions.

So, focused growth with some diversity in business and geographical scope seems like the appropriate recipe. Collins found little evidence to suggest that lack of innovation was a cause for the fall of great companies. Instead he confirmed what he refers to as "Packard's Law," named after the founder of Hewlett-Packard: "A great company is more likely to die of indigestion from too much opportunity than starvation from too little." Furthermore, his study of failing companies suggests that "exceptional enterprise depends first and foremost upon having self-managed and self-motivated people."[35] In other words, it points toward a focus on corporate business development supported by a few core competencies operated within a structure of engaged participation by key employees with freedom to pursue initiatives that can respond to emerging business opportunities. The corporate focus is also supported by what Simons referred to as belief systems and boundary systems (see Chapter 4). The belief systems derive from core values revealed in the corporate culture that pinpoint what the firm is about, what it prioritizes, and what the common aspirations are for organizational members. All these things are normally expressed as part of a mission statement. The boundary systems outline the risks to avoid and the type of activities and transactions the firm expressly will not entertain. The content to both of these systems derives from the rational analytical strategy process discussed in Chapter 2 as part of a central planning approach and thus provides important guidance and direction for organizational members when they act and respond in the face of emerging risks and opportunities.

It is not surprising, then, when Zook and Allen find that employee loyalty and commitment are driven by "a belief in the values of the management team and the organization's strategy" and that this is important to achieve sustainable performance. They generally find that successful firms are characterized by developed systems to learn from experimentation that drives continuous improvement across the business activities. These approaches can be repeated and transferred in corporations that have a focus on related businesses activities.[36] IKEA, the Swedish home products company, Tetra Pak, the Swedish food packaging and processing company, LEGO Systems, the Danish toy manufacturing company, Nike, the US-based clothing, footwear, sportswear, and equipment supplier, and Apple are all used to exemplify these types of successful companies. One common trait is that they stay close to their core activities and gain sustainable performance through gradual expansion of business activities and continuous improvement in product offerings and internal processes. If they diverge from the focused approach, this has adverse performance effects. However, one should keep in mind that particularly in overseas expansion it can be quite challenging to transpose an existing, well-functioning business model developed in a familiar market context onto another region where the economic infrastructure and behaviors are different. Consider, for example, the challenges associated with Dell Computer's forays into the Chinese market and Wal-Mart's business expansion in South America and Europe.

Hence, it makes sense to shed distracting business activities that are outside the scope of what the core competencies can support, and many firms fail when they digress into unrelated activities, even though it may be done in the name of pursuing new, innovative paths.[37] Durable business activities must come from within, driven by people engaged in the daily transactions and who can see where the corporate capabilities make a difference while trying out new approaches and solutions as the surroundings change. So, learning from responsive initiatives pursued throughout the organization can bring important experiential insights and form viable solutions that become strategic options for future corporate maneuvering. That is, frontline employees can become an important source of updated strategic information that any company can obtain, if they manage it consciously.[38] Accordingly, the strategic leadership challenge is associated with an ability to enable decentralized experimentation within a framework of direction and core values while at the same time exploiting good solutions found through trial and error, supported by central, forward-looking strategy considerations. This also

entails the use of appropriate management controls, such as
interactive control systems proposed by Simons that can create
a dynamic interaction between insights gained from dispersed
initiatives and central planning considerations (see Chapter 4).
The corporate structure should be supported by technology-driven
communication and information-processing capabilities to
facilitate the informal interaction between central analytical
processes and responsive peripheral processes in many parts of
the organization.

Apart from setting up the appropriate structure, processes, and
systems that can support effective managerial decision making
at all levels and parts of the organization, it is necessary to focus
on the belief systems and core values that guide these human
interventions throughout the firm. The corporate culture largely
determines accepted behaviors in the organization and is
influenced and even shaped by executive behaviors.[39] So, acting
according to the prescribed principles is an essential part of the
strategic leadership challenge. That is, the priorities preached and
practiced by executives reflect the particular leadership style
and in turn shape the organizational climate that circumscribes the
way operating activities are carried out in the firm. Among other
things, this reflects whether top management instills a culture
that seeks active participation, allows individual experimentation,
and encourages creativity, new ideas, and collaborative learning
while accepting that failure is possible as a way to learn and
improve. It also reflects a management control and monitoring
system that is proactive and linked to incentive practices
that reward people accordingly. The development of these
underlying values, priorities, and strategic aspirations is implied
in formulating a mission statement as the initial steps of the
central planning process (Figure 6.2).

While structure, processes, and systems will affect the way
people can act and interact throughout the organization, the
cultural and behavioral aspects play an important role as well.
Adair suggests that good leaders balance three basic needs in
organizations: task accomplishment, group unity, and individual
human needs.[40] Since the needs are overlapping, improvements in
one area will affect the other areas and the system can become
self-reinforcing. That is, achieving common goals and aspirations

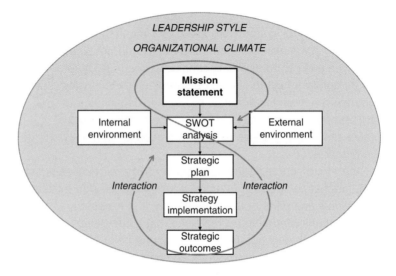

Figure 6.2 Creating the appropriate corporate context

raises morale and motivation, the ensuing team spirit and good internal communication increase individual satisfaction, which in turn enhances performance to achieve better outcomes, etc.

Based on Charles Darwin's theories about human evolution, Lawrence argues that human beings are designed to work in groups and that we evolved as a successful social species through collective learning by trusting, protecting, and caring for each other to the benefit of all. Hence, the motivation and creative engagement of individuals depend on whether all the elements of this social structure are nurtured, which implicitly speaks to the strategic leadership challenge. Those who climb to the leadership positions of higher formal authority as members of the top management team and the board of directors should take this into account. According to Lawrence, then, good leadership tries to satisfy four essential human drives: to acquire, to comprehend, to bond, and to defend. That is, human needs go beyond acquiring wealth and material things as may typically be the focus in rational economic analyses. Human curiosity and social needs, including an inherent sense of justice and fairness, must also be considered to create a proper context for sustainable value creation based on human contributions. The ability to fulfill the four drives for everyone will affect the way all individuals in the organization act and contribute. Hence, *bad leadership* arises when top managers satisfy their own four drives but disregard the needs of the followers and all the dependent organizational members.[41] Since the real organizational actions happen deep within and around the edges of the organization based on things performed by individual employees, these concerns are important. Employees perform the things that enact strategic aims as they deal with external stakeholders such as customers, suppliers, partners, and competitors, and deal with other internal stakeholders to perform the operating processes that ensure efficient delivery and handling of products and services.

In discussing *good leadership* around the Manhattan Project that developed the atomic bomb during World War Two, Bennis and Biederman explain how Oppenheimer, who led the scientific work, "created an atmosphere of excitement, enthusiasm, and high intellectual and moral purpose."[42] This provided an important organizational context that was conducive to a successful engagement with exceptional contributions from the knowledgeable individuals involved in the project. In other words, striving for a higher moral purpose has motivational effects, and accordingly a focus on responsible behavior can also motivate stronger individual efforts. Conversely, allowing "irresponsible" corporate behaviors and pushing hard for short-term gains can have adverse economic effects, at least as time goes by. Not only will it demotivate employees but it also has direct economic downsides. If, for example, the gains have been obtained at the expense of other stakeholders, one can be pretty sure that these relationships will turn sour sooner or later. Just think about how in 1999 Coca-Cola's reputation and sales suffered in Europe when people, mostly schoolchildren, fell ill in Belgium after drinking contaminated products. Similarly, if immediate economic benefits are obtained through diseconomies, such as polluting the environment, that impose future costs on society, it can create significant economic liabilities. Consider, for example, how the Swiss–Swedish engineering giant ABB (Asea Brown Boveri) was on the brink of insolvency in 2002 due to the asbestos liabilities of its US business unit, Combustion Engineering, acquired in 1999. In addition, there may be potential benefits in the form of economic gains derived from improved energy efficiencies, sustainable access to key resources, and general benefits ascribed to higher reliability among customers and public trust. (See Box 6.1 *Strategic leadership in the Danish maritime sector.*)

The *United Nations Global Compact* is a policy initiative committed to inducing corporate businesses to abide by ten universal principles in the areas of human rights, labor conditions, environment, and anti-corruption.[43] It asks for compliance with basic human rights and that there is freedom of association, no forced labor, no child labor, no discrimination, and no corruption. It further pleads for adopting precautionary environmental approaches and promoting greater environmental responsibility that encourages the use of environmentally friendly technologies. However, environmental protection is often seen as an extra burden to business, but the expenses to reduce pollution may be partly or completely offset by higher revenues from differentiated quality products and reduced costs of materials, energy, capital, and labor.[44] In general, adopting the broader concerns for responsible corporate behaviors into strategy analysis can help reduce potential costs in the future by taking better precautions and imposing better strategic risk-management efforts (see Chapter 2). Some recent studies have indeed found that improved environmental risk management has associated benefits reflected in lower cost of capital.[45]

Hence, it is argued that contemporary organizations must be "adaptable, innovative, and socially responsible, as well as operationally excellent."[46] This requires a corporate context or an organizational environment where all employees are given the freedom to collaborate, innovate, and excel. In this context the strategic leadership role of top management is to create purpose, direction, and supportive values, but it is not to formulate strategy and detailed plans for others to follow. Rather it has to do with creating the conditions whereby new strategic initiatives can emerge and evolve through the engagement of individual employees within the organization. This obviously calls for organizational backing in the form of appropriate structure, processes, and systems, combined with a leadership style that supports engagement, experimentation, and learning from failure. It implies that power is dispersed to lower-level decision nodes

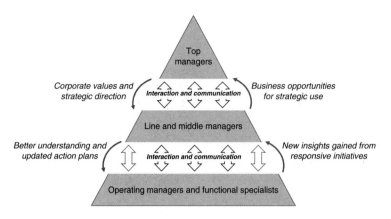

Figure 6.3 Leading the strategic interaction loops

closer to where the real actions take place. It implies that the decentralized decision-making processes are enhanced by effective communication and information-processing capabilities. It also implies the adoption of interactive management control systems that facilitate faster updates to central strategy considerations from current responses taken in the local entities. Hence, it generally implies that there is an interacting loop between the overarching purpose and aims of top management, expressed as corporate values and strategic direction, and the business opportunities identified by operating managers in the functional entities as potential strategic solutions (Figure 6.3).

There is also an interacting loop between the line and middle managers who report to the top management team and the operational managers and functional specialists who operate throughout the different parts of the organization. The middle managers are involved in the ongoing interpretation of the overarching strategic direction as they pan out in updated action plans for all intended activities based on new insights obtained from open communication with lower-level managers who are close to the daily transactions. Hence, there is an important role to be played by all managers within the organization at all levels and all locations to participate actively in the decision-making processes and engage in frequent communication and exchange of updated information.[47] That is, in larger organizations there is a need to actively engage layers of operational and middle managers who can link top management to the operational activities within the organization and all the way to the actions and initiatives taken by the frontline employees close to the external stakeholders.

While we present this as a primary responsibility of top managers, we should not forget that all CEOs, at least in principle, depend on their board of directors. That is, corporate governance matters. It is important to have a diverse and balanced membership in the board that can engage and challenge the thinking of the executive decision makers and thereby avoid the most blatant effects of potential cognitive biases and flaws.[48] We have argued for the importance of involving key managers in strategic decisions as well as staying updated on dispersed responsive initiatives taken by lower-level employees as potential sources for new emerging strategies. However, for this to work properly also requires understanding among board directors, many of whom continue to see strategic management as a high-level command-and-control exercise. The board of directors should be equally interested in receiving frequent updates on environmental interpretations from the ongoing experimental activities pursued throughout the organization rather than primarily letting strategy discussions center around what has recently been heard in other high-echelon circles.

Unfortunately, the often singular focus on aligning the interests between top management and the company shareholders as the essential stakeholder group, for example, by issuing stock options and the like, provides a limiting view of the strategic leadership challenge. In the worst of cases this will lead to Mintzberg's caricature of strategic leadership where "the CEO decrees the desired results, and everyone else has to run around meeting them – no matter what the consequences."[49] So, we need to move toward a governance system where both top management and board members on behalf of the owners engage in open and fruitful strategy discussions involving operating managers broadly informed by updated insights from the frontline employees who execute the corporate business activities. This should give access to more nuanced and relevant information to challenge conventional wisdom that may color executive decisions. According to Pfeffer and Sutton: "Most corporate disasters … happened not simply because these people were greedy, immoral, or unethical people, but because such people were in leadership positions with so much control that no one could challenge them or raise questions."[50]

So, what can we say to round off the strategic management topic in a proper manner? Well, borrowing from Rumelt, we can argue that "bad strategy abounds" where top managers fail to identify and deal with the real issues but rather pursue visionary goals without logical underpinnings and garnered with catchy buzzwords.[51] We suggest that adherence to a rational analytical and facts-based strategy formulation process can help avoid the major pitfalls of this kind of false strategizing. In fact, this framework can be applied as the analytical backdrop to all major resource-committing decisions and as a way to deal with identified strategic issues. The empirical evidence clearly indicates that there are benefits associated with forward-looking analytical thinking as a basis for forming strategic direction and focus with a common understanding of the competitive situation, particularly under turbulent business conditions. However, there also needs to be broad inclusion of relevant internal managerial insights and expertise around important decisions, with sufficient leeway to allow individual initiatives in response to emerging risks and opportunities that eventually will uncover the solutions for tomorrow. Particularly the dynamic interaction between central, forward-looking strategic reasoning and updated insights gained from dispersed business initiatives should be emphasized as a way to identify relevant adaptive moves that can renew the corporate strategy in response to changing environmental conditions. It also provides the underlying integrating processes to streamline corporate activities and coordinate adaptive responses assumed to achieve the overarching strategic aims.

Conclusion

Strategic leadership is often equated with executive ambition, excellence, passion, vision, foresight, or a well-articulated plan with a meticulous outline of the necessary steps to success. However, this is false. The central feature of *strategic leadership* is rather to establish an organizational setting that is conducive to an effective integrative strategy-making process. Hence, the strategic leadership role is to create an interactive dynamic where a central, forward-looking understanding of the strategic direction embedded in genuine analyses can guide decentralized strategy making where alternative voices are heard and autonomous initiatives are encouraged as a way to explore new ways. This organizational setting builds on structure, processes, and systems that provide frequent updates to the central strategy interpretation and facilitates ongoing responses to emerging events and circumstances.

Box 6.1 Strategic leadership in the Danish maritime sector

The Danish maritime sector fell upon hard times in the 1970s as high oil prices and slow international economic growth imposed new challenges on industry players. However, the companies in the industry were able to respond to the challenge and made substantial changes over the next three decades to significantly enhance the status of the sector. The following reflects some observations to explain this development.

The leading Danish shipping companies showed an ability to respond to new market opportunities with a willingness to invest in business expansion. Investments were tailored to specific segments and to develop related activities in infrastructure such as ports, terminals, cargo handling, logistics, ground transportation, document and administrative systems. The expansion built on strong relationships with international partners through personal friendships, giving insights and knowledge across the global maritime industry. Alliances with partners created cultural compatibility and better integration of cross-border acquisitions. Corporate values emphasized customer focus, modesty, humbleness, trustworthiness, credibility, professionalism, reliability, and quality, with room for individuality and cultural differences. Openness for change made it possible to make swift and smooth business transitions. The leadership style was trust-based, with personal relationships across important stakeholder groups where empathetic traits allowed inclusion of helpful expertise.

The good results were favored by some foresight and doses of good "luck" where luck may be more manageable than we think as it often comes to those who pursue it. Hence, we can learn to live with uncertainty by dropping the "illusion of control" and accepting uncertain conditions as a future full of opportunities.[1] So, foresight and luck may be related to a particular leadership style of dealing with the unknown. Lucky people seem to maintain strong networks because that is how new opportunities arise and are discovered.[2] They appear to be calm, which increases their chances of seeing and identifying opportunities, and they are open to new experiences. That is, they are open to learn and experiment and thereby find new ways to conduct business and deal with change, which is commensurate with a leadership style conducive to exploring and exploiting opportunities.

The companies had strong corporate values, with clear ideas of an overarching purpose setting priorities for preferred practices and inspiring constructive efforts to advance business activities. Another leadership trait was an inclusive international pursuit of business opportunities based on collaboration between related sectors with complementary operations. These activities formed a regional center for commercial ship operations based on commercial interactions among brokers, charterers, shipyards, component suppliers, service providers, etc. This helped the development of an industry cluster with diverse maritime services, including environmental technologies and instruments, radio transmission and satellite communication, shipbroker services, logistics systems, maintenance, base supplies, etc.

The positive results seem to derive from leadership traits that consider a broad set of constituents and engaging them in business networks around common value-creating aims through inclusion. The premise is that we as human beings accomplish things in groups where both the need for relationships and a craving to understand are essential drivers of human activity. The ability to learn and evolve is associated with ongoing decision-making and action outcomes in all parts of the organization and in all segments of the industry. So, many people must be involved and motivated as durable results depend on collaboration between people who can bond across a broader set of activities and experiences. Hence, good leadership influences important stakeholders to take actions toward certain ends while ensuring a balance between the core needs and drivers of all the constituents.

Source: T. J. Andersen (2011) *Lessons from Corporate Leadership in the Danish Maritime Sector*, The Danish Maritime Foundation.

[1] S. Makridakis, R. Hogarth, A. Gaba (2009) *Dance with Chance: Making Luck Work for You,* Oneworld Publications: Oxford.

[2] R. Wiseman (2004) *The Luck Factor,* Arrow Books: London.

Notes

1 S. Wetlaufen, Organizing for empowerment: An interview with AES's Roger Sant and Dennis Bakke, *Harvard Business Review* 77(1): 111–123, 1999.

2 M. M. Hamilton, AES's new power center: Struggling utility overhauls corporate (lack of) structure, *Washington Post*, Monday, June 2, 2003.

3 T. J. Andersen, D. Minbaeva, The role of human resource management in strategy making, SMG Working Paper, Copenhagen Business School, 2012.

4 K. Sawyer, Hanging up on a network of satellites, *Washington Post*, Tuesday, August 29, 2000.

5 B. R. Agle *et al.*, Does CEO charisma matter? An empirical analysis of the relationships among organizational performance, environmental uncertainty, and top management team perceptions of CEO charisma, *Academy of Management Journal* 49(1): 161–174, 2006.

6 A. M. Grant *et al.*, Reversing the extraverted leadership advantage: The role of employee proactivity, *Academy of Management Journal* 54(3): 528–550, 2011.

7 Lehman's CEO Richard Fuld was among the highest paid executives in America and actually received a bonus of US$22 million six months before the bank collapsed. See T. J. Andersen, Case: Lehman Brothers (B), Copenhagen Business School (available through the European Case Clearing Corporation – ECCH), 2010.

8   J. Collins, M. T. Hansen, *Great by Choice: Uncertainty, Chaos, and Luck – Why Some Thrive Despite Them All*, Random House Business Books: London, 2011.

9   H. Mintzberg, Opinon: Productivity is killing American enterprise, *Harvard Business Review* 85(4): 25, 2007.

10 H. Mintzberg, *Managing*, FT Prentice Hall: Harlow, 2009.

11 C. A. Montgomery, Putting leadership back into strategy, *Harvard Business Review* 86(1): 54–60, 2008.

12 J. Collins, M. T. Hansen, *Great by Choice: Uncertainty, Chaos, and Luck – Why Some Thrive Despite Them All*, Random House Business Books: London, 2011.

13 P. Sims, *Little Bets: How Breakthrough Ideas Emerge from Small Discoveries*, Random House Business Books: London, 2011; J. A. Schlesinger, C. F. Kiefer, *Just Start: Take Action, Embrace Uncertainty, Create the Future*, Harvard Business Review Press: Boston, MA, 2012.

14 See, for example, H. Mintzberg, *The Nature of Managerial Work*, Harper & Row: New York, 1973.

15 H. Mintzberg *et al.*, *The Strategy Process: Concepts, Contexts, Cases* (fourth edn.), Pearson Prentice Hall: Upper Saddle River, NJ, 2003.

16 H. Mintzberg, *Managing*, FT Prentice Hall: Harlow, 2009.

17 It is argued that *acting* and *creating* are the proper ways to engage in entrepreneurial strategy making. See J. A. Schlesinger, C. F. Kiefer, *Just Start: Take Action, Embrace Uncertainty, Create the Future*, Harvard Business Review Press: Boston, MA, 2012.

18 J. R. Pisapia, *The Strategic Leader: New Tactics for a Globalizing World*, IAP – Information Age Publishing: Charlotte, NC, 2009.

19 G. Gavetti, J. W. Rivkin, How strategists really think: Tapping the power of analogy, *Harvard Business Review* 83(4): 54–63, 2005.

20 A. Campbell *et al.*, Why good leaders make bad decisions, *Harvard Business Review* 87(2): 60–66, 2009.

21 S. S. Torp, Employee stock ownership: Effect on strategic management and performance, PhD dissertation, Copenhagen Business School, 2011.

22 J. Pfeffer, R. I. Sutton, *Hard Facts, Dangerous Half-Truths and Total Nonsense*, Harvard Business School Press: Boston, MA, 2006.

23 M. Goold, A. Campbell, Desperately seeking synergy, *Harvard Business Review* 76(5): 131–143, 1998.

24 M. W. Blenko *et al.*, *Decide & Deliver: 5 Steps to Breakthrough Performance in Your Organization*, Harvard Business School Press: Boston, MA, 2010.

25 S. Caudron, The amoeba corporation, *Business Finance*, April 1, 2000.

26 M. Goold, A. Campbell, Desperately seeking synergy, *Harvard Business Review* 76(5): 131–143, 1998.

27 This obviously does not imply that top management should refrain from monitoring and controlling performance developments throughout the organization, but it rather suggests that the management control systems are used in an interactive manner.

28 Reuben Mark joined the company in 1963 and became vice-president for Far East Operations and president before he assumed the role of CEO in 1984. That

is, he grew up from within the organization and learned a lot about the actual doings of the firm over two decades prior to his appointment to lead the entire enterprise. See, for example, Colgate-Palmolive's Reuben Mark: On leadership and "moving the bell curve," Knowledge@Wharton.

29 J. Lardner, Features: In praise of the anomymous CEO, *Business 2.0*, magazine article, September, 2002.

30 K. Iverson, *Plain Talk: Lesson from a Business Maverick*, Wiley: New York, 1998.

31 J. Chambers, B. Fryer, T. A. Stewart, The HBR Interview: Cisco sees the future, *Harvard Business Review* 86(11): 72–79, 2008.

32 M. James. McKinsey conversations with global leaders: John Chambers, *McKinsey Quarterly* 4: 80–87, 2009.

33 C. Zook, J. Allen, *Profit from the Core: A Return to Growth in Turbulent Times*, Harvard Business Press: Boston, MA, 2010.

34 See, for example, T. J. Andersen, Multinational risk and performance outcomes: Effects of knowledge intensity and industry context, *International Business Review* 21(2): 239–252, 2012.

35 J. Collins, *How the Mighty Fall: And Why Some Companies Never Give In*, Random House Business Books: London, 2009.

36 C. Zook, J. Allen, *Repeatability: Build Enduring Businesses for a World of Constant Change*, Harvard Business Review Press: Boston, MA, 2012.

37 J. Collins, *How the Mighty Fall: And Why Some Companies Never Give In*, Random House Business Books: London, 2009.

38 C. Zook, J. Allen, *Repeatability: Build Enduring Businesses for a World of Constant Change*, Harvard Business Review Press: Boston, MA, 2012.

39 See, for example, E. H. Schein, *Organizational Culture and Leadership* (third edn.), Jossey-Bass: San Francisco, CA, 2004.

40 J. Adair, *Effective Leadership: How to Be a Successful Leader*, Pan Books: London, 2009; J. Adair, *Effective Motivation: How to Get the Best Results from Everyone*, Pan Books: London, 2009.

41 P. R. Lawrence, *Driven to Lead: Good, Bad, and Misguided Leadership*, Jossey-Bass: San Francisco, CA, 2010.

42 W. Bennis, P. W. Biederman, *Organizing Genius: The Secrets of Creative Collaboration*, Basic Books: New York, 1997.

43 See the UN Global Compact's ten principles online [www.unglobalcompact.org].

44 S. Ambec, P. Lanoi, Does it pay to be green? A systematic overview, *Academy of Management Perspectives* 22(4): 45–62, 2008.

45 M. P. Sharfman, C. S. Fernando, Environmental risk management and the cost of capital, *Strategic Management Journal* 29(6): 569–592, 2008.

46 G. Hamel, Moon shots for management, *Harvard Business Review* 87(2): 91–98, 2009.

47 H. Mintzberg, *Managing*, FT Prentice Hall: Harlow, 2009.

48 A. Campbell *et al.*, Why good leaders make bad decisions, *Harvard Business Review* 87(2): 60–66, 2009.

49 H. Mintzberg, Opinon: Productivity is killing American enterprise, *Harvard Business Review* 85(4): 25, 2007.

50 J. Pfeffer, R. I. Sutton, *Hard Facts, Dangerous Half-Truths and Total Nonsense*, Harvard Business School Press: Boston, MA, 2006.

51 R. Rumelt, The perils of bad strategy, *McKinsey Quarterly* (1): 30–39, 2011; R. Rumelt, *Good Strategy/Bad Strategy: The Difference and Why It Matters*, Profile Books: London, 2011.

References

Adair J. (2009). *Effective Leadership: How to Be a Successful Leader*, Pan Books: London.

Adair J. (2009). *Effective Motivation: How to Get the Best Results from Everyone*, Pan Books: London.

Adner R., Helfat C. E. (2003). Corporate effects and dynamic managerial capabilities, *Strategic Management Journal* 24(10): 1011–1025.

Agarwal R., Helfat C. E. (2009). Strategic renewal of organizations, *Organization Science* 20(2): 281–293.

Agle B. R., Nagarajan N. J., Sonnenfeld J. A., Srinivasan D. (2006). Does CEO charisma matter? An empirical analysis of the relationships among organizational performance, environmental uncertainty, and top management team perceptions of CEO charisma, *Academy of Management Journal* 49(1): 161–174.

Ambec S., Lanoie P. (2008). Does it pay to be green? A systematic overview, *Academy of Management Perspectives* 22(4): 45–62.

Ambos T. C., Andersson U., Birkinshaw J. (2010). What are the consequences of initiative-taking in multinational subsidiaries? *Journal of International Business Studies* 41(7): 1099–1118.

Andersen M. M., Poulfelt F. (2006). *Discount Business Strategies: How the New Market Leaders are Redefining Business Strategy*, Wiley: Chichester.

Andersen T. J. (2000). Real options analysis in strategic decision making: An applied approach in a dual options framework, *Journal of Applied Management Studies* 9(2): 235–255.

Andersen T. J. (2000). Strategic planning, autonomous actions and corporate performance, *Long Range Planning* 33(2): 184–200.

Andersen T. J. (2001). Information technology, strategic decision making approaches and organizational performance in different industrial settings, *Journal of Strategic Information Systems* 10(2): 101–119.

Andersen T. J. (2001). A real options approach to strategy making: Applications in the global semiconductor, pharmaceutical, and astronautics industries, *Strategic Management Society Annual International Conference*, San Francisco.

Andersen T. J. (2002). How to reconcile the strategy dilemma? *European Business Forum* 9(1): 32–35.

Andersen T. J. (2004) Integrating decentralized strategy making and strategic planning processes in dynamic environments, *Journal of Management Studies* 41(8): 1271–1299.

Andersen T. J. (2004). Integrating the strategy formation process: An international perspective, *European Management Journal* 22(3): 263–272.

Andersen T. J. (2005). The performance effect of computer-mediated communication and decentralized strategic decision making, *Journal of Business Research* 58(8): 1059–1067.

Andersen T. J. (2006). *Global Derivatives: A Strategic Risk Management Perspective*, FT Prentice Hall: Harlow.

Andersen T. J. (2008). The performance relationship of effective risk management: Exploring the firm-specific investment rationale, *Long Range Planning* 41(2): 155–176.

Andersen T. J. (2008). Multinational performance relationships and industry context, SMG Working Paper 15/2008, Copenhagen Business School.

Andersen T. J. (2009). Effective risk management: Exploring effects of innovation and capital structure, *Journal of Strategy and Management* 2(4): 352–379.

Andersen T. J. (2010). *Case: Lehman Brothers (B)*, Copenhagen Business School (available through the European Case Clearing Corporation – ECCH).

Andersen T. J. (2010). *Case: Porsche (D)*, Copenhagen Business School (available through the European Case Clearing Corporation – ECCH).

Andersen T. J. (2010). *Case: Samsung Electronics Corporation*, Copenhagen Business School.

Andersen T. J. (2010). Combining central planning and decentralization to enhance effective risk management outcomes, *Risk Management* 12(2): 101–115.

Andersen T. J. (2011). Corporate relationship management as driver of socially responsible behavior, *Nordic Symposium for Corporate Social Responsibility*, Copenhagen Business School.

Andersen T. J. (2011). Risk implications of multinational enterprise, *International Journal of Organizational Analysis* 19(1): 49–70.

Andersen T. J. (2012). Multinational risk and performance outcomes: Effects of knowledge intensity and industry context, *International Business Review* 21 (2): 239–252.

Andersen T. J., Bettis R. A. (2006). The risk-return effects of strategic responsiveness: A simulation analysis, Chapter 3 in Andersen T. J. (ed.) *Perspectives on Strategic Risk Management*, CBS Press: Copenhagen.

Andersen T. J., Foss N. J. (2005). Strategic opportunity and economic performance in multinational enterprises: The role and effects of information and communication technology, *Journal of International Management* 11(2): 293–310.

Andersen T. J., Fredens K. (2011). Strategy as complementary interaction between central and peripheral processes, *Strategic Management Society Annual International Conference*, Miami, FL.

Andersen T. J., Joshi M. P. (2008). Strategic orientations of internationalizing firms: A comparative analysis of firms operating in technology intensive and common goods industries, SMG Working Paper (WP 11/2008), Copenhagen Business School.

Andersen T. J., Minbaeva D. (2012). The role of human resource management in strategy making, Working Paper, Copenhagen Business School.

Andersen T. J., Nielsen B. B. (2009). Adaptive strategy making: The effects of emergent and intended strategy modes, *European Management Review* 6(2): 94–106.

Andersen T. J., Schrøder P. W. (2010). *Strategic Risk Management Practice*, Cambridge University Press.

Andersen T. J., Segars A. H. (2001). The impact of IT on decision structure and firm performance: Evidence from the textile and apparel industry, *Information & Management* 39(2): 85–100.

Andersen T. J., Denrell J., Bettis R. A. (2007). Strategic responsiveness and Bowman's risk-return paradox, *Strategic Management Journal* 28: 407–429.

Anderson C. (1997). Values-based management, *Academy of Management Executive* 11(4): 25–46.

Andrews K. R. (1971). *The Concept of Corporate Strategy*, Dow-Jones Irwin: Homewood, IL.

Andrews K. R. (1987). *The Concept of Corporate Strategy* (custom edition), McGraw-Hill: New York (originally published in 1971).

Ansoff I. (1965). *Corporate Strategy*, McGraw-Hill: New York.

Ansoff H. I. (1980). Strategic issue management, *Strategic Management Journal* 1: 131–148.

Ansoff I. (1987). *Corporate Strategy* (update edition), Penguin Books: London (first published by McGraw-Hill in 1965).

Ansoff H. I. (1987). The emerging paradigm of strategic behavior, *Strategic Management Journal* 8(6): 501–515.

Ansoff I. (1991). Critique of Henry Mintzberg's The Design School: Reconsidering the basic premises of strategic management, *Strategic Management Journal* 12(6): 449–461.

Antonenko P., Paas F., Grabner R., van Gogh T. (2010). Using electroencephalography to measure cognitive load, *Educational Psychology Review* 22: 425–438.

Bain J. S. (1956). *Barriers to New Competition*, Harvard University Press: Cambridge, MA.

Barnard C. I. (1968). *The Functions of the Executive* (thirtieth anniversary edn.), Harvard University Press: Cambridge, MA (first published in 1938).

Barney J. B. (1986). Strategic factor markets: Expectations, luck, and business strategy, *Management Science* 32(19): 1231–1241.

Barney J. B. (1991). Firm resources and sustained competitive advantage, *Journal of Management* 17: 99–120.

Barney J. B. (1997). *Gaining and Sustaining Competitive Advantage*, Addison-Wesley, Reading, MA.

Barney J. B. (2002). *Gaining and Sustaining Competitive Advantage* (second edn.), Prentice Hall: Upper Saddle River, NJ.

Bartlett C. A., Ghoshal S. (1998). *Managing Across Borders: The Transnational Solution* (second edn.), Random House: London.

Bartlett C. A., Ghoshal S., Birkinshaw J. (2004). *Transnational Management: Text, Cases, and Readings in Cross-Border Management* (fourth edn.), McGraw-Hill/Irwin: Boston, MA.

Bazerman M. H., Moore D. A. (2009). *Judgment in Managerial Decision Making* (seventh edn.), Wiley: Hoboken, NJ.

Bazerman M. H., Watkins M. D. (2008). *Predictable Surprises: The Disasters You Should Have Seen Coming, and How to Prevent Them*, Harvard Business Press: Boston, MA.

Beamish P., Morrison A., Rosenzweig P., Inkpen A. (2000). *International Management: Text and Cases* (fourth edn.), Irwin McGraw-Hill: Homewood, IL.

Bennis W., Biederman P. W. (1997). *Organizing Genius: The Secrets of Creative Collaboration*. Basic Books: New York.

Besnako D., Dranove D., Shanley M., Schaefer S. (2010). *Economics of Strategy* (fifth edn.), Wiley: Hoboken, NJ.

Bettis R. A. (1981). Performance differences in related and unrelated diversified firms, *Strategic Management Journal* 2(4): 379–393.

Bettis R. A., Hitt M. A. (1995). The new competitive landscape, *Strategic Management Journal* 16: 7–19.

Bettis R. A., Prahalad C. K. (1995). The dominant logic: Retrospective and extension, *Strategic Management Journal* 16(1): 5–14.

Bilton C., Cummings S. (2010). *Creative Strategy: Reconnecting Business and Innovation*, Wiley: Chichester.

Birkinshaw J., Gibson C. B. (2004). Building ambidexterity into an organization, *MIT Sloan Management Review* Summer: 47–55.

Birkinshaw J., Morrison A., Hulland J. (1995). Structural and competitive determinants of global integration strategy, *Strategic Management Journal* 16(8): 17–31.

Blenko M. W., Mankins M. C., Rogers P. (2010). *Decide & Deliver: 5 Steps to Breakthrough Performance in Your Organization*, Harvard Business School Press: Boston, MA.

Blenko M. W., Mankins M. C., Rogers P. (2010). The decision-driven organization, *Harvard Business Review* 88(6): 54–62.

Bojadziev G., Bojadziev M. (2007). *Fuzzy Logic for Business, Finance, and Management* (second edn.), World Scientific Publishing: Singapore.

Bourgeois L. J. (1980). Performance and consensus, *Strategic Management Journal* 1(3): 227–248.

Bourgeois L. J. (1980). Strategy and environment: A conceptual integration, *Academy of Management Review* 5(1): 25–39.

Bourgeois L., Brodwin D. (1986). Strategic implementation: Five approaches to an elusive phenomenon, *Strategic Management Journal* 5(3): 241–264.

Bower J. (1986). *Managing the Resource Allocation Process*, Harvard Business School Press: Boston, MA (first published in 1970).

Bower J. L., Gilbert C. G. (eds.) (2005) *From Resource Allocation to Strategy*, Oxford University Press: New York.

Bower J. L., Gilbert C. G. (2007). How managers' everyday decisions create or destroy your company's strategy, *Harvard Business Review* 82(5): 72–79.

Bowman E. H., Hurry D. (1993). Strategy through the options lens: An integrated view of resource investments and the incremental-choice process, *Academy of Management Review* 18(4): 760–782.

Brandenburger A. M., Nalebuff B. J. (1996). *Co-opetition*, Currency Doubleday: New York.

Brealey R. A., Myers S. C. (2000). *Principles of Corporate Finance* (sixth edn.), Irwin McGraw-Hill: Boston, MA.

Bromiley P. (2005). *The Behavioral Foundations of Strategic Management*, Blackwell Publishing, Malden, MA.

Buckley P. (1988). The limits of explanation: Testing the internalization theory, *Journal of International Business Studies* 19(2): 181–194.

Buckley P. J., Casson M. C. (1976). *The Future of the Multinational Enterprise*, Macmillan: London.

Burgelman R. A. (1983). A model of the interaction of strategic behavior, corporate context, and the concept of strategy, *Academy of Management Review* 8(1): 61–70.

Burgelman R. A. (1983). A process model of internal corporate venturing in the diversified major firm, *Administrative Science Quarterly* 28(2): 223–244.

Burgelman R. A. (1996). A process model of strategic business exit: Implications for an evolutionary perspective on strategy, *Strategic Management Journal* 17 (S1): 193–214.

Burgelman R. A. (2005). The role of strategy making in organizational evolution, Chapter 3 in Bower J. L. and Gilbert C. G. (eds.) *From Resource Allocation to Strategy*, Oxford University Press: New York.

Burgelman R. A., Grove A. S. (1996). Strategic dissonance, *California Management Review* 38(2): 8–28.

Burgelman R. A., Grove A. S. (2002). *Strategy Is Destiny: How Strategy-Making Shapes a Company's Future*, Free Press: New York.

Burgelman R. A., Grove A. S. (2007). Let chaos reign, then rein in chaos – repeatedly: Managing strategic dynamics for corporate longevity, *Strategic Management Journal* 28(10): 965–979.

Burrough B., Helyar J. (1990). *Barbarians at the Gate: The Fall of RJR Nabisco*, Harper & Row: New York.

Campbell A., Whitehead J., Finkelstein S. (2009). Why good leaders make bad decisions, *Harvard Business Review* 87(2): 60–66.

Campbell-Hunt C. (2000). What have we learned about generic competitive strategy? A meta-analysis, *Strategic Management Journal* 21(2): 127–154.

Caves R. E. (1971). Industrial corporations: The industrial economics of foreign investment, *Economica* 38(149): 1–27.

Chambers J., Fryer B., Stewart T. A. (2008). The HBR Interview: Cisco sees the future, *Harvard Business Review* 86(11): 72–79.

Chandler A. D. (1990). *Strategy and Structure: Chapters in the History of Industrial Enterprise*, The MIT Press: Cambridge, MA (first published in 1962).

Chandler A. D. (1991). The functions of the HQ unit in the multibusiness firm, *Strategic Management Journal* 12(WSI): 31–50.

Chapman C., Ward S. (2004). *Project Risk Management: Processes, Techniques and Insights*, Wiley: Chichester.

Child J., McGrath R. G. (2001). Organizations unfettered: Organizational form in an information-intensive economy, *Academy of Management Journal* 44(6): 1135–1148.

Christensen C. M. (1997). *The Innovator's Dilemma: When New Technologies Cause Great Firms to Fail*, Harvard Business School Press: Boston, MA.

Clausewitz C. von (1997). *On War*, Wordsworth Classics: London (written before 1831).

Cohen M. D., March J. G., Olsen J. P. (1972). A garbage can model of organizational choice, *Administrative Science Quarterly* 17(1): 1–25.

Collins J. (2001). *Good to Great: Why Some Companies Make the Leap … and Others Don't*, Random House Business Books: London.

Collins J. (2009). *How the Mighty Fall: And Why Some Companies Never Give In*, Random House: London.

Collins J., Hansen M. T. (2011). *Great by Choice: Uncertainty, Chaos, and Luck – Why Some Thrive Despite Them All*, Random House Business Books: London.

Collins J., Porras J. (1994). *Built to Last: Successful Habits of Visionary Companies*, Random House: London.

Collis D. J., Montgomery C. A. (1997). *Corporate Strategy: Resources and the Scope of the Firm*, Irwin McGraw-Hill: Boston, MA.

Collis D. J., Montgomery C. A. (1998). Creating corporate advantage, *Harvard Business Review* 76(3): 71–83.

Courtney H., Kirkland J., Viguerie P. (1997). Strategy under uncertainty, *Harvard Business Review* 75(6): 67–79.

Cyert R. M., March J. G. (1963). *A Behavioral Theory of the Firm*, Prentice Hall: Englewood Cliffs, NJ.

Damodaran A. (2001). *Corporate Finance*, Wiley: New York.

Das T. K. (1987). Strategic planning and individual temporal orientation, *Strategic Management Journal* 8(2): 203–209.

D'Aveni R. A. (1994). *Hypercompetition: Managing the Dynamics of Strategic Maneuvering*, Free Press: New York.

D'Aveni R. (1999). *Strategic Supremacy: How Industry Leaders Create Growth, Wealth, and Power through Spheres of Influence*, Free Press: New York.

D'Aveni R. A. (1999). Strategic supremacy through disruption and dominance, *Sloan Management Review* Spring: 127–135.

Davenport T. H., Leibold M., Voelpel S. (2006). *Strategic Management in the Innovation Economy: Strategy Approaches and Tools for Dynamic Innovation Capabilities*, Publicis Corporate Publishing and Wiley-VCH Verlag: Erlangen, Germany.

De Kluyver C. A. (2000). *Strategic Thinking: An Executive Perspective*, Prentice Hall: Upper Saddle River, NJ.

Denrell J. (2005). Selection bias and the perils of benchmarking, *Harvard Business Review* 83(4): 114–119.

Dess G. G., Beard D. W. (1984). Dimensions of organizational task environments, *Administrative Science Quarterly* 29(1): 52–73.

Dess G. G., Davis P. S. (1984). Porter's (1980) generic strategies as determinants of strategic group membership and organizational performance, *Academy of Management Journal* 27(3): 467–488.

Dess G. G., Lumpkin G. T., Taylor M. L. (2005). *Strategic Management: Creating Competitive Advantage* (second edn.), McGraw-Hill Irwin: Boston, MA.

Dess G. G., Lumpkin G. T., Eisner A. B. (2008). *Strategic Management: Creating Competitive Advantages*, McGraw-Hill: Boston, MA.

de Wit R., Meyer R. (2004). *Strategy – Process, Content, Context*, Thomson: London.

Dill W. (1958). Environment as an influence on managerial autonomy, *Administrative Science Quarterly* 2(2): 409–443.

Dixit A. K., Nalebuff B. J. (2008). *The Art of Strategy: A Game Theorist's Guide to Success in Business and Life*, Norton: New York.

Doz Y. L., Bartlett C. A., Prahalad C. K. (1981). Global competitive pressures and host country demands: Managing the tensions in MNCs, *California Management Review* 23(3): 63–74.

Doz Y. L., Santos J., Williamson P. (2001). *From Global to Metanational: How Companies Win in the Knowledge Economy*, Harvard Business School Press: Boston, MA.

Drucker P. F. (1967). The effective decision, *Harvard Business Review* 45(1): 92–98.

Dunning J. H. (1973). The determinants of international production, *Oxford Economic Papers* 25(3): 289–336.

Dunning J. H. (2001). The eclectic (OLI) paradigm of international production: Past, present and future, *International Journal of the Economics of Business* 2: 173–190.

Dutta P. K. (1999). *Strategies and Games: Theory and Practice*, MIT Press: Cambridge, MA.

Egelhoff W. (1988). Strategy and structure in multinational corporations: A revision of the Stopford and Wells model, *Strategic Management Journal* 9(1): 1–14.

Eisenhardt K. M. (1989). Making fast strategic decisions in high-velocity environments, *Academy of Management Journal* 32(3): 543–576.

Eisenhardt K. M., Brown S. L. (1999). Patching: Restitching business portfolios in dynamic markets, *Harvard Business Review* 77(3): 72–82.

Eisenhardt K. M., Martin J. A. (2000). Dynamic capabilities: What are they? *Strategic Management Journal* 21(5): 1105–1121.

Ejler N., Poulfelt F., Czerniawska F. (2011). *Managing the Knowledge-Intensive Firm*, Routledge: London.

Fahey L. (2003). How corporations learn from scenarios, *Strategy & Leadership* 31(2): 5–15.

Fahey L., King W., Narayanan V. (1981). Environmental scanning and forecasting in strategic planning – the state of the art, *Long Range Planning* 14(1): 32–39.

Fiegenbaum A., Hart S., Schendel D. (1996). Strategic reference point theory, *Strategic Management Journal* 17(2): 219–235.

Fine C. H. (1998). *Clock Speed: Winning Industry Control in the Age of Temporary Advantage*, Basic Books: New York.

Finkelstein S. (2003). *Why Smart Executives Fail: And What You Can Learn from Their Mistakes*, Penguin Books: New York.

Finkelstein S., Hambrick D. C., Canella A. A. (2009). *Strategic Leadership: Theory and Research on Executives, Top Management Teams, and Boards*, Oxford University Press: New York.

Fisher L. (2008). *Rock, Paper, Scissors: Game Theory in Everyday Life*, Hay House: London.

Forsgren M. (2008). *Theories of the Multinational Firm: A Multidimensional Creature in the Global Economy*, Edward Elgar: Cheltenham.

Freeman R. E. (1984). *Strategic Management: A Stakeholder Approach*, Cambridge University Press.

Freeman R. E., Harrison J. S., Wicks A. C., Parmar B. L., de Colle S. (2010). *Stakeholder Theory: The State of the Art*, Cambridge University Press.

Galbraith J. R. (1977). *Organization Design*, Addison-Wesley: Reading, MA.

Galbraith J. R., Kazanjian R. K. (1986). *Strategy Implementation: Structure, Systems and Processes*, West Publishing: St. Paul, MN.

Gavetti G., Levinthal D. (2000). Looking forward and looking backward: Cognitive and experiential search, *Administrative Science Quarterly* 45(1): 113–137.

Gavetti G., Rivkin J. W. (2005). How strategists really think: Tapping the power of analogy, *Harvard Business Review* 83(4): 54–63.

Ghemawat P. (2002). Semiglobalization and international business strategy, *Journal of International Business Studies* 34(2): 138–152.

Gibson C. B., Birkinshaw J. (2004). The antecedents, consequences, and mediating role of organizational ambidexterity, *Academy of Management Journal* 47(2): 209–226.

Gilad B. (2004). *Early Warning: Using Competitive Intelligence to Anticipate Market Shifts, Control Risk, and Create Powerful Strategies*, American Management Association (AMACOM): New York.

Goold M., Campbell A. (1998). Desperately seeking synergy, *Harvard Business Review* 76(5): 131–143.

Goold M., Quinn J. J. (1990). The paradoxes of strategic controls, *Strategic Management Journal* 11(1): 43–57.

Goold M., Campbell A., Alexander M. (1994). *Corporate Level Strategy: Creating Value in the Multibusiness Company*, Wiley: New York.

Govindarajan V., Gupta A. K. (2001). *The Quest for Global Dominance: Transforming Global Presence into Global Competitive Advantage*, Jossey-Bass: San Francisco.

Granovetter M. S. (1973). The strength of weak ties, *American Journal of Sociology* 78(6): 1360–1380.

Grant A. M., Gino F., Hofmann D. A. (2011). Reversing the extraverted leadership advantage: The role of employee proactivity, *Academy of Management Journal* 54(3): 528–550.

Grant J. H., King W. R. (1982). *The Logic of Strategic Planning*, Little, Brown and Company, Boston, MA.

Grant R. M. (1996). Toward a knowledge based theory of the firm, *Strategic Management Journal* 17 (winter special issue): 109–122.

Grant R. M. (2002). *Contemporary Strategy Analysis* (fourth edn.), Blackwell Publishing: Malden, MA.

Grant R. M. (2003). Strategic planning in a turbulent environment: evidence from the oil majors, *Strategic Management Journal* 24(6): 491–517.

Grant R. M. (2008). *Contemporary Strategy Analysis* (sixth edn.). Blackwell Publishing: Malden, MA.

Grove A. S. (1996). *Only the Paranoid Survive: How to Exploit the Crisis Points that Challenge Every Company and Career*, HarperCollins Business: London.

Gulati R., Nohria N., Zaheer A. (2000). Strategic networks, *Strategic Management Journal* Special Issue 21(3): 203–215.

Guth W. D., Macmillan I. C. (1986). Strategy implementation versus middle management self-interest, *Strategic Management Journal* 7(4): 313–327.

Habib M. M., Victor B. (1991). Strategy, structure, and performance of US manufacturing and service MNCs: A comparative analysis, *Strategic Management Journal* 12(8): 589–606.

Halin C., Andersen T. J., Tveterås S. (2012). Executive expectations and forecasts versus employee sensing: An unequal prediction contest? Working Paper, Copenhagen Business School.

Hambrick D. C. (1983). High profit strategies in mature capital goods industries: A contingency approach, *Academy of Management Journal* 26(4): 687–707.

Hambrick D. C. (1989). Putting top managers back in the strategy picture, *Strategic Management Journal* 10: 5–15.

Hambrick D. C., Cannella A. A. (1989). Strategy implementation as substance and selling, *Academy of Management Executive* 3: 278–285.

Hambrick D. C., Mason P. A. (1984). Upper echelons: The organization as a reflection of its top managers, *Academy of Management Review* 9(2): 193–206.

Hamel G. (2000). *Leading the Revolution*, Harvard Business School Press: Boston, MA.

Hamel G. (2009). Moon shots for management, *Harvard Business Review* 87(2): 91–98.

Harrison E. F. (1995). *The Managerial Decision-Making Process*, Houghton Mifflin: Boston, MA.

Harrison E. F. (1999). *The Managerial Decision-Making Process*, Houghton Mifflin: Boston, MA.

Harrison J. S. (2003). *Strategic Management of Resources and Relationships*, Wiley: New York.

Hart S. L. (1992). An integrative framework for strategy making processes, *Academy of Management Review* 17: 327–351.

Hart S. L., Banbury C. (1994). How different strategy-making processes can make a difference, *Strategic Management Journal* 15: 251–269.

Harzing A. (2000). An empirical analysis and extension of the Bartlett and Ghoshal typology of multinational companies, *Journal of International Business Studies* 31(1): 101–120.

Hatch M. J. (2006). *Organization Theory* (second edn.), Oxford University Press.

Hayes J. (2007). *The Theory and Practice of Change Management* (second edn.), Palgrave Macmillan: Hampshire.

Helfat C. E., Finkelstein S., Mitchell W., Peteraf M. A., Singh H., Teece D. J., Winter S. G. (2007). *Dynamic Capabilities: Understanding Strategic Change in Organizations*, Blackwell Publishing: Malden, MA.

Hendry J. (2000). Strategic decision making, discourse and strategy as a social practice, *Journal of Management Studies* 37(7): 955–977.

Hill C. W., Jones G. R. (2001). *Strategic Management Theory: An Integrated Approach*, Houghton Mifflin: Boston, MA.

Hill S., Martin R., Harris M. (2000). Decentralization, integration and the post-bureaucratic organization: The case of R&D, *Journal of Management Studies* 37(4): 563–585.

Himes T. (1987). Left brain/right brain mythology and implications for management and training, *Academy of Management Review* 12(4): 600–606.

Hornsby A. S. (1974). *Oxford Advanced Learner's Dictionary of Current English*, Oxford University Press.

House C. H., Price R. L. (2009). *The HP Phenomenon: Innovation and Business Transformation*, Stanford University Press.

Hrebiniak L. G. (2005). *Making Strategy Work: Leading Effective Execution and Change*, Wharton School Publishing, Pearson Education: Upper Saddle River, NJ.

Hymer S. H. (1976). *A Study of Foreign Direct Investment*, MIT Press: Cambridge, MA.

Ilinitch A. Y., Zeithaml C. P. (1995). Operationalizing and testing Galbraith's center of gravity theory, *Strategic Management Journal* 16(5): 401–410.

Ireland R. G., Covin J. G., Kuratko D. F. (2009). Conceptualizing corporate entrepreneurship strategy, *Entrepreneurship Theory and Practice* 33(1): 19–46.

Iverson K. (1998). *Plain Talk: Lesson from a Business Maverick*, Wiley: New York.

James M. (2009). McKinsey conversations with global leaders: John Chambers, *McKinsey Quarterly* 4: 80–87.

Janis I. L. (1971). Groupthink, *Psychology Today* 5(6): 43–46.

Jarrell G. A., Brickley J. A., Netter J. M. (1988). The market for corporate control: The empirical evidence since 1980, *Journal of Economic Perspective* 2(1): 49–68.

Jarzabkowski P., Balogun J. (2009). The practice and process of delivering integration through strategic planning, *Journal of Management Studies* 46(8): 1255–1288.

Jensen M., Meckling W. (1976). Theory of the firm: Managerial behavior, agency costs, and ownership structure, *Journal of Financial Economics* 3: 305–360.

Johanson J., Vahlne J. E. (1977). The internationalization process of the firm: A model of knowledge development and increasing foreign commitments, *Journal of International Business Studies* 8(1): 23–32.

Johnson G., Melin L., Whittington R. (2003). Micro strategy and strategizing: Towards an activity-based view, *Journal of Management Studies* 40(1): 3–22.

Johnson G., Scholes K., Whittington R. (2006). *Exploring Corporate Strategy*, FT Prentice Hall: Harlow.

Johnson G., Langley A., Melin J., Whittington R. (2007). *Strategy as Practice: Research Directions and Resources*, Cambridge University Press.

Johnson J. (1995). An empirical analysis of the integration-responsiveness framework: US construction equipment industry firms in global competition, *Journal of International Business Studies* 26: 621–635.

Jones G. R., Hill C. W. L. (1988). Transaction cost analysis of strategy-structure choice, *Strategic Management Journal* 9(2): 159–172.

Kahneman D. (2011). *Thinking Fast and Slow*, Farrar, Straus and Giroux: New York.

Kaplan R. S., Norton D. P. (2001). *The Strategy-Focused Organization: How Balanced Scorecard Companies Thrive in the New Business Environment*, Harvard Business School Press: Boston, MA.

Kaplan R. S., Norton D. P. (2004). *Strategy Maps: Converting Intangible Assets into Tangible Outcomes*, Harvard Business School Press: Boston, MA.

Kaplan R. S., Norton D. P. (2006). *Alignment: Using the Balanced Scorecard to Create Corporate Synergies*, Harvard Business School Press: Boston, MA.

Kaplan R. S., Norton D. P. (2008). *The Execution Premium: Linking Strategy to Operations for Competitive Advantage*, Harvard Business School Publishing: Boston, MA.

Karim S., Mitchell W. (2004). Innovating through acquisition and internal development: A quarter-century of boundary evolution at Johnson & Johnson, *Long Range Planning* 37(6): 525–547.

Kaufman H. (1991). *Time, Chance, and Organization: Natural Selection in a Perilous Environment* (second edn.), Chatham House: Chatham, NJ.

Kelso J. A. S., Engstrøm D. A. (2006). *The Complementary Nature*, MIT Press: Cambridge, MA.

Kiechel W. (2010). *The Lords of Strategy: The Secret Intellectual History of the New Corporate World*, Harvard Business Press, Boston, MA.

Kim W. C., Mauborgne R. (2005). *Blue Ocean Strategy: How to Create Uncontested Market Space and Make the Competition Irrelevant*, Harvard Business School Press: Boston, MA.

Knight F. H. (2006). *Risk, Uncertainty and Profit*, Dover Publications: Mineola, NY (originally published in 1921).

Kobrin S. J. (1991). An empirical analysis of the determinants of global integration, *Strategic Management Journal* 12(S1): 17–37.

Kogut B. (1985). Designing global strategies: Profiting from operational flexibility, *Sloan Management Review* Fall: 27–38.

Kogut B., Kulatilaka N. (1994). Operating flexibility, global manufacturing and the open value of a multinational network, *Management Science* 40: 123–138.

Kogut B., Zander U. (1993). Knowledge of the firm and the evolutionary theory of the multinational corporation, *Journal of International Business Studies* 15: 151–168.

Korem Y. (1983). *Computer Control of Manufacturing Systems*, McGraw-Hill: New York.

Kuratko D. F., Morris M. H., Covin J. G. (2011). *Corporate Innovation & Entrepreneurship: Entrepreneurial Development within Organizations* (third edn.), International edn: South-Western: Nashville, TN.

Kytle B., Ruggie J. G. (2005). Corporate social responsibility as risk management: A model for multinationals, Working Paper No. 10, John F. Kennedy School of Government, Harvard University.

Lawrence P. R. (2010). *Driven to Lead: Good, Bad, and Misguided Leadership*, Jossey-Bass: San Francisco, CA.

Lawrence P. R., Lorsch J. W. (1967). Differentiation and integration in complex organizations, *Administrative Science Quarterly* 12: 1–47.

Learned E., Christensen C. R., Andrews K. R., Guth W. D. (1965). *Business Policy: Text and Cases*, Irwin: Homewood, IL.

Lechner C., Floyd S. W. (2007). Searching, processing and practicing – key learning activities in exploratory initiatives, *Long Range Planning* 40(1): 9–29.

Leong S., Tan C. (1993). Managing across borders: An empirical test of the Bartlett and Ghoshal (1989) organizational typology, *Journal of International Business Studies* 24(3): 449–464.

Leuhrman T. (1998). Strategy as a portfolio of real options, *Harvard Business Review* 76(5): 89–99.

Levinthal A. D., March J. G. (1993). The myopia of learning, *Strategic Management Journal* Special Issue 14: 95–112.

Levy S. (2011). *In The Plex: How Google Thinks, Works, and Shapes Our Lives*, Simon & Schuster: New York.

Liker J. K. (2004). *The Toyota Way: 14 Management Principles from the World's Greatest Manufacturer*, McGraw-Hill: New York.

Linstone H. A. (1984). *Multiple Perspectives for Decision Making: Bridging the Gap between Analysis and Action*, Elsevier: New York.

Linstone H. A., Turoff M. (1975). *The Delphi Method: Techniques and Applications*, Addison-Wesley: Reading, MA.

Lord M. D., Ranft A. L. (2000). Organizational learning about new international markets: Exploring the internal transfer of local market knowledge, *Journal of International Business Studies* 31(4): 573–589.

Lu J. W., Beamish P. W. (2004). International diversification and firm performance: The S-curve hypothesis, *Academy of Management Journal* 47(4): 598–609.

Lubatkin M. H., Lane P. J. (1996). The merger mavens still have it wrong, *Academy of Management Executive* 10(1): 21–39.

Lubatkin M. H., Rogers R. C. (1989). Diversification, systematic risk, and shareholder return: A capital market extension of Rumelt's 1974 study, *Academy of Management Journal* 32(2): 454–465.

Makridakis S., Hogarth R., Gaba A. (2009). *Dance with Chance: Making Luck Work for You*, Oneworld Publications: Oxford.

Manas J. (2006). *Napoleon on Project Management: Timeless Lessons in Planning, Execution, and Leadership*, Nelson Business: Nashville, TN.

March J. G. (1962). The business firm as a political coalition, *The Journal of Politics* 24(4): 662–678.

March J. G. (1991). Exploration and exploitation in organizational learning, *Organization Science* 2(1): 71–87.

March J. G. (1995). The future, disposable organizations and the rigidities of imagination, *Organization* 2(3/4): 427–440.

Markides C. C. (1992). Consequences of corporate refocusing: Ex ante evidence, *Academy of Management Journal* 35(2): 398–412.

Markides C. C. (2008). *Game Changing Strategies: How to Create New Market Space in Established Industries by Breaking the Rules*, Jossey-Bass: San Francisco, CA.

McArthur T. (1981). *Longman Lexicon of Contemporary English*, Longman: Harlow.

McGee J., Thomas H., Wilson D. (2005). *Strategy: Analysis & Practice*, McGraw-Hill: London.

Miller A., Dess G. G. (1993). Assessing Porter's model in terms of its generalizability, accuracy, and simplicity, *Journal of Management Studies* 30(4): 553–585.

Miller C. C., Cardinal L. B. (1994). Strategic planning and firm performance: A synthesis of more than two decades of research, *Academy of Management Journal* 37(6): 1649–1665.

Miller D. (1986). Configurations of strategy and structure: Towards a synthesis, *Strategic Management Journal* 7(3): 233–249.

Miller D. (1990). *The Icarus Paradox: How Exceptional Companies Bring About Their Own Downfall*, Harper Business: New York.

Miller D., Friesen P. (1984). *Organizations: A Quantum View*, Prentice Hall: Englewood Cliffs, NJ.

Miller D., Friesen P. H. (1986). Porter's (1980) generic strategies and performance: An empirical examination with American data. Part II: Testing Porter, *Organization Studies* 7(3): 255–261.

Miller J. (2003). *Game Theory at Work: How to Use Game Theory to Outthink and Outmaneuver Your Competition*, McGraw-Hill: New York.

Miller K. D., Waller H. G. (2003). Scenarios, real options, and integrated risk management, *Long Range Planning* 36: 93–107.

Miller S., Wilson D., Hickson D. (2004). Beyond planning strategies for successfully implementing strategic decisions, *Long Range Planning* 37: 201–218.

Mintzberg H. (1973). *The Nature of Managerial Work*, Harper & Row: New York.

Mintzberg H. (1973). Strategy making in three modes, *California Management Review* 16(2): 44–54.

Mintzberg H. (1976). Planning on the left side and managing on the right, *Harvard Business Review* 54(4): 49–58.

Mintzberg H. (1978). Patterns in strategy formation, *Management Science* 24(9): 934–948.

Mintzberg H. (1979). *The Structuring of Organizations*, Prentice Hall: Englewood Cliffs, NJ.

Mintzberg H. (1983). *Structures in Fives: Designing Effective Organizations*, Prentice Hall: Englewood Cliffs, NJ.

Mintzberg H. (1990). The Design School: Reconsidering the basic premises of strategic management, *Strategic Management Journal* 11(3): 171–195.

Mintzberg H. (1991). Learning 1, Planning 0, Reply to Igor Ansoff, *Strategic Management Journal* 12(6): 463–466.

Mintzberg H. (1994). The fall and rise of strategic planning, *Harvard Business Review* 72(1): 107–114.

Mintzberg H. (1994). *The Rise and Fall of Strategic Planning*, Prentice Hall: Upper Saddle River, NJ.

Mintzberg H. (2007). Opinon: Productivity is killing American enterprise, *Harvard Business Review* 85(4): 25.

Mintzberg H. (2009). *Managing*, FT Prentice Hall: Harlow.

Mintzberg H., McHugh A. (1985). Strategy formation in an adhocracy, *Administrative Science Quarterly* 30(2): 160–197.

Mintzberg H., Waters J. A. (1982). Tracking strategy in an entrepreneurial firm, *Academy of Management Journal* 25(3): 465–499.

Mintzberg H., Waters J. A. (1985). Of strategies, deliberate and emergent, *Strategic Management Journal* 6: 257–272.

Mintzberg H., Raisinghani D., Theoret A. (1976). The structure of "unstructured" decision processes, *Adminstrative Science Quarterly* 21(2): 246–274.

Mintzberg H., Lampel J., Quinn J. B., Ghoshal S. (2003). *The Strategy Process: Concepts, Contexts, Cases* (fourth edn.), Pearson Prentice Hall: Upper Saddle River, NJ.

Mintzberg H., Ahlstrand B., Lampel J. (2009). *Strategy Safari: Your Complete Guide through the Wilds of Strategic Management* (second edn.), FT Prentice Hall: Harlow.

Mitroff I. I., Silvers A. (2010). *Dirty Rotten Strategies: How We Trick Ourselves and Others into Solving the Wrong Problems Precisely*, Stanford Business Books: Stanford, CA.

Montgomery C. A. (2008). Putting leadership back into strategy, *Harvard Business Review* 86(1): 54–60.

Morck R., Shleifer A., Vishny R. W. (1990). Do managerial objectives drive bad acquisitions? *Journal of Finance* 45(1): 31–48.

Morgan M., Levitt R. E., Malek W. (2007). *Executing Your Strategy: How to Break It Down and Get It Done*, Harvard Business School Press: Boston, MA.

Morris W. (ed.) (1980). *The Houghton Mifflin Canadian Dictionary of the English Language*, Houghton Mifflin Canada: Markham, Ontario.

Murray A. I. (1988). A contingency view of Porter's "generic strategies," *Academy of Management Review* 13(3): 390–400.

Nahapiet J., Ghoshal S. (1998). Social capital, intellectual capital, and the organizational advantage, *Academy of Management Review* 23(2): 242.

Narayanan V. K., Fahey L. (1982). The micro-politics of strategy formulation, *Strategic Management Journal* 7(1): 25–34.

Noble C. H. (1999). The eclectic roots of strategy implementation research, *Journal of Business Research* 45(2): 119–134.

Noda T., Bower J. (1996). Strategy making as integrated processes of resource allocation, *Strategic Management Journal* 17 (special issue): 159–192.

Nonaka I. (1988). Toward middle-up-down management: accelerating information creation, *Sloan Management Review* 29(3): 9–18.

Nonaka I., Takeuchi H. (1995). *The Knowledge Creating Company*, Oxford University Press: New York.

Osterwalder A., Pigneur Y. (2010). *Business Model Generation*, Wiley: Hoboken, NJ.

Ouchi W. G. (1979). A conceptual framework for the design of organizational control mechanisms, *Management Science* 25(9): 833–848.

Ouchi W. G. (1980). Market, bureaucracies, and clans, *Administrative Science Quarterly* 25(1): 129–141.

Owen G. (2010). *The Rise and Fall of Great Companies: Courtaulds and the Reshaping of the Man-Made Fibers Industry*, Oxford University Press: New York.

Paas F., Goghvan T., Sweller J. (2010). Cognitive load theory: New conceptualizations, specifications, and integrated research perspectives, *Educational Psychology Review* 22: 115–121.

Packard D. (1995). *The HP Way: How Bill Hewlett and I Built Our Company*, HarperCollins: New York.

Page S. E. (2007). *The Difference: How the Power of Diversity Creates Better Groups, Firms, Schools, and Societies*, Princeton University Press.

Palich L. E., Cardinal L. B., Miller C. C. (2000). Curvilinearity in the diversification-performance linkage: An examination of over three decades of research, *Strategic Management Journal* 21(2): 155–174.

Pascale R. M. (1984). Perspectives on strategy: The true story behind Honda's success, *California Management Review* 26(3): 47–72.

Pascale R. M. (1990). *Managing on the Edge*, Simon & Schuster: New York.

Pascale R. M. (1996). Reflections on Honda, *California Management Review* 38(4): 112–117.

Penrose E. (2009). *The Theory of the Growth of the Firm* (fourth edn.), Oxford University Press: Oxford (first published in 1959).

Perrow C. (1999). *Normal Accidents: Living with High-Risk Technologies*, Princeton University Press.

Pfeifer R., Bongard J. (2009). *How the Body Shapes the Way We Think: A New View of Intelligence*, MIT Press: Cambridge, MA.

Pfeffer J., Salancik G. R. (2003). *The External Control of Organizations: A Resource Dependence Perspective*, Stanford Business Classics: Stanford, CA (first published in 1978).

Pfeffer J., Sutton R. I. (2006). *Hard Facts, Dangerous Half-Truths and Total Nonsense: Profiting from Evidence-Based Management*, Harvard Business School Press: Boston, MA.

Pine J. (1992). *Mass Customization: The New Frontier in Business Competition*, Harvard Business School Press: Boston, MA.

Pine J., Victor B., Boynton A. C. (1993). Making mass customization work, *Harvard Business Review* 72(6): 108–119.

Pisapia J. R. (2009). *The Strategic Leader: New Tactics for a Globalizing World*, IAP – Information Age Publishing: Charlotte, NC.

Porter M. E. (1979). How competitive forces shape strategy, *Harvard Business Review* March–April: 137–145.

Porter M. E. (1985). *Competitive Advantage: Creating and Sustaining Superior Performance*, Free Press: New York.

Porter M. E. (1987). From competitive advantage to corporate strategy, *Harvard Business Review* 65(3): 43–59.

Porter M. E. (1990). *The Competitive Advantage of Nations*, Free Press: New York.

Porter M. E. (1996). What is strategy? *Harvard Business Review* November–December: 61–78.

Porter M. E. (2004). *Competitive Strategy: Techniques for Analyzing Industries and Competitors* (export edn.), Free Press: New York (first published in 1980).

Porter M. E. (2008). The five competitive forces that shape strategy, *Harvard Business Review* 86(1): 78–93.

Prahalad C. K., Bettis R. A. (1986). The dominant logic: A new linkage between diversity and performance, *Strategic Management Journal* 7(6): 485–501.

Prahalad C. K., Doz Y. L. (1987). *The Multinational Mission: Balancing Local Demands and Global Vision*, Free Press: New York.

Prahalad C. K., Hamel G. (1990). The core competence of the corporation, *Harvard Business Review* 68(3): 79–91.

Quinn J. B. (1978). Strategic change: "logical incrementalism," *Sloan Management Review* 20(1): 7–21.

Quinn J. B. (1980). *Strategies for Change: Logical Incrementalism*, Irwin: Homewood, IL.

Raiffa H. (1968). *Decision Analysis: Introductory Lectures on Choices under Uncertainty*, Addison-Wesley: Reading, MA.

Rainey D. L. (2010). *Enterprise-Wide Strategic Management*, Cambridge University Press.

Ralston B., Wilson I. (2006). *The Scenario Planning Handbook*, Thomson/South-Western: Mason, OH.

Ramirez R., Selsky J. W., van der Heijden K. (2008). *Business Planning for Turbulent Times: New Methods for Applying Scenarios*, Earthscan: London.

Roll R. (1986). The hubris hypothesis of corporate takeovers, *Journal of Business* 59 (2): 197–216.

Romanelli E., Tushman M. L. (1986). Organizational transformation as punctuated equilibrium, *Academy of Management Journal* 37(5): 1141–1166.

Roth K., O'Donnell S. (1996). Foreign subsidiary compensation strategy: An agency theory perspective, *Academy of Management Journal* 39(3): 678–703.

Roubin N., Mihm S. (2010). *Crisis Economics: A Crash Course in the Future of Finance*, Penguin Books: London.

Royer P. S. (2002). *Project Risk Management: A Proactive Approach*, Management Concepts: Vienna, VA.

Rugman A. M. (1981). *Inside the Multinational: The Economics of International Markets*, Croom Helm: London.

Rumelt R. P. (1974). *Strategy, Structure, and Economic Performance*, Harvard University Press: Boston, MA.

Rumelt R. (2011). The perils of bad strategy, *McKinsey Quarterly* 1: 30–39.

Rumelt R. (2011). *Good Strategy/Bad Strategy: The Difference and Why It Matters*, Profile Books: London.

Salancik G. R., Pfeffer J. (1977). Who gets power – and how they hold on to it: A strategic contingency model of power, *Organizational Dynamics* 5(3): 3–21.

Saloner G., Sheppard A., Podolny J. (2001). *Strategic Management*, Wiley: New York.

Sarasvathy S. (2008). *Effectuation: Elements of Entrepreneurial Expertise*, Edward Elgar: Cheltenham.

Sathe V. (2003). *Corporate Entrepreneurship: Top Managers and New Business Creation*, Cambridge University Press.

Scharfstein D. (1988). The disciplinary role of takeovers, *Review of Economic Studies* 55: 185–199.

Schein E. H. (2004). *Organizational Culture and Leadership*, Jossey-Bass: San Francisco, CA.

Schendel D., Hofer C. (1979). *Strategic Management: A New View of Business Policy and Planning*, Little, Brown: Boston, MA.

Schlesinger L. A., Kiefer C. F. (2012). *Just Start: Take Action, Embrace Uncertainty, Create the Future*, Harvard Business Review Press: Boston, MA.

Schoemaker P. J. H. (2003). Scenario planning: A tool for strategic thinking, *Sloan Management Review*, Winter: 25–40.

Schumpeter J. A. (1975). *Capitalism, Socialism and Democracy*, Harper & Row: New York (originally published in 1942).

Schumpeter J. A. (2008). *The Theory of Economic Development: An Inquiry into Profits, Capital, Credit, Interest, and the Business Cycle*, Transaction Publishers: New Brunswick, NJ (originally published in 1934).

Schwaber K. (2004). *Agile Project Management with Scrum*, Microsoft Press: Redmond, WA.

Schwenk C. R. (1984). Cognitive simplification processes in strategic decision-making, *Strategic Management Journal* 5(2): 111–128.

Scott W. R., Davis G. F. (2007). *Organizations and Organizing: Rational, Natural, and Open Systems Perspectives*, Pearson Education: Upper Saddle River, NJ.

Selznick P. (1984). *Leadership in Administration: A Sociological Interpretation* (California Paperback edn.), University of California Press: Berkeley, CA (first published by Harper & Row in 1957).

Shaker S. M., Gembicki M. P. (1999). *The WarRoom Guide to Competitive Intelligence*, McGraw-Hill: New York.

Sharfman M. P., Fernando C. S. (2008). Environmental risk management and the cost of capital, *Strategic Management Journal* 29(6): 569–592.

Sharp S. (2009). *Competitive Intelligence Advantage: How to Minimize Risk, Avoid Surprises, and Grow Your Business in a Changing World*, Wiley: Hoboken, NJ.

Sheffi Y. (2007). *The Resilient Enterprise: Overcoming Vulnerability for Competitive Advantage*, MIT Press: Cambridge, MA.

Sidhu I. (2010). *Doing Both: How Cisco Captures Today's Profit and Drives Tomorrow's Growth*, FT Press: Upper Saddle River, NJ.

Simon H. A. (1997). *Administrative Behavior: A Study of Decision-Making Processes in Administrative Organizations* (fourth edn.), Free Press: New York (first published in 1945).

Simon H. A., Dantzig G. B., Hogarth R., Plott C. R., Raiffa H., Schelling T. C., Shepsle K. A., Thaler R., Tversky A., Winter S. (1987). Decision making and problem solving, *Interfaces* 17(5): 11–31.

Simons R. (1990). The role of management control systems in creating competitive advantage: New perspectives, *Accounting, Organization and Society* 15(1/2): 127–143.

Simons R. (1991). Strategic orientation and top management attention to control systems, *Strategic Management Journal* 12(1): 49–62.

Simons R. (1994). How top managers use control systems as levers of strategic renewal, *Strategic Management Journal* 15(3): 169–189.

Simons R. (1995). *Levers of Control: How Managers Use Innovative Control Systems to Drive Strategic Renewal*, Harvard Business School Press: Boston, MA.

Sims P. (2011). *Little Bets: How Breakthrough Ideas Emerge from Small Discoveries*, Random House Business Books: London.

Slyvotsky A. J. (1996). *Value Migration: How to Think Several Moves Ahead of the Competition*, Harvard Business School Press: Boston, MA.

Slyvotsky A. J., Morrison D. J. (1997). *The Profit Zone: How Strategic Business Design Will Lead You to Tomorrow's Profits*, Wiley: Chichester.

Spekuland R. (2009). *Beyond Strategy: The Leader's Role in Successful Implementation*, Jossey-Bass: San Francisco, CA.

Stabell C. B., Fjeldstad Ø. D. (1998). Configuring value for competitive advantage, *Strategic Management Journal* 19(5): 413–437.

Stevenson H. H., Jarillo-Mossi J. C. (1986). Preserving entrepreneurship as companies grow, *Journal of Business Strategy* 10: 76–89.

Stopford J. M., Wells L. T. (1972). *Managing the Multinational Enterprise*, Basic Books: New York.

Sun Tsu (2005). *The Art of War*, Shambhala Publications: Boston, MA, translated by Thomas Cleary (first compiled well over two thousand years ago).

Sutton R. S., Barto A. (1998). *Reinforcement Learning*, MIT Press: Cambridge.

Sweller J. (1988). Cognitive load during problem solving: Effect on learning, *Cognitive Science* 12(2): 257–285.

Taggart J. H. (1997). Strategy shifts in MNC subsidiaries, *Strategic Management Journal* 19(7): 663–681.

Taleb N. N. (2007). *The Black Swan: The Impact of the Highly Improbable*, Allen Lane, Penguin: London.

Teece D. J. (1981). The multinational enterprise: Market failure and market power considerations, *Sloan Management Review* Spring: 3–17.

Teece D. J. (2007). Explicating dynamic capabilities: The nature and microfoundations of (sustainable) enterprise performance, *Strategic Management Journal* 28(13): 1319–1350.

Teece D. J. (2009). *Dynamic Capabilities and Strategic Management: Organizing for Innovation and Growth*, Oxford University Press: New York.

Teece D. J., Pisano G., Shuen O. (1997). Dynamic capabilities and strategic management, *Strategic Management Journal* 18(7): 509–533.

Thompson A. A., Strickland A. J., Gamble J. E. (2005). *Crafting and Executing Strategy: The Quest for Competitive Advantage*, McGraw-Hill Irwin: New York.

Thompson J. (1967). *Organizations in Action*, McGraw-Hill: New York.

Tolio T. (2009). *Design of Flexible Production Systems – Methodologies and Tools*, Springer: Berlin.

Torp S. S. (2011). Employee stock ownership: Effect on strategic management and performance, PhD dissertation, Copenhagen Business School.

Tushman M. L., O'Reilly C. A. (1996). Ambidextrous organizations: Managing evolutionary and revolutionary change, *California Management Review* 38(4): 8–30.

Veniak S., Midgley D. F., Devinney T. M. (2004). A new perspective on the integration-responsiveness pressures confronting multinational firms, *Management International Review* 44: 15–48.

Volberda H. W. (1996). Toward the flexible form: How to remain vital in hypercompetitive environments, *Organization Science* 7(4): 359–374.

Wally S., Baum R. (1994). Personal and structural determinants of the pace of strategic decision-making, *Academy of Management Journal* 37(4): 932–956.

Waterman R. H. (1982). The seven elements of strategic fit, *Journal of Business Strategy* 2(3): 69–73.

Weihrich H. (1982). The TOWS matrix – A tool for situational analysis, *Long Range Planning* 15(2): 54–66.

Werbach A. (2009). *Strategy for Sustainability: A Business Manifesto*, Harvard Business School Press: Boston, MA.

Wernerfelt B. (1984). A resource-based view of the firm, *Strategic Management Journal* 5(2): 171–180.

White R. E., Hamermesh R. G. (1981). Toward a model of business unit performance: An integrative approach, *Academy of Management Review* 6(2): 213–223.

Whittington R. (2008). Alfred Chandler, founder of strategy: Lost tradition and renewed inspiration, *Business History Review* 82(2): 267–277.

Wiseman R. (2004). *The Luck Factor*, Arrow Books: London.

Womack J. P., Jones D. T. (2005). *Lean Solutions: How Companies and Customers Can Create Value and Wealth Together*, Simon & Schuster: London.

Yip G. S. (1995). *Total Global Strategy*, Prentice Hall: Upper Saddle River, NJ.

Zaheer S. (1996). Overcoming the liabilities of foreignness, *Academy of Management Journal* 38(2): 341–363.

Zaheer S., Musakowski E. (1997). The dynamics of the liability of foreignness: A global study of survival in financial services, *Strategic Management Journal* 18: 439–464.

Zook C., Allen J. (2012). *Repeatability: Build Enduring Businesses for a World of Constant Change*, Harvard Business Review Press: Boston, MA.

Index